WHAT AMERICANS BUILD AND WHY

What Americans Build and Why examines five areas of America's built environment: houses, health care facilities, schools, workplaces, and shopping environments. Synthesizing information from both academic journals and the popular press, this book examines the relationships of size and scale in the way Americans live their lives and how their way of life is fundamentally shaped by the highway system, cheap land, and incentives. This book is timely because, although Americans say they crave community, they continue to construct buildings such as McMansions and big box stores that make creating community a challenge. Furthermore, in many ways, the movement toward teleworking, discussed in the chapter on office environments, also challenges the traditional place-based formation of community. Although focused on the United States, this book includes reference to other parts of the world, especially regarding the retail environment.

Ann Sloan Devlin is the May Buckley Sadowski '19 Professor of Psychology and college marshal at Connecticut College. She has taught at Connecticut College since 1973 and received the John S. King Faculty Teaching Award (2006) and the Student Government Association Excellence in Teaching Award (1991). In the spring of 2009, she taught at the Pantheon Institute in Rome in a Study Away Teach Away (SATA) program sponsored by Connecticut College. While in Rome, she was invited to present a seminar at La Sapienza (University of Rome). She is on the editorial review board of the journal *Environment and Behavior* and has been a board member and secretary of the Environmental Design Research Association. She is a Fellow of Division 34, Population and Environmental Psychology of the American Psychological Association. She is the author of two previous books: *Mind and Maze: Spatial Cognition and Environmental Behavior* (2001) and *Research Methods: Planning, Conducting, and Presenting Research* (2006). Her articles appear in journals such as *Environment and Behavior,* the *Journal of Environmental Psychology,* and the *EDRA* (Environmental Design Research Association) *Proceedings.*

What Americans Build and Why

PSYCHOLOGICAL PERSPECTIVES

Ann Sloan Devlin

Connecticut College

CAMBRIDGE
UNIVERSITY PRESS

CAMBRIDGE UNIVERSITY PRESS
Cambridge, New York, Melbourne, Madrid, Cape Town, Singapore,
São Paulo, Delhi, Dubai, Tokyo, Mexico City

Cambridge University Press
32 Avenue of the Americas, New York, NY 10013-2473, USA

www.cambridge.org
Information on this title: www.cambridge.org/9780521734356

First published 2010

Printed in the United States of America

A catalog record for this publication is available from the British Library.

Library of Congress Cataloging in Publication data

Devlin, Ann Sloan, 1948–
What Americans build and why : psychological perspectives / Ann Sloan Devlin.
   p.   cm.
Includes bibliographical references and index.
ISBN 978-0-521-51657-0 (hardback) – ISBN 978-0-521-73435-6 (pbk.)
1. Architecture and society – United States.   2. Space (Architecture) – United
States – Psychological aspects.   3. Architecture – United States – Psychological
aspects.   4. Architecture – United States – Human factors.   I. Title.
NA2543.S6D48   2010
720.1′030973 – dc22   2009050319

ISBN 978-0-521-51657-0 Hardback
ISBN 978-0-521-73435-6 Paperback

For Sloan. Carpe diem!

CONTENTS

LIST OF FIGURES

PREFACE

This book expresses my ongoing fascination with the built environment. It is also a chance to incorporate many of the ideas I discuss in the course I teach in environmental psychology at Connecticut College. For those who are unfamiliar with the discipline of environmental psychology, it examines the relationship between human behavior and the environment. In the approach I take, I focus on the built environment (e.g., the benefits of high- vs. low-rise housing for the elderly), although a portion of the practitioners in this field focus on the natural environment. In this discipline, we often look at such traditional variables as crowding, personal space, and territoriality, or newer concerns such as recycling and sustainability. My approach to this topic has been somewhat different, focusing first on the facility type (e.g., health care facilities or schools) and then exploring a variety of behavioral manifestations within those building types, wherever the research led me.

What Americans Build and Why takes that "facility-first" approach; it presents chapters on five different types of facilities – our houses, health care facilities, schools, workplaces, and shops – essentially, places where Americans live their lives. Coverage of these topics combines research literature and popular media with personal reflection; I describe my approach as one of synthesis. Eminent environmental psychologist Robert Sommer described this approach best in his book on farmers markets of America when he said: "I have never believed that social research need be dull or celebration should ignore facts or figures."[1] I couldn't agree more.

Begun in 2007, this project has taken me about three years to complete. In that time, much has happened to affect America's landscape. Who knew

---

[1] Sommer, R. (1980). *Farmers markets of America: A renaissance.* Santa Barbara, CA: Capra Press, p. 8.

anything about credit default swaps three years ago (for that matter, who really understands them now)? Where appropriate, I have tried to incorporate data on some of the effects of this downturn – for example, in the number of retail establishments that have closed in the past year or so.

In addition, over the three-year period, one particular personal journey has greatly impacted my view of America. This personal journey began in spring 2009, the semester I spent teaching in Rome, Italy. I had traveled abroad but had never lived abroad. Nor had I ever lived in a city. The experience of living in a city, Rome in particular, has given me a new understanding of America, specifically, how vast and young its built environment is. I have also acquired an even greater understanding of the impact of the highway system, the creation and expansion of suburbs, and the role of legislation on almost every aspect of American life. My reflections on Rome, as they relate to America's built landscape, are part of this book.

ACKNOWLEDGMENTS

I owe Connecticut College a debt of gratitude for the semester sabbatical in 2007 during which this book was launched and for the study-abroad teaching experience in 2009 that propelled it to its finish. The interlibrary loan staff, headed by Emily Aylward at the College, does a tremendous job supporting faculty and student needs; without their help, this book could not have been written. A number of other librarians (information specialists) deserve special thanks. One of them is my sister, Elizabeth Sloan Smith, who on many occasions looked up information for me, as well as helped me take a number of photographs for the book, on the "fly." For instance, she drove and I snapped photographs, or vice versa, of the elephant statues at the Northland Center. A responsive librarian from the Ann Arbor District Library reference staff answered my email query on whether it was a Sears or Montgomery Ward on Main Street in Ann Arbor during the 1950s (I was less than confident of my memory); her check of the 1952 city directory revealed that it was a Sears. My daughter Sloan also deserves a special thank-you for photographing the pods of the DuBois organic chemistry lab at Stanford. Tek-wah King of the Department of East Asian Language and Culture at Connecticut College graciously translated the Chinese characters in the "Medicine No Fakes" sign I describe in Chapter 2. I also want to thank the experts who shared their views on various aspects of the built environment: Marie Cox, Jennifer Gallagher, John Sloan, Robert Sloan, C. Wesley Greenleaf, Elizabeth Gianacoplos, Eric Ward, Ellen Bruce Keable, and Daniel Sargis.

At the Psychology Department of Connecticut College, my colleague Stuart Vyse was helpful and encouraging about this project, particularly in urging me to use my own "voice" and to incorporate personal anecdotes to illustrate the shapes of the built landscapes in this country.

In Rome, my SATA (study away teach away) students could not have been a better group of travelers during our adventures in the eternal city. I had no idea how much that experience would mean to me, personally and professionally, and how much it would shape a number of chapters in this book. I also want to thank Jesse Smeal, the student services coordinator and onsite administrator of the Pantheon Institute. The institute was housed in a renovated convent (Sant' Agnese in Agone) overlooking the Piazza Navona, where we lived and worked. At La Sapienza (University of Rome), I was fortunate to be in contact with environmental psychologists Mirilia Bonnes and Marino Bonaiuto, who invited me to give a seminar at La Sapienza and shared with me a number of wonderful meals. I also want to thank Elena Bilotta and Giuseppe Tronu, two of the program's doctoral students, who extended their friendship to me. Also, to the familiar strangers pouring my cappuccinos at Tor Millina, my neighborhood café, thank you.

I would like to thank Simina Calin and her assistant Jeanie Lee of Cambridge University Press, who took on the task of bringing my manuscript to its publishable form. During the production phase, Eleanor Umali's help was invaluable. I also want to thank Eric Schwartz, now with Princeton University Press, who gave me the encouragement to move forward with the publication process. My thanks also go to the anonymous reviewers who responded positively to the draft of my first chapter on housing, as well as to my final manuscript. Finally, special thanks to Sloan and David, my fellow travelers on life's great adventure.

1

The Landscape of Housing: Suburbia, New Urbanism, and McMansions

When I first visited Seabrook, Maryland, the home of a college friend, I felt like Gertrude Stein describing Oakland, California. "That can't be a town," I said, "because there is no there, there." Seabrook was off the Beltway surrounding Washington, D.C., about 12 miles east of the city. Primarily residential, Seabrook was developed during the 1950s to provide housing for employees in government agencies, such as the Goddard Space Flight Center and the National Security Agency, where my friend's father worked. I came from a different residential experience. I grew up in a university town, Ann Arbor, Michigan, which definitely had a "there, there," and I was less accustomed to using the car. I walked to high school in good weather, to Burns Park, to the Food and Drug Mart (a small grocery/convenience store), the Ann Arbor Bank (for my Christmas Club account), and the Dairy Queen, all important destinations. In all honesty, mothers with five children in the 1950s (as was true for my mother) were probably more willing to let their children wander a far distance from home than they would let them today!

When my spouse and I bought our house, we looked for a place where we could walk downtown. More than 30 years later, we still live in that house on Elm Street in that small town: Mystic, Connecticut. Settled in the 1650s along the banks of the Mystic River, Mystic has one main street (Main Street) and about 4000 residents, according to the 2000 Census. Mystic is not actually an independent municipality; rather, it sits within the towns of Groton (west of the Mystic River) and Stonington (east of the Mystic River). Despite its inclusion in two different towns, Mystic has a definite and integrated sense of place. Long before I understood the intellectual and planning implications of my need to live in a walkable small town such as Mystic, I understood it on an emotional level.

1

When we first moved to Mystic, the downtown had a shoe repair shop, a bookstore, a number of drycleaners, a post office, at least two independently owned pharmacies, an A&P grocery store and liquor store, a sporting goods store, many other independent retailers, and a variety of restaurants. Today the shoe repair and sporting goods stores are gone, and the pharmacies vanished when CVS took over the A&P location after the A&P built a much larger grocery store about a mile away. The post office and A&P liquor store are still there, and an independent bookstore is holding on. Many independent clothing retailers are also holding on, although these are different businesses than they were 30 years ago.

A portion of the residential area surrounding downtown is part of a historic district, with strict guidelines about what modifications can be approved (e.g., the Historic District Commission takes a dim view of plans to eliminate decorative trim and replace it with aluminum siding). Despite its age, Mystic might be considered the model for one of the important current residential trends in this country, new urbanism or neo-traditionalism.

The urban planning concepts of new urbanism, neo-traditional design, and traditional neighborhood development, terms often used interchangeably, emerged in the 1980s with the work of Peter Calthorpe, Peter Katz, Robert Davis, and the team of Andres Duany and Elizabeth Plater-Zyberk. These architects and planners talked about an alternative to urban sprawl that might provide the kind of spatial arrangement that could foster a sense of community. Perhaps the defining feature of new urbanism is its goal of creating walkable communities. The implications of a walkable community are many. Among them is the need to have destinations that can be reached on foot, including work, or at least a transit stop to take you to work. New urbanism also promotes mixed use of functions (i.e., not exclusively residential), neighborhoods with higher densities than one sees in typical suburbs, and streets that bring neighbors into contact with one another. New urbanism is one reaction to the sprawl created in post–World War II America.

Neo-traditional design refers to neighborhoods that emphasize compactness, traditional street patterns, the role of the front porch and stoop, and walkability. Essentially, this is what is meant by new urbanism. And the final term, traditional neighborhood development, usually abbreviated as TND, describes a

> comprehensive planning system that includes a variety of housing types and land uses in a defined area. The variety of uses permits educational facilities, civic buildings and commercial establishments to be located

within walking distance of private homes. A TND is served by a network of paths, streets and lanes suitable for pedestrians as well as vehicles. This provides residents the option of walking, biking or driving to places within their neighborhood.[1]

This definition from the home page of The Town Paper, a Web site that promotes traditional neighborhood developments, also features images of Celebration, Florida, and The Kentlands, Maryland, two communities almost always given as examples of new urbanism. In this chapter, the term new urbanism is used for the kind of developments that emphasize a spatial arrangement intended to promote walking, contact, and in turn, community.

But there is an enormous difference between living in a small town that has evolved over time and a community that has been planned and built essentially at one time, as is the case with many new urbanist developments. Creating "Mystic" is a difficult if not impossible planning challenge for reasons explained in this chapter. Yet communities surrounding Mystic are trying to do just that. Recently an article appeared in the local newspaper about a floating zone that proposes a mixed use of shopping and housing in Groton, which is contiguous with Mystic. A floating zone is legitimate, but its existence may not have been included in a formal zoning map.[2] The idea of a floating zone is useful when a development is proposed for a location not specified in advance. The article dealing with floating zones began, "Imagine the village feel of Mystic and Noank – where people live, shop and do business all in one place – transported to other parts of Groton."[3] The use of a floating zone as a planning tool is getting more popular nationally. Two other terms are important to understand in our discussion of development. Greenfield development refers to development in unoccupied areas (e.g., agricultural areas), typically at the perimeter of a community. Infill development refers to development occurring in core areas where structures already exist.

At the same time the physical core of Mystic is being preserved, new residential areas are being built at its perimeter that include houses that might euphemistically be described as "large." Some would call them Mc-Mansions. The McMansion stereotype is that it is a very large house, offers little variety within the context of its neighbors, and often sits on a plot

---

[1] http://www.tndtownpaper.com/neighborhoods.htm (para. 1).

[2] http://www.co.tompkins.ny.us/planning/vct/tool/floatingzones.html.

[3] Warchut, K. (2007). In Groton, "floating zone" proposal envisions mix of shopping, housing. *The New London Day*, p. B2.

of land where all the original vegetation has been cut. Recent research[4] addresses the extent of McMansions in the United States and the degree to which communities have tried to regulate the impact of such housing. Using newspaper articles as a data source, research indicates that between 1998 and 2004, at least 40 communities had taken the step of creating policies to address some aspect of McMansions, for example by controlling house size or lot coverage. Further, by surveying the 50 largest cities in the United States, the authors found that more than 60 percent reported the development of McMansions. In other words, McMansions are not an isolated phenomenon.

As I look at home sale prices in the Mystic area, I see that there are comparable residential choices, in terms of price, for both well-preserved homes in the historic district of Mystic and in developments of McMansions on the perimeter of the community. In the new homes, the square footage is often greater, and these homes frequently include what is called a "bonus" room (often unfinished) over the garage. Many historic homes in the Mystic area have no garages in the formal sense and thus no opportunity for such bonus space. For example, my own home has a barn/shed that is used as a one-car garage. There are many choices in the centrally located historic home and the less centrally located McMansion. A fair number of people, though certainly not all, seem more eager to embrace the new rather than the charm, history, and walkability of houses in the core. School choice, often related to housing prices (a better school system is associated with higher housing prices), is essentially irrelevant in these decisions. The middle school and high school are the same for both residential types in the Mystic area (on the Groton side of the Mystic River). What does the existence of these two kinds of residential choices say about us as a culture? Who selects which option, and why?

In the United States there are currently a number of residential trends. My goal in this chapter and in the book is to understand the forces that have shaped our built landscape, from our houses to our hospitals to our malls. Often these trends have to do with size, and in particular an increase in size. The core of Mystic represents smallness, especially in house size and proximity to neighbors, and the prototype of what is being called new urbanism. The McMansion represents bigness. These two forms reflect as much about the immediate area surrounding the house (i.e., the proximity of neighbors) as they do about the actual form of the residence.

Why are many people trying to find alternatives to suburbia, to return to a spatial sense of community linked to the traditional neighborhood form

---

[4] Nasar, J. L., Evans-Cowley, J. S., & Mantero, V. (2007). McMansions: The extent and regulation of supersized houses. *Journal of Urban Design, 12*, 339–358.

in America at the beginning of the 20th century, to find new "Mystics," if you will? Who is attracted to new urbanism? Who buys a McMansion? What does research tell us about the effects of living in such places? What do these types of residences say about American design and about Americans?

I'M FROM THE GOVERNMENT AND I'M HERE TO HELP YOU

To understand why the new urbanist movement and an emphasis on small-ness and community exist when the trend in America has been to "build big," we need to look at the developments in the highway system and hous-ing during the early to middle parts of the 20th century. The interstate highway system and decent housing for Americans, essentially in the form of suburbs, seemed like good ideas in the early 20th century and put mil-lions of people to work, but today we are overwhelmed by our highways and suburbs.

A short history might help explain how we arrived at this predicament and why new urbanism exists. In 1994, when Philip Langdon, senior editor of *New Urban News*, wrote his book *A Better Place to Live: Reshaping the American Suburb*,[5] he reported that more than 95 percent of Americans lived in metropolitan areas. Of those, more than two-thirds resided in the suburbs. This distribution was a world apart from the turn of the 20th century, when about one-third of the U.S. population lived on small, family-owned farms.[6]

A confluence of what seemed like good ideas is largely responsible for the suburban predicament in which we find ourselves. This predicament involves spatial isolation and loss of community in the suburbs, longer commutes to work, a reliance on the automobile, and a paucity of mass transit options. From the beginning through the middle of the 20th century, the federal government passed several pieces of legislation dealing with transportation and housing that had profound effects on the shape of our communities and the way we lead our lives.

Our Roads

First, let's consider roads. Many contend that the 1956 legislation during the Eisenhower administration had a profound impact on our roads, homes, and cities. The Interstate Highway Act of 1956 was responsible for creating

[5] Langdon, P. (1994). *A better place to live: Reshaping the American suburb.* Amherst, MA: The University of Massachusetts Press.
[6] Kunstler, J. H. (1993). *The geography of nowhere: The rise and decline of America's man-made landscape.* New York: Simon and Schuster.

more than 41,000 miles of roads in this country that established the interstate highway system and linked cities of at least 50,000 with beltways around them. At an initial cost of $26 billion in 1956 dollars, the federal government covered 90 percent, with the states contributing 10 percent.[7] One justification for this system, initiated during the cold war, was the movement of troops and material (as well as citizens) in the event of a nuclear strike. Prior to the Interstate Highway Act, there were fewer than 500 miles of freeways in urban areas.[8] With these transportation acts, the government moved "toward a transportation policy emphasizing and benefiting the road, the truck, and the private motorcar."[9] As Andres Duany, an influential designer in the new urbanism movement, notes, "money spent on roads is called 'highway investment,' while money spent on rails is called 'transit subsidy.'"[10] Thus, we *invested* in our highways, a positive connotation, but we *subsidized* our transit system, with the negative connotations a subsidy suggests.

At least one author argues that the outcome might have been different if there had been support for a form of public transportation, the streetcar, when both the electric streetcar and the automobile were introduced from 1890 to 1915.[11] Instead, federal dollars went to the automobile, the streetcar had no public funding, and ultimately the support of highways, and by default of automobiles, with tax dollars contributed to reliance upon the automobile and to suburban sprawl. Although an urban myth blames General Motors for the streetcar's demise, General Motors was hardly responsible for the change in our transportation system. For the interested reader, a careful deconstruction of this myth, its origins and permutations, is provided by Cliff Slater in an article in the journal *Transportation Quarterly*.[12] The reasons for the change in our transportation system are described in architecture and planning critic Jane Holtz Kay's book *Asphalt Nation*.[13] As she explains, funding ratios discriminated against mass transit. In the case of railroads, for every dollar spent on railroads, 20 were spent on roads. Lower densities in residential neighborhoods were

[7] Jackson, K. T. (1985). *Crabgrass frontier: The suburbanization of the United States.* New York: Oxford University Press, pp. 249–250.

[8] Kay, J. H. (1997). *Asphalt nation: How the automobile took over America and how we can take it back.* Berkeley, CA: The University of California Press, p. 232.

[9] Jackson (1985), p. 191.

[10] Duany, A., Plater-Zyberk, E., & Speck, J. (2000). *Suburban nation: The rise of sprawl and the decline of the American dream.* New York: North Point Press, p. 96.

[11] Kunstler (1993).

[12] http://www.lava.net/cslater/TQOrigin.pdf.   [13] Kay (1997).

associated with the dominance of the roadway system, and there was (and is) an intimate connection between the development of the road system and the development of the spatial character of our communities.

Another impact of this country's roads on the formation (or lack) of community is the width of streets. Duany and his colleagues argue that wide streets promote speed, called "unimpeded flow."[14] Twelve-foot lanes (24-foot total width) are typically required for new streets. One explanation for the width of streets was the cold war; wide streets promoted timely evacuation in the event of a nuclear strike. Fire trucks also play a role, as streets are supposed to be built wide enough to enable fire trucks to turn around without using reverse, and cul-de-sacs are paved to a width of 30 feet to accommodate this maneuver.[15] Another explanation for wide streets is offered by planner Michael Southworth, who focuses on the impact of what seem to have become inflexible engineering standards.[16] Widely adopted standards from the Institute of Transportation Engineers were ostensibly aimed at livability, but the prescriptions emphasized traffic control at the expense of functional accessibility, according to Southworth. Today's street standards prescribe wide streets. As the early work of researchers Donald Appleyard and Mark Lintell[17] demonstrated, streets with substantial amounts of traffic, often a function of synchronized traffic lights, make neighboring behavior more difficult.

Two groups particularly impacted by sprawl in a negative way are teenagers and the elderly, both of whom struggle with autonomy in suburbia. Duany et al. talk about "the child who lives as a prisoner of a thoroughly safe and unchallenging environment."[18] Without nearby neighborhood facilities, such as the kind of corner store I experienced growing up, children and young teenagers in suburbia have few places to visit on their own. In a sense, suburbia stifles the emergence of independence in children. Children are prisoners of the carpool at the same time that their mothers are imprisoned in the role of chauffeur. For the elderly in suburbia, driving becomes increasingly challenging as their visual acuity and mental sharpness decline. When they are unable to drive, they become prisoners in their own homes without walkable destinations, as is true of children and young teenagers.

---

[14] Duany et al. (2000), p. 65.   [15] Ibid., p. 66.

[16] Southworth, M., & Ben-Joseph, E. (1995). Street standards and the shaping of suburbia. *Journal of the American Planning Association, 61*(1), 65–81.

[17] Appleyard, D., & Lintell, M. (1972). The environmental quality of city streets: The residents' viewpoint. *Journal of the American Institute of Planners, 38*, 84–101.

[18] Duany et al. (2000), p. 116.

My Interstate Highway Experience

In the summer of 2006, my daughter and I drove more than 2000 miles of these roads on I-80 from Mystic, Connecticut, to Palo Alto, California, where she began graduate school. A number of things struck me about the drive and my own family experiences. My older brother went to college in California in 1963. My family of origin lived (and still lives) in Ann Arbor, Michigan. My parents, with their five children, put my older brother, the eldest, on the train and sent him to California by himself with his footlocker. Parenting has changed since the early 1960s, as has outfitting a dorm room. Most families today, if they are able, find a way to personally deliver their offspring to college (and beyond). Thus it was that I drove my daughter to graduate school. It was not an easy drive, and with a used Subaru that had been purchased for the trip and graduate school and a lack of mechanical skill, the two of us were nervous about the adventure. But we made it.

It was a long trip; America is a vast country. Many parts of this country remain uninhabited relative to the coasts. I think the worst day for me was leaving Rawlins, Wyoming, in the morning, determined to make Reno by dinnertime. When we passed through Salt Lake City around noon and I saw the road sign that said "Reno, NV 500 miles" I wanted to give up. We did make it to Reno that "day," helped by gaining an hour when we passed through a time zone, but dinner turned out to be around 9 p.m. that night. What I remember of that day was the relative density of Salt Lake City compared to its outskirts; the emptiness of the Bonneville Salt Flats; and the casino in Wendover, Nevada, essentially in the middle of nowhere as soon as you passed the state line leaving Utah (no legal gambling) to enter Nevada (plenty of gambling). On the last day of our trip, a Friday, most striking was coming out of the mountains from Lake Tahoe in the early afternoon and hitting bumper-to-bumper traffic that seemed to have no explanation, such as an accident or too many merges. There were cars as far as the eye could see. This bumper-to-bumper situation was the first bona fide traffic jam we had seen since day 2 of driving, when we tried to get around Chicago, a nightmare with all of its road construction.

Yes, this country has employed millions of workers constructing roads and residences, but the products have handicapped us in many respects. During the New Deal, upward of 80 percent of that period's expenditures involved "roads and construction."[19] In the decade 1930 to 1940, there was a doubling in mileage of surfaced roads to more than 1.3 million.[20] And

---

[19] Kay (1997), p. 199.   [20] Ibid.

a concept called induced traffic suggests that building more lanes only increases traffic volume.[21]

Some smart person said, "You get what you reward." What that phrase means here is that by rewarding the building of roads, however laudable some stated reasons may be (such as national defense and employment), what we got was more roads. With more roads came houses that were farther apart because the land was available and cheaper at the perimeter. Now, couple what happened to the road system with what was reinforced in terms of housing development.

Housing Policy

In her influential book *Asphalt Nation*, Kay argues that building highways and taking homes through the urban renewal process was a disaster for this country. In addition to the legislation creating the interstate highway system and other roadways, the government heavily invested in housing during the 20th century and provided opportunities for private developers to do so as well. The Home Owners Loan Corporation (HOLC) created in 1933 addressed urban housing ills, provided self-amortizing long-term mortgages, and set up the mortgages with uniform payments spread throughout the length of the loan. With the HOLC came mortgage guarantees, although discrimination came as well. Neighborhoods judged risky, typically those in inner cities and those that housed low-income families and families in racially segregated neighborhoods, were those in Category D. Category D was at the bottom of the A (green), B (blue), C (yellow), D (red) classification, hence the term redlining for discrimination involving those areas judged least worthy of support. "The lasting damage done by the national government was that it put its seal of approval on ethnic and racial discrimination and developed policies which had the result of the practical abandonment of large sections of older, industrial cities."[22] Moreover, banks and savings-and-loans also practiced this kind of discrimination based on location.

Prior to the Depression, you needed a down payment of between 30 percent and 50 percent to purchase a house, and a long-term loan was 10 years. With the Federal Housing Administration established by the National Housing Act of 1934, and the addition of the GI Bill of 1944, creating the Veterans Administration, came an impetus for private developers to build homes because the loans were guaranteed. A small down payment

---

[21] Duany et al. (2000), p. 89. [22] Jackson (1985), p. 217.

(not more than 10 percent) sufficed, and the loan length could be 20–30 years.[23] With the Housing Act of 1949, which promised a "decent home and a suitable living environment for every American family,"[24] came urban renewal as well. For example, when the Cross Bronx Expressway was built, the homes of some 5000 people were taken, and 113 streets and 159 buildings were sacrificed.[25]

A passing reference to Robert Moses seems in order when talking about the transformation of the American landscape, at the crossroads of highway and housing policy. When you look around New York City today, you see his imprint on the infrastructure, on bridges such as the Triborough and Verrazano Narrows, on parkways such as the Henry Hudson, and on expressways such as the Brooklyn-Queens and the Cross Bronx. You also see his imprint on recreational and civic developments, such as Jones Beach and Lincoln Center. His additions were said to include as many as 658 playgrounds and 17 swimming pools to the New York City park system.[26] His reach was vast, and he held up to 12 positions in municipal offices at one time.[27] In a sense Moses embodied the dominance of the automobile over other forms of transportation seen nationwide, although his domain was New York City. It has been argued that *The Death and Life of Great American Cities*[28] by urbanist Jane Jacobs was a challenge to Moses's contention that the city was the domain of the automobile and traffic. For Jacobs, the primary planning concept was the neighborhood and its functional diversity.[29] She initially became involved in her battle with Moses over his desire to put a four-lane road through Washington Square Park in Greenwich Village. As has been noted, "In taking on Greenwich Village, Moses had found his Opposite."[30]

[23] Jackson (1985); Kunstler (1993).

[24] Anderson, M. (1964). *The federal bulldozer: A critical analysis of urban renewal, 1949–1962.* Cambridge, MA: The MIT Press, p. 4.

[25] Kay (1997), p. 230.

[26] Goldberger, P. (2007, February 5). Eminent Dominion: Rethinking the legacy of Robert Moses. *The New Yorker.* http//www.newyorker.com/arts/critics/skyline/2007/02/05/070205crsk_skyline_goldberger.

[27] Purrington, G. (1999, June 30). Robert Moses: A tribute to the man and his impact on the borough. *The Queens Gazette.* http://www.qgazette.com/News/1999/0630/Feature_Story/.

[28] Jacobs, J. (1961). *The death and life of great American cities.* New York: Random House.

[29] Jackson, K. T. (2007). Robert Moses and the rise of New York: The power broker in perspective. In H. Ballon & K. T. Jackson (Eds.), *Robert Moses and the modern city: The transformation of New York* (pp. 67–71). New York: W. W. Norton & Company.

[30] Fishman, R. (2007). Revolt of the urbs: Robert Moses and his critics. In H. Ballon & K. T. Jackson (Eds.), *Robert Moses and the modern city: The transformation of New York* (pp. 124–129). New York: W. W. Norton & Company, p. 124.

All federal legislation we have discussed had the potential for benefit. And many people had good reason to want to leave the city and its dirt, pollution, congestion, and crime, typified by the slum housing described in Lewis Mumford's works.[31,32] But the problem with the legislation was its one-sidedness. Although new single-family houses were endorsed, the legislation did not support the inner city, either in terms of apartments or money to rehabilitate existing houses. The outcome was an equation where home ownership = suburbia, with all the associated dependence on the automobile.[33]

An additional factor that fueled the purchase of single-family dwellings was the Levitt family's construction of inexpensive housing. Kenneth Jackson, professor of history at Columbia University, argues that the Levitt family had the "greatest impact on postwar housing in the United States,"[34] ultimately building more than 140,000 houses. Although the family originally built houses for upper-middle-income families, a government contract for workers' housing in Norfolk, Virginia, was the beginning of mass market housing for the family. Preassembling walls and laying many concrete slab foundations in a day led to big volume construction. At the peak of production of Levittown housing, more than 30 structures appeared in a single day.[35] These houses provided more space than apartments in cities and were affordable; they were priced within reach. That affordability had not previously been the case for middle-income Americans.

In Levittown on Long Island the most popular style initially was the Cape Cod, a four-room house on a 60 × 100 foot lot with the kitchen and living room toward the front of the house, making the street the focus. Mothers in the kitchen could look out at their children playing in the street. The Cape Cod was priced at $6990, and later at $7990. When the ranch style was introduced in 1949, the living room faced the rear of the house and the family's focus became the backyard and common areas created because the Levitts prohibited fences.

As a quintessential postwar suburb, Levittown possessed five characteristics: peripheral location, low density relative to city dwellings, architectural similarity, financial feasibility, and economic and racial homogeneity.[36] Rate of growth in suburbs was outpacing that of central cities by about 10 to 1 by

---

[31] Mumford, L. (1968). *The urban prospect*. New York: Harcourt, Brace & World.

[32] Mumford, L. (1938). *The culture of cities*. New York: Harcourt, Brace & World.

[33] Gratz, R. B. (with N. Mintz). (1998). *Cities: Back from the edge; New life for downtown*. New York: John Wiley & Sons, p. 144.

[34] Jackson (1985), p. 234.   [35] Ibid., p. 235.

[36] Ibid., pp. 238–241.

1950.[37] And in the decade between 1946 and 1956, more than 95 percent of all new single-family dwellings were detached; row housing was a thing of the past except in central cities.[38]

Another factor contributing to the separation of city and suburb was legislation that legalized single-use zoning. In the 1926 decision Village of Euclid v. Ambler Realty Co., the Supreme Court ruled in favor of the Village of Euclid, Ohio, which in 1922 had passed a zoning code dividing the village into six districts by use: three residential types (single-family, two-family, and apartment houses) and three nonresidential types (retail–wholesale stores, commercial, and industrial).[39] Ultimately the Supreme Court was persuaded by arguments that such zoning was reasonable as a kind of nuisance control, which in turn justified expansion of the Village's police power.

Thus, many factors contributed to the development of single-family dwellings in the suburbs. Was there a downside? Indeed. But as Jackson poignantly states, what was happening in the central cities, its people and its buildings, was of little concern to those in the suburbs: "They were concerned about their hopes and their dreams. They were looking for good schools, private space, and personal safety, and places like Levittown could provide those amenities on a scale and at a price that crowded city neighborhoods, both in the Old World and in the new, could not match."[40] James Kunstler, who writes on the causes of urban sprawl, says that this suburban dream was cruel, however, because suburbia lacked the cultural institutions of the city and provided little in the way of the nature of the countryside. "The main problem with it was that it dispensed with all the traditional connections and continuities of community life, and replaced them with little more than cars and television."[41]

The spread of the automobile, in terms of the number of people owning cars, spread out the population as well, and this was true in suburbia. In areas accessible only by automobiles, the price of land was cheaper than in areas where there was streetcar service. The building lot size in suburbs served by automobiles was about 5000 sq. ft., whereas for those served by streetcars, it was about 3000 sq. ft.[42] Very simply, when lots are larger, people are farther apart. It is difficult to make community visible when people are invisible. In a charming book *City Comforts: How to Build an Urban Village*,

[37] Ibid., p. 238.   [38] Ibid., p. 239.
[39] http://www.planning.org/pathways/details/euclid.htm.
[40] Jackson (1985), p. 244.   [41] Kunstler (1993), p. 105.
[42] Jackson (1985), pp. 184–185.

David Sucher[43] essentially emphasizes points made by urbanists Jane Jacobs (*The Death and Life of Great American Cities*[44]) and William Whyte (*The Social Life of Small Urban Spaces*[45]) – that buildings need to be close to the street to make community permeable: "Conversation between buildings, as among humans, is a poignant sign of neighborliness."

In the process of creating suburbia and extending commuting times, America has lost what urban sociologist Ray Oldenburg[46] calls her third places – not the home, not the workplace, but the bar, café, deli, any place that is inclusive, accessible, has regulars, is homey, and homelike. Newer environments lack such third places: "Where once there were places, we now find nonplaces."[47]

But some observers, such as *Washington Post* journalist Joel Garreau,[48] talk about sprawl positively, in the form of new edge cities. Edge cities form when you add commercial, entertainment, and work activities to suburban areas that previously just supported housing. Another new form is what is called a boomburb,[49] which describes a type of fast-growing (double-digit population growth over a number of years) suburban city that has more than 100,000 residents, is incorporated, but is not the largest city in that given metropolitan area. Examples of such boomburbs include Mesa, Arizona, Gilbert, Arizona, and Santa Ana, California. As horizontal entities (growing out rather than up), the boomburbs' major competitive edge came through their spatial qualities as greenfields.[50] Ironically, at least one writer contends that the future of landlocked boomburbs may "depend on the success of urban design movements – such as the New Urbanism – in introducing more traditional, city-like development into the suburbs."[51] In contrast to the relatively positive view of edge cities and boomburbs, a more typical

---

[43] Sucher, D. (1995). *City comforts: How to build an urban village.* Seattle, WA: City Comforts Press, p. 101.

[44] Jacobs (1961).

[45] Whyte, W. (1980). *The social life of small urban spaces.* Washington, D.C.: The Conservation Foundation.

[46] Oldenburg, R. (1989). *The great good place: Cafes, coffee shops, community centers, beauty parlors, general stores, bars, hangouts, and how they get you through the day.* New York: Paragon House.

[47] Ibid., p. 205.

[48] Garreau, J. (1991). *Edge city: Life on the new frontier.* New York: Doubleday.

[49] Lang, R. E., & Simmons, P. A. (2003). Boomburbs: The emergence of large, fast-growing suburban cities. In B. Katz & R. E. Lang (Eds.), *Redefining urban and suburban America: Evidence from Census 2000* (pp. 101–116). Washington, D.C.: Brookings Institution Press.

[50] Lang, R. E. (2004, October). Are the boomburbs still booming? Fannie Mae Foundation, Census Note 15.

[51] Ibid., p. 4.

outlook is expressed in *Cities: Back from the Edge: New Life for Downtown.* In this book Roberta Gratz of the Center for the Living City at Purchase College describes what has happened to our social environment in a manner similar to the new urbanists: "The highways and parking lots built since the 1950s have so separated, segregated, and isolated the American people that we have become pockets of hostile aliens."[52] We have lost what it means to share community. We need to create ways to rediscover community. Can we change the way we build in America to create the opportunity for a sense of community to develop? Can we build more new urbanist communities or reduce America's predilection for bigness? Can we at the very least provide options for those who favor increased density and smallness?

NEW TOWNS: WHAT'S NOT TO LIKE?

Levittown, a planned community, had a tremendous impact on the development of residential patterns in the United States. Some people refer to such planned communities as a kind of new town. The term new town has been used to describe entities that vary in scale from a large suburb (e.g., Columbia, Maryland) to a city (e.g., Brasilia, Brazil, or Chandigarh, India). What these entities have in common is that they are built "brand new" and attempt to provide all the functions and services you would find in an existing town. By the time the second Levittown was built in Pennsylvania in the 1950s, athletics fields, greenbelts, and a shopping center were provided, arguably creating a more bona fide new town than the first Levittown on Long Island. William Levitt said about the Levittown in Pennsylvania, "We planned every foot of it – every store, filling station, school, house, apartment, church, color, tree and shrub."[53]

Before focusing specifically on new urbanism and McMansions, it seems important to examine new towns and their impact, as new towns have much in common with new urbanism, and yet new urbanists try to avoid some of the drawbacks identified in earlier planned communities. Some new urbanists avoid the term new town altogether, arguing that the phrase has a negative connotation.[54]

One of my college roommates lived for a time in Columbia, Maryland, considered one of the new towns in the United States. Located between Baltimore and Washington, D.C., Columbia is a planned community of about 22 square miles. The goal for Columbia was about 30,000 residences,

[52] Gratz (1998), p. 33.   [53] Jackson (1985), p. 237.
[54] Calthorpe, P. (1994). The region. In P. Katz, *The new urbanism: Toward an architecture of community* (pp. xi–xvi). New York: McGraw-Hill.

organized in a pattern of smaller neighborhoods (1200–2000) comprising larger villages of 6,000–10,000 residents. There were different house styles, in different colors, but it was clear to the observer that a grand plan had dictated the outcome. My roommate told me that the regulations were extensive, even to the point of dictating what kind of trees could be planted.

The Rouse Company developed Columbia in the 1960s. The Rouse Company is probably best known for its urban malls up and down the East Coast. Perhaps most famous is its Quincy Market development in Boston. My view is that its approach creates generic experiences, and I am not alone in this view. Calvin Trillin[55] wrote eloquently in *The New Yorker* about this lack of individual sense of place in his article "Thoughts brought on by prolonged exposure to exposed brick."

In an earlier book[56] I spent a good portion of one chapter talking about new towns, briefly recounting their history and including international examples of Brasilia, Brazil, and Chandigarh, India, as well as a number of American models including Levittown, New Jersey, and Columbia, Maryland. The new town movement is sometimes traced to the work of Ebenezer Howard, who wrote a book entitled *Garden Cities of To-morrow*[57] to describe a form he thought would address the problems of British cities, primarily lack of room to house an expanding population. This form was known as a satellite garden city because English cities had no room to grow. As might be expected given the role of the English landscape in British history and culture, the creation of developments that showed sympathy toward the natural environment is viewed as an advantage of the Garden City movement.

Perhaps the most influential new town in terms of its history in America is the third Levittown in Willingboro, New Jersey. The social scientist Herbert Gans wrote about this community in his book *The Levittowners: Ways of Life and Politics in a New Suburban Community.*[58] The houses in the third Levittown were ready for purchase in 1958, making this Levittown a contemporary of both Brasilia and Chandigarh. Gans was an insider, a resident observer, and documented the development of the community as he lived there for 2 years. There were three basic house styles: Cape Cod,

---

[55] Trillin, C. (1977, May 16). U.S. journal: New England. Thoughts brought on by prolonged exposure to exposed brick. *The New Yorker*, pp. 101–102, 104–107.

[56] Devlin, A. S. (2001). *Mind and maze: Spatial cognition and environmental behavior.* Westport, CT: Praeger.

[57] Howard, E. (1898/1945). *Garden cities of to-morrow.* London: Faber and Faber.

[58] Gans, H. (1969). *The Levittowners: Ways of life and politics in a new suburban community.* New York: Vintage.

Ranch, and Colonial. Each street was to have a mixture of these designs. By varying two possible elevations, three different house styles, and different exterior colors, only about every 150th house was a duplicate. Even with this apparent diversity, Levittown was criticized for its uniformity of architecture and people. Gans was unsympathetic to the criticism.

He felt that the critics didn't have the perspective of residents; rather they had the perspective of tourists who seek visual interest and cultural diversity. But in his response to the critics of Levittown, when he mentions their desire for places to wander, for the charm of a medieval village, and for the architectural variety synonymous with high-income suburbs, he might be describing what new urbanists attempt to provide.

In critiquing the success of new towns, particularly their ability to meet psychological needs, I earlier wrote that two criteria new towns must meet for success are those that apply to any urban community: diversity and legibility. And a tension between diversity and legibility often exists. Diversity is a term familiar to most of us that refers to variety: variety of building types, both residential and commercial; variety of spaces for meandering; variety of people. Legibility is a term used by the late urban planner Kevin Lynch. It refers to the idea that an environment must make sense or be readable, in the way that handwriting must be legible. In his landmark book *The Image of the City*[59] and later in *A Theory of Good City Form*,[60] Lynch describes urban design principles that promote legibility.

What new town planned environments seem to lack is the mixed-up quality of different functions that can contribute to both diversity and legibility. And many critics of such planned communities as Levittown fault their architectural uniformity. We see this mixing of different functions in European cities, and it is one of the aspects we like about such cities. This is how Kevin Lynch described the European cities many Americans love: "We have a great affection for these towns. They seem secure, legible, proportioned to the human scale, and charged with life, even if at times a little oppressive."[61] For me, the example of such a city is Riva del Garda, Italy, at the northern end of Lake Garda (essentially north of Verona). I have had the good fortune to travel internationally, accompanying my daughter to sailing regattas in many out-of-the-way places, including Split, Croatia, and Cagliari, Sardinia. Riva del Garda is one place I remember with extraordinary fondness (see Figure 1.1). My daughter and I went to the

[59] Lynch, K. (1960). *The image of the city*. Cambridge, MA: The MIT Press.
[60] Lynch, K. (1981). *A theory of good city form*. Cambridge, MA: The MIT Press.
[61] Ibid., p. 407.

FIGURE 1.1. Riva del Garda, Italy

market every day to get food for her lunch on the water (and mine on shore), and each day involved considerable walking from the hotel to the regatta site. Most streets in the inner core of the small city prohibited automobile traffic because they were so narrow. In many respects, it is the qualities of places like Riva del Garda that planners want to incorporate in their models of new urbanism.

In contrast to Riva del Garda, Columbia, Maryland, Greenbelt, Maryland, and several other new towns, including the Levittowns, have on occasion been criticized for a lack of visual and functional interest. Even a strong supporter of Columbia has suggested that its place-making vitality may be limited.[62] Plans to renovate Columbia emphasize new urbanist principles such as walkability and a street pattern that connects, rather than segregates, functions.[63] Some advocates of new urbanism avoid the term "new town" precisely because of its association with such limitations. The challenge for new towns is that they must meet the criteria of diversity and legibility from the outset; there is no incremental growth that invariably brings change.

Critical to the argument about diversity and legibility is the work of architect and theorist Christopher Alexander, especially in his paper "A city is not a tree."[64] What Alexander says echoes the advice of Jane Jacobs in her book *The Death and Life of Great American Cities.*[65] Alexander argues that the richness and texture of cities emerges out of growth over time, and that you cannot plan such richness (or diversity) at one time. A tree has separate, nonoverlapping branches. What Alexander calls a semilattice (borrowing a term from mathematics) has many crossovers and intersections that come when two functions or activities happen by chance to overlap. Alexander argues that new towns such as Columbia fit into his notion of being a tree rather than offering the overlap of a semilattice. He even provides a mathematical tree graph to document the "treeness" of Columbia, Maryland, as a spatial entity.

Alexander talks about the fact that designers are trapped in a tree; what they and we cannot do is imagine multiple categories simultaneously. Humans are limited cognitively in this respect. In Alexander's article he talks about the overlap of functions emerging in a way that could not have been planned. The diversity is genuine and functional, not artificial. In fact, Alexander uses the terms natural and artificial to differentiate between

[62] Avin, U. P. (2004, February). Should we copy Columbia? *Planning, 70*(2), 27–29.

[63] Dennis, S. T. (2005, August). Columbia, Maryland steps toward walkability. *Planning, 71*(8), 49.

[64] Alexander, C. (1965, April, May). A city is not a tree. *Architectural Forum, 1,* 58–62, p. 2.

[65] Jacobs (1961).

cities that provide spatial semilattices (natural) versus those that are spatial trees (artificial).

Overlaps or semilattices are much more common in Europe than in the United States, perhaps because of the age and incremental growth of the communities where they occur. Through the semilattices or overlaps, these European towns provide the opportunity for interaction that most American planned communities lack.[66] A number of designers[67] have commented that the closest we come in America in new construction to creating these opportunities for engagement is in malls! In the days of the baby boomer generation and their parents, opportunities for engagement took place in a variety of other locales, from parks and corner stores to the post office and the public library. Malls may have a number of virtues, but it is a sad commentary on American design that there are so few functional options for engagement.

THE ALLURE OF SMALL TOWNS

What is it that many Americans love about real small towns? And what attracts the Americans who can afford it to travel to the heart of such European cities as Florence or Venice or Paris? One of my colleagues spent a semester on a Fulbright Fellowship in Durham, England. He and his wife and two teenage daughters lived within walking distance of all their daily functions. Transportation was the public transit system or their own two feet. They loved walking to the market, and their daughters walked to the school they attended. This experience in England changed their lives. When they returned to the United States, they sold their home in a locale that was halfway between the work destination of each spouse and moved to a community where they bought a house within walking distance of the schools of both daughters and of downtown. Admittedly one spouse now has a longer commute than before (and one a much shorter commute), but they believe the benefits gained by being close to a downtown and using neighborhood schools were a trade-off well worth this major change in their lives. To be sure, there are wonderful sections of large cities that take on the character of small towns. It is these sections of cities that often capture the imagination, whether Greenwich Village in New York City, Back Bay in Boston, or even Greektown in Detroit. Many small towns embody the qualities of these sections.

[66] Halpern, K. (1978). *Downtown USA: Urban design in nine American cities.* New York: Whitney Library of Design.

[67] Francaviglia, R. V. (1977, Spring-Summer). Main Street USA: The creation of a popular image. *Landscape*, pp. 18–22.

The small towns of America are attractive, and we seem drawn to the main street, whether it is called Main Street or Market Street or Front Street or South University Avenue (~SouthU). These main streets are manageable in size, and they typically contain all the basic functions we need. Toy manufacturers, such as Fisher Price, have capitalized on these quintessential elements in their playset of a small town. The main street of a prototypical small play town contains a bank, market, post office, fire station, and often an ice cream parlor (now perhaps a Starbucks).

Disneyland has capitalized on the draw of Main Street as well, as revealed in a book on Disney architecture by Beth Dunlop. She writes "Main Street, U. S. A. (Disney edition), is not an official address, but it is nonetheless one of the most influential streets in America."[68] Americans seek places like Disney World's Main Street to replace the small towns that have been lost. A number of writers, most prominently Jane Jacobs,[69] point to urban renewal as the culprit in the loss of the integrity of our cities and towns. What Main Street provided that is so hard to recapture is a sense of place and identity.[70] New urbanist communities are essentially what Walt Disney was trying to create in his model of Main Street in Disneyland (and subsequently Disney World); he was trying to recapture the essence of small-town America (in truth an idealized form of that small town) at the turn of the 20th century. Moving beyond theme parks, the Disney Company incorporated this notion of Main Street and the principles of new urbanism in its town of Celebration, near Orlando, Florida. Celebration is a focus later in this chapter. We will revisit the concept of Main Street in the context of retail environments in the last chapter.

If the forms of early new towns such as Levittown and Columbia are now avoided because of their limited visual interest, lack of variety, and challenging legibility, are the new urbanist communities, which ostensibly remind us of such places as Mystic, an improvement in terms of diversity and legibility? Do such communities provide a better spatial framework to create a sense of community than modern suburbs?

THE HISTORY AND PRINCIPLES OF NEW URBANISM

During the last quarter of the 20th century, new ideas about residential community design were introduced. These new models were prompted

---

[68] Dunlop, B. (1996). *Building a dream: The art of Disney architecture*. New York: Abrams, p. 117.

[69] Jacobs (1961).

[70] Rifkind, C. (1977). *Main Street: The face of urban America*. New York: Harper Colophon.

by the social isolation, spatial isolation, lengthy commuting times, and depletion of natural resources associated with the suburban way of life. The new urbanists introduced many of these changes. To appreciate what new urbanists are trying to accomplish, a good starting point is a short history and their statement of goals and principles.

By the early 1990s, the concept of new urbanism was beginning to emerge. Plans for a number of communities cited as examples of new urbanism, including Seaside, Florida, and The Kentlands, Maryland, date to the 1980s. Design and marketing consultant Peter Katz's book *The New Urbanism: Toward an Architecture of Community*[71] does a nice job of articulating the principles and spirit of new urbanism through essays by Peter Calthorpe, Andres Duany, and Elizabeth Plater-Zyberk, among others.

In fact, Peter Katz played a pivotal role in the development of new urbanist principles. Katz was a staff member of the Local Government Commission, a private nonprofit group in Sacramento, California, and helped organize a group of architects and planners to address the problems of urban sprawl and respond with appropriate land planning principles. In 1991 what were called the Ahwahnee Principles emerged from a meeting organized and held at the Ahwahnee Hotel in Yosemite National Park, hence the Ahwahnee label. Among the attendees were Peter Calthorpe, Andres Duany, and Elizabeth Plater-Zyberk. The goals of the Ahwahnee Principles were to identify the patterns of development that degraded our quality of life, including loss of sense of community, and to propose measures to change these patterns.[72]

Many of those instrumental in the development of the Ahwahnee Principles went on to found the Congress for the New Urbanism (CNU), first based in Chicago.[73] This group developed The Charter of the New Urbanism, which looks at the "erosion of society's built heritage as one interrelated community-building challenge."[74] This charter was ratified in 1996 at the 4th-annual Congress for the New Urbanism. The complete charter can be found on the CNU Web site.[75] The Web site shows the complete list of principles provided to direct public policy, urban planning, and design. These principles are reminiscent of Kevin Lynch's ideas in *A Theory of Good City Form* and Christopher Alexander's in *A Pattern Language*.[76] The

---

[71] Katz, P. (1994). *The new urbanism: Toward an architecture of community.* New York: McGraw-Hill.

[72] http://www.lgc.org/ahwahnee/principles.html.

[73] http://www.cnu.org/history.   [74] http://www.cnu.org/charter.

[75] http://cnu.org/sites/files/charter.english.pdf.

[76] Alexander, C., Silverstein, M., & Ishikawa, S. (1977). *A pattern language: Towns, buildings, construction.* New York: Oxford University Press.

CNU has been influential and has played a role in design specifications for rebuilding communities along the Gulf Coast ravaged by Hurricane Katrina.[77]

The tenets of new urbanism are often distilled into the following 10 principles[78]:

1. walkability
2. connectivity
3. mixed use and diversity
4. mixed housing
5. quality architecture and urban design
6. traditional neighborhood structure
7. increased density
8. smart transportation
9. sustainability
10. quality of life

The principles suggest that by promoting walking, encouraging contact between people through buildings of mixed use, and structuring the arrangement of houses to include public sidewalks (which in turn promote contact), a *community* will emerge. Reflecting the ideas of legibility, the traditional neighborhood structure often possesses short blocks and grids.[79] The concepts of coherence, human scale, and legibility are embedded in the tenets of new urbanism. Further, the principles imply that experiencing such a community should enhance our quality of life.

A concept closely linked to the new urbanist principles is the pedestrian pocket, linked to the work of Peter Calthorpe and Doug Kelbaugh.[80] Calthorpe and others argue that mixed-use areas consisting of a balance of housing, retail space, and office space and supported by a light rail system can decrease reliance on the car without eliminating its use entirely. To be successful, these mixed-use areas need to be within a 5-minute walking radius of transit options.

In Katz's book he explains his belief that the paradigm of planning, manifested in the form of suburbia that dominated this country during the

---

[77] McKee, B. (2005, November 24). To restore or reinvent? *The New York Times*, pp. F1–F2.

[78] http://www.newurbanism.org/newurbansim/principles.html.

[79] Ford, L. R. (1999). Lynch revisited: New urbanism and theories of good city form. *Cities*, 16(4), 247–257.

[80] Kelbaugh, D. (Ed.)(1989). *The pedestrian pocket book: A new suburban design strategy*. New York: Princeton Architectural Press.

1940s and 1950s, could not "sustain another generation of growth."[81] Katz also reminds us that earlier models of city planning, particularly those that stress the neighborhood from the period 1900–1920, serve as models for new urbanism. But he points out that new urbanists move beyond a mere revival of these earlier principles because they must address aspects of life, such as the automobile and big box stores, that were not part of the culture of early–20th-century America.

One of the central components of new urbanism is the *neighborhood*, and what the layout and plan of a traditional neighborhood make possible. In their essay for Katz's book, Duany and Plater-Zyberk focus on the role of the neighborhood. They argue that neighborhoods as we traditionally understand them have a center, but also an edge (suggesting that neighborhoods are bounded). Further, neighborhoods have a particular size, and Duany and Plater-Zyberk say that the distance from center to edge should be about one-quarter mile. Reminiscent of some of the work of Christopher Alexander about what makes cities lively, neighborhoods should have a mixture of activities – not just residences, but schools and places to shop, to work, to play, and to worship.[82]

Of particular importance, in my view, is what Duany and Plater-Zyberk say about the relationship of the physical form to the social form. They suggest that the "center" is fundamental to community. The center contains a public space, for example, a park, square, or even a significant intersection. In their view, this legible spatial form, with its center and limit or boundaries, can set the stage for a sense of community. When I say I live in Mystic, people familiar with the area know what I mean. These people know Mystic's defining physical characteristics. The focus or center is the downtown, with its drawbridge, and the community is bounded by interstate I-95 on the north and Noank Village on the south, the top of Fort Hill on the west, and the A&P on Rte. 1 on the east. On the other hand, if I say I live in Groton, Connecticut, even those from this area have no idea where I might actually live. Groton, like Seabrook, Maryland, which is described at the beginning of this chapter, has "no there, there." Groton has no true center.

The emphasis on the center as a place to meet and greet can be contrasted with what some writers have mentioned in describing exurbia (contracted from extra-urban), the current suburban ring farthest from the urban core,

[81] Katz (1994), p. ix.

[82] Duany, A., & Plater-Zyberk, E. (1994). The neighborhood, the district and the corridor. In P. Katz (Ed.), *The new urbanism: Toward an architecture of community* (pp. xvii–xx), p. xvii.

another residential form in America experiencing growth. Writing about exurbia in the Sunday *New York Times Magazine*, David Brooks states:

> In these new, exploding suburbs, the geography, the very landscape of life, is new and unparalleled. In the first place, there are no centers, no recognizable borders to shape a sense of geographic identity. Throughout human history, most people have lived around some definable place – a tribal ring, an oasis, a river junction, a port, a town square. But in exurbia, each individual has his or her own polycentric nodes – the school, the church and the office park.[83]

But Brooks argues we need not pity those who live the exurban life. In fact, he argues that exurbia is the American Dream in its most current iteration. To give us some idea of the scale of exurbia, and also of its driving principle of ample parking, he provides a wonderful image. Talking about the parking lots of big box stores, he says: "These parking lots are so big that you could recreate the Battle of Gettysburg in the middle and nobody would notice at the stores on either end."[84]

Exurbia seems a far cry from the new urbanists and their emphasis on small scale and the neighborhood as a fundamental principle. And although physical layout can set the stage for communication to develop, it cannot create neighbors in the emotional sense of the word. Neighbors have to create neighborliness. The physical form cannot in and of itself create social interaction. But it can certainly make interaction more or less likely. In an article describing Americans' search for community as they "rethink the suburbs," Barbara Flanagan provides a telling statement by Plater-Zyberk. In this statement Plater-Zyberk discusses the importance of mixing housing types to avoid geographical enclaves by income level: "What started out as an aesthetic idea, has become social engineering."[85] In my judgment, that quotation attributes more determinism to architecture than physical form deserves.

It is too early to tell whether the design codes established by Duany, Plater-Zyberk, and others will promote the social interaction they advocate, and it is too early to tell whether the form of new urbanism permits enough flexibility for the richness of semilattices to develop. But many don't seem to care if we look at the interest in such communities as Celebration, Florida,

[83] Brooks, D. (2004, April 4). Our sprawling supersize utopia. *The New York Times Magazine*, pp. 46–51, p. 48.
[84] Ibid., p. 49.
[85] Flanagan, B. (1992, March). The search for the new hometown: Yearning for community, Americans rethink the suburbs. *Metropolitan Home*, pp. 55–58, 60–61, 111, p. 58.

where a lottery was required to select initial residents given the overflow of applicants!

To better understand new urbanist principles in action, let's take a closer look at three classic examples of new urbanism: Seaside, Celebration, and The Kentlands.

Seaside, Florida

The first new urbanist community that seems to have caught the public's imagination was Seaside, Florida. You cannot call Seaside a city, or even perhaps a town. It is not even a municipality. And it is fundamentally a resort community. Seaside is only about 80 acres, and the initial plan called for about 350 houses to be built (construction was to occur at a slow pace), with apartments and hotel rooms providing accommodations for about another 300. The "downtown" or civic focus was to include a town hall, school, open air market, post office, and some offices and retail space. The plan for Seaside emerged from the work of Andres Duany and Elizabeth Plater-Zyberk, the husband and wife planning duo (DPZ), and developer Robert Davis. There is a certain irony that much of the movie *The Truman Show* was filmed at Seaside, and the perfectly predictable Truman Burbank lived in this perfectly predictable and completely planned town. Fees from the movie shoot were used to pay for the school building.[86]

At Seaside, the town center is at the intersection of the North–South axis, which emphasizes its importance or prominence in the plan. Some argue that there is insufficient variety within the housing vocabulary established in the master plan, but think back to the limited number of housing types at Levittown. Although some critics describe Seaside as cute, such criticism has been balanced by considerable praise: "it is the master planners' subtler urban traditionalism – the town center, the civic buildings, the street grid and narrow streets, the lot sizes, alleys, and setbacks – that distinguishes Seaside from scores of instantly erected ersatz-old-fashioned places."[87] Thinking of such instant places, what comes to mind is a development I saw in Crystal Beach, Ontario. Near the sailing venue where my

---

[86] http://www.seasidefl.com/communityCharterSchool.asp.

[87] Andersen, K. (1991). Is Seaside too good to be true? In D. Mohney & K. Easterling (Eds.), *Seaside: Making a town in America* (pp. 42–47). Princeton, NJ: Princeton Architectural Press, p. 44.

daughter was staying was a Seaside-like development that seemed totally out of place in this aging rural community. The structures look like those at Seaside, but the development reflected no attention to the relationship of the houses to the street or sidewalks.

In fact, what has been lost in so many new towns, like Roosevelt Island or Chandigarh or Brasilia, is the relationship to the street. Seaside has this. Seaside is predicated on this relationship. Most houses in Seaside have porches, and the small front yards bring those enjoying their porches into close contact with those using the sidewalks. "Destinations" such as the post office and town hall are designed to be a 5-minute walk. All of the home sites were sold by the time of the publication in 1994 of Katz's book, and he reports that 225 houses were built by that time. Echoing my comments earlier about whether communities will actually develop from the new urbanist template, Katz wonders whether a fully functioning community will develop when construction of the commercial and public buildings is finished.[88]

In addition to its small size, Seaside differs from what most would consider the template of a new urbanist community in terms of price. A search of the real estate listings for Seaside in July 2007[89] revealed that all of the house listings were well over $1 million, with many of them nearing $3 million. The homesites (where construction had not occurred) varied from half a million dollars to almost $4 million, depending on proximity to the ocean. The housing listings are identified by such names as "Ivy," "Lemon Tree Resort," "Apple Pie & A La Mode," "Brickwalk," and "Equinox," names that certainly contribute to the idea of a community that communicates a certain sense of being practically perfect in every way. Although prices have dropped with the economic downturn, the real estate listings in July 2009 revealed that most of the homes were still more than $1 million, with "Wilder by the Sea" on the Gulf front (4 bedrooms, $3\frac{1}{2}$ baths, and 2331 sq. ft.) topping the list at $4,850,000. The affordability of new urbanist developments continues to spark comment and concern,[90] and the Congress for the New Urbanism has established an Affordability Initiative to promote a discussion of ways to increase the affordability of such developments.[91]

---

[88] Katz (1994), p. 4.

[89] http://seasidefl.com/realEstateListingsDetailsv2.asp?salesID=1177.

[90] See, for example, Walker, R. (2007, October). The affordability paradox. New urbanism is great in concept, but can it be affordable? http://www.tndtownpaper.com/Volume9/affordability_paradox.htm; and Can we afford new urbanism (2006, August 26). *Pine Magazine.* http://www.pinemagazine.com/site/article/can-we-afford-new-urbansim-103.

[91] Congress for the new Urbanism (2007). *Affordable Housing Initiative.* http://www.cnu.org.

Celebration, Florida

In November 2003, one of my students sent me a large Norman Rockwell-esque postcard illustrating Celebration. She said on the card, "It is incredible! The town is picture perfect, the residents are very friendly, and the whole place is wonderful to be in. [The] only problem [is] that I can't find information about the town because there are no more residences for sale. But I had to send you a postcard."

At one time, the official Web site of Celebration read as if Norman Rockwell *had* written it. In July 2007 these descriptions of Celebration were part of a Celebration real estate Web site.[92] The official Web site now takes you to a page headed "Front Porch: Celebration Community Web Site."[93] The earlier home pages themselves may have seemed a bit over the top. Judge for yourself:

> Take the best ideas from the most successful towns of yesterday and the technology of the new millennium, and synthesize them into a close-knit community that meets the needs of today's families. The founders of CELEBRATION started down a path of research, study, discovery, and enlightenment that resulted in one of the most innovative communities of the 20th century.
>
> A place where memories of a lifetime are made, it's more than a home; it's a community rich with old-fashioned appeal and an eye on the future. Homes are a blend of traditional southeastern exteriors with welcoming front porches and interiors that enhance today's lifestyles.
>
> A showcase for some of the world's leading architects, MARKET STREET at CELEBRATION is a unique collection of charming shops and tempting eateries nestled around a dazzling lakeside promenade. Always on the menu at MARKET STREET are flavorful styles, distinctive ambiance, and patio dining. Whether you're shopping or dining, MARKET STREET is cause for Celebration.
>
> In the spirit of neighborliness, CELEBRATION residents gather at front porches, park benches, recreational areas, and downtown events celebrating a place they call home. CELEBRATION is a community built on a foundation of cornerstones: Community, Education, Health, Technology, and a Sense of Place.

Celebration, a Disney development, is just less than 5000 acres; unlike Seaside, it qualifies as a "new town." When fully built out, the plan for

[92] http://www.celebrationfl34747.com/about_celebration.htm.
[93] http://www.celebration.fl.us.

Celebration was to accommodate about 20,000 people in 8,000 housing units; the original investment was slated to be about $2.5 billion. The 2000 U.S. Census reported 2376 residents with just more than 1000 housing units, and one of the official Celebration Web pages reported about 9000 residents, with 3500 homes and condominiums sold, 1.1 million sq. ft. of commercial office space, 49 businesses, and 17 restaurants on July 7, 2007.[94] Thus, the initial plan of 20,000 residents is far from realized. In fact, on one of the official Web site pages in July 2007, the current completed size of Celebration is anticipated to be 12,000 residents.[95]

The idea of mixed community is inherent in the plan, because single-family dwellings, townhouses, and apartments, along with much more expensive estate homes, are in the same neighborhood. At the same time, individual streets tend to be uniform in the type of housing they offer. The original prices for the homes, which have since skyrocketed, varied from apartments at the lower end ranging from monthly rents of $575–$1,125 and village houses from $200,000–$315,000 to estate houses from $350,000–$750,000. Real estate listings on July 5, 2007, showed a variety of prices, with a Mediterranean-style home with four bedrooms listed at $2,500,000. In July 2007, the lowest home prices started in the $300,000s, with the final phase, Artisan Park, offering 600 homes and condominiums on 160 acres.[96] Offering a range of housing options is laudable and critical to the concept of a mixed-income community, but the success of the development has pushed up the entry-level costs for all housing options.

Celebration is a kind of small town USA, with garages behind the houses and everything within walking distance. But reminiscent of Columbia, Maryland, and Levittown, there are prescribed styles, here six of them (Classical, Victorian, Colonial Revival, Coastal, Mediterranean, and French), and design restrictions, which could be viewed as limiting the visual richness many find engaging. Although the six styles, defined by a pattern book, are intermingled to create diversity, there is a heavy-handedness to this kind of visual effect. Yet the architecture of the civic buildings is a powerful display of creativity, as Celebration reflects the Disney Company's patronage of star architects. At the time of its development, Celebration was a veritable who's who of American architecture. Contributors include Graham Gund, the late Philip Johnson, Michael Graves, Venturi, Scott Brown & Associates, Cesar Pelli, the late Charles Moore, and Robert Stern.

[94] http://www.celebration.fl.us/celpress/celebrationpress.pdf.
[95] Ibid.   [96] Ibid.

The downtown has a main street, Market Street, with restaurants, civic buildings like a town hall and post office, a preview center for home sales in the community, and a cinema. There are some shops, although these tend to be fairly upscale and not particularly functional in nature – more gift shopping than dry cleaning. In 2005, a new 120,000-sq.-ft. retail center, Water Tower Place, was added, which provided more basic amenities like a gas station and video rental store. This retail space was developed by Unicorp.[97] There is also a school, set on a 26-acre campus initially including grades K–12, as well as a teaching academy to attract educators from around the nation for seminars to take place in this "model" of education. Some guidance for the curriculum at the school was also provided by the University of Minnesota Center for Cooperative Learning, and there have been teaching interns from a variety of universities (e.g., Stetson, Auburn, and the University of Central Florida). Having a school promotes the idea of a sustainable community.

Like Seaside, an image of Celebration as precious, cute, and practically perfect exists in the public's imagination. For example, in describing the problems with Al Gore's 2000 presidential campaign, Michael Tomasky wrote in a column on the national interest in *New York Magazine*, "It's the Celebration, Florida, of political campaigns, simulated with precision on the advice of the greatest minds in America down to the last (supposedly) randomly placed cobblestone but recognizable as false goods in an instant, evanescent, forgettable, even rather embarrassing."[98] This is not faint praise; it reflects considerable disdain for the concept of such a completely planned community. My brother John and his family recently visited Celebration over the winter holidays. Someone told them there would be "snow" in Celebration. Snow did, in fact, arrive in the form of something like Ivory Snow flakes blown on Market Street. The flakes may have created a picture-perfect moment in a completely planned community, but my brother said that his eyes began to burn!

From October 6, 1998, to January 10, 1999, the Cooper-Hewitt National Design Museum in New York City held an exhibit entitled "The Architecture of Reassurance: Designing the Disney Theme Parks." The phrase "architecture of reassurance" speaks to the idea that Disney theme parks are a place for families, a place for peace of mind. The phrase "the architecture of reassurance" applies to Celebration as well. The exhibit "explores the

[97] Ibid.
[98] Tomasky, M. (1999, November 8). The wrong stuff. *New York Magazine*, p. 26.

connections between the real world and fantasy in shaping an architecture of pleasure."[99] Many goals articulated for the theme parks, such as creating an environment for pedestrians, are at work in Celebration. The Main Street of the theme park is critical to its identity, just as Market Street is to Celebration. Under a section titled "Main Street, U. S. A." in the exhibit brochure, it says: "Drawings of Main Street, U. S. A. present a streetscape based on Walt Disney's memories of his childhood town of Marceline, Missouri. With its scaled-down street fronts, Main Street evokes an ideal town as seen from the perspective of a child. Walt Disney intended visitors to be filled with a sense of mastery, as if playing with model trains and dollhouses."[100] In many ways, towns like Celebration are about mastery as well. They may provide a sense of reassurance and control in what has become an unpredictable world, even more so than at the time the town was conceived.

The exhibition culminates with a look at Disneyland's impact on the real world – its influence on shopping malls, restaurants, and city planning – as well as at Disney's place in our collective psyche. Disney's original experimental community, EPCOT, or Experimental Prototype Community of Tomorrow, which had been planned for Florida, was not constructed. But in a sense Celebration has become the embodiment of a community of tomorrow, based on the concept of Main Street and new urbanism.

I visited Celebration with an Environmental Design Research Association (EDRA) tour when the annual conference was held in Orlando in 1999. Our tour guide was a resident selected to show us the town and its housing (see Figure 1.2), so the sense of satisfaction he expressed about living there needs to be put in the context of his position as a "selected" insider. But while we were walking around we spoke to a number of teenagers who lived in the community (who happened to be walking by and were not preselected). When we asked what they liked about the community, they commented favorably on the proximity to friends by walking or bicycling.

Celebration has experienced backlash in the press, much of it concerned with what were considered failings of the school to meet the needs of all children who attended. A book entitled *The Celebration Chronicles*[101] by Andrew Ross spends a good deal of time on the issue of the school and its shortcomings, including the disconnection between parents' expectations about how an orderly school should be run and theorists' interest in how the

---

[99] *The architecture of reassurance: Designing the Disney theme parks.* (1998/1999). New York: Cooper-Hewitt National Design Museum, Exhibit brochure, p. 1.
[100] Ibid., p. 2
[101] Ross, A. (1999). *The Celebration chronicles: Life, liberty, and the pursuit of property value in Disney's new town.* New York: Random House.

FIGURE 1.2. Celebration housing

process of learning occurs (see also Frantz and Collins's *Celebration, U. S. A.: Living in Disney's Brave New Town*[102]). There were also problems with such practical issues as low pay for teachers. The school is actually operated by the Osceola County School District in Florida, not by Disney. In response to parents' dissatisfaction, more structure has been added to the curriculum, and grades are now awarded in the high school because parents argued that portfolios limited their children's competitiveness in applying to colleges. But the biggest change was brought about by economic issues – pressure of the growth of the student population in Osceola County and the projected growth in Celebration. In an arrangement that served both the Celebration Company and the school district, the Celebration Company was to donate

---

[102] Frantz, D., & Collins, C. (1999). *Celebration, U. S. A.: Living in Disney's brave new town.* New York: Henry Holt and Co.

50 acres to the county to build a new high school, in the process saving itself the cost of building more schools as Celebration's population increases. But this agreement meant abandoning the K–12 concept as Celebration's high school students would attend the new regional high school.[103] The original Celebration school would serve students in grades K–8. In 2008, the Osceola County School District Web site listed both a Celebration multilevel school and a Celebration high school.[104]

Beyond difficulties with the school, other criticisms have involved a failure to achieve racial diversity in the community. For example, Jayson Blair[105] writes in *The New York Times* that the community failed to achieve its goals of diversity.[106] The 2000 Census data essentially reflect such a claim. Osceola County, home to Celebration, had a population of 79.9 percent White and 15 percent Black (of those classified as one race).[107] In Celebration, using CDP (Census designated place data), the 2736-person population as reflected in the 2000 Census is 93.6 percent White and 1.7 percent Black.[108] Disney is given credit for trying to make diversity a reality, but Blair notes that achieving such diversity is much more difficult in reality than in a plan. Blair argues that one of the difficulties may have been linked to a recruiting strategy that was not sufficiently aggressive. He noted that few Blacks or Hispanics attended the open houses, nor did these racial groups sign up for the housing lottery. In this article, Celebration is contrasted with Columbia, Maryland, which is acknowledged as more successful in establishing diversity, perhaps because the founder, James Rouse, described as a "socially conscious" developer, wanted to create a community with diversity in race as well as age and class.[109] Reflecting his vision that Columbia should be a garden where people thrive, the community logo represents people

[103] Frantz, D. (1999, August 1). The Nation: Disney's brave new town; Trouble at the happiest school on earth. *The New York Times*. http://www.nytimes.com/1999/08/01/weekinreview/the-nation-disney-s-brave-new-town-trouble-at-the-happiest-school-on-earth.html.

[104] http://www.osceola.k12.fl.us/Pages_2004/02_01Calendars.asp.

[105] Although Blair is, in fact, the Jayson Blair, a former writer for the *New York Times* who was discredited for fabricating stories, I include his perspective but provide data from the Census that I looked up separately from his article. He reports being born in Columbia, Maryland, which figures in the article.

[106] Blair, J. (2001, September 23). Failed Disney vision: Integrated city. *The New York Times*, National Report, A21.

[107] http://factfinder.census.gov (Florida by County – GCT – PL. Race and Hispanic or Latino: 2000).

[108] http://factfinder.census.gov (Celebration CDP. Florida – Fact Sheet – American FactFinder).

[109] Burkhart, L. C. (1981). *Old values in a new town: The politics of race and class in Columbia, Maryland*. New York: Praeger, p. v.

with their arms upstretched, emerging from a common base.[110] Columbia was opened in the late 1960s, and the first decennial U.S. Census data for Columbia are available for 1970. These data show that in Howard County, where Columbia is located, the percentage of African Americans and other races (one category in the 1970 Census) was 8.6 percent (within a population of 61,911). By contrast, the 1970 data for Columbia (unincorporated) were 14.1 percent for the category African American and other races (within a population of 8,815).[111] Blair comments that it may be much harder today to establish the kind of diversity Columbia achieved because there may be less idealism than in the 1960s. Further, he reports on a trend of at least a decade for the suburbs to be segregated, especially in the South and the Sun Belt, according to demographers.

The pressure of perfection in every realm may have been one reason Disney seems to have tried to separate itself from Celebration, or at least its commercial core. In 2004, the Celebration Company, Disney's real estate development division, sold the 18-acre town center to Lexin Capital, a private real estate investment company.

As may be the case with many planned communities, a particular type of person is drawn to the idea of living in an environment with a certain uniform quality of maintenance or presentation. In other words, there is a substantial component of self-selection in this kind of housing choice. Such self-selection may be associated with a high level of satisfaction for residents. We will examine this issue of self-selection and its impact later in the chapter when we turn to the research available on new urbanist communities.

The Kentlands, Maryland

Like Seaside, The Kentlands involved the design work of Andres Duany and Elizabeth Plater-Zyberk, who participated in a design charrette for the master plan of the 350+ acre site on Kent Farm near Gaithersburg, Maryland. A design charrette typically involves an intense period of activity, focused on a particular design problem (e.g., revitalizing a downtown). Often designers and the community stakeholders or clients meet for a period of days to work on the project.

Seaside is often regarded as a seasonal resort community. The Kentlands, on the other hand, presents a better test of year-round new urbanist concepts. The master plan includes a retail center, at the juncture of two busy

---

[110] Ibid., p. 20.

[111] U.S. Bureau of the Census (1973). *Census of Population: 1970. Volume 1, Characteristics of the Population. Part 22, Maryland*. Washington, D.C.: U.S. Government Printing Office.

routes, and six distinct neighborhoods that include a mix of elements, from housing to civic structures and green space. The elementary school is appropriately named after Rachel Carson, the well-known environmentalist. A variety of housing options is presented in each neighborhood (single-family dwellings, rental apartments, carriage houses, and townhouses). The community was not created by a single builder, and participation by a range of developers has been argued to contribute to the community's architectural diversity. The master plan calls for 1600 residential units slated for 5000 residents.[112] The Kentlands has been the focus of at least one major research project to contrast it with a more typical suburb,[113] and this study will be discussed in the section on research on new urbanist communities. A particularly nice array of photographs of The Kentlands, taken over a period of 4 years, is available on the Web.[114] The site illustrates the urban center emphasis of Market Street, its retail focus, and the variety of housing types available, with row houses cited as the most prevalent form.

In June 2007, the community hired a consulting firm to conduct a telephone poll of 300 households in The Kentlands about their views of the development.[115] This survey provides a positive image of the community. When residents were asked to provide words that would communicate to friends what The Kentlands "is really like," 25 percent cited "friendly, caring community," 23 percent cited "small town appeal," and another 21 percent said "great place to live." The description "unique community" was offered by 14 percent.[116] To the statement "I think having architectural standards are (sic) important to maintaining the new urban lifestyle we have here in The Kentlands," 88 percent agreed.[117] In general people were satisfied with the maintenance of common facilities. Many of the questions in the survey focused on the source of the news that people would prefer to obtain information about the community, with some form of a community newsletter far and away preferred over a Web site (although 80 percent reported having a high-speed Internet connection). Of the respondents, 64 percent do not have children under the age of 18 living at home; 39 percent have lived at The Kentlands 9 or more years; 37 percent for 4–8 years; 42 percent lived in a house; 23 percent in a townhouse;

---

[112] Katz (1994).

[113] Kim, J., & Kaplan, R. (2004). Physical and psychological factors in sense of community: New urbanist Kentlands and nearby Orchard Village. *Environment and Behavior, 36,* 313–340.

[114] http://www.beyonddc.co/features/kentlands.html.

[115] http://kentlandsusa.com/kentlands/docs/survey_2007_presentation.pdf.

[116] Ibid., p. 4.   [117] Ibid., p. 5.

27 percent in a condominium; and 89 percent were owners as opposed to renters.

The issue of who is attracted to such new urbanist communities begins to be revealed in such data about Seaside, Celebration, and The Kentlands. Certainly one theme emerging is that new urbanist communities, at least the ones consistently featured in the media, are expensive and financially out of reach of most American families.

A National Phenomenon?

Although Seaside, Celebration, and The Kentlands are essentially East Coast locations, the new urbanist phenomenon is widespread. Whereas this chapter focuses on the United States, new urbanist communities have taken hold in England, Australia, Canada, Portugal, and even in Bhutan. If you enter the words "new urbanism" into the database LexisNexis, which primarily covers newspapers and magazines, you get a sense of how widespread the new urbanist concept is in the United States. There are news articles about developments in such places as St. Charles, Missouri, where the president of Whittaker Homes, Greg Whittaker, states that his company's development The New Town at St. Charles is his most successful.[118] "In the hectic atmosphere of today's world, people seem to be craving a more comfortable atmosphere reminiscent of towns in days gone by," Whittaker says.[119] Whittaker used DPZ as the planners, who in turn used the charrette format to involve residents. Whittaker's development company took what it had learned in the process of this development and packaged "the process they painstakingly went through in turning their vision into reality. Called 'New Town in a Box,' it contains the processes for marketing, product testing, floor plans, legal documents and other pertinent material for recreating a TND like New Town."[120] I think Christopher Alexander would shudder at the thought of a new town in a box!

There are hundreds of new urbanist communities spanning the coasts of the United States. These communities take a number of different forms, from those that can be described as infill mixed use to those developed at the perimeter of communities as a kind of edge development. Some of these communities also reflect a greater range of affordability than is true for Seaside, Celebration, and The Kentlands. In the section on McMansions we will see a parallel to McMansions described as oversized houses in

[118] Jarasek, M. (2006, October 1). http://www.housingzone.com/article/CA6377004.html.
[119] Ibid., para. 3.   [120] Ibid., para 19.

existing neighborhoods (infill) and such houses developed in new areas (greenfields). Infill essentially involves the redevelopment of areas where construction already exists. Crawford Square in Pittsburgh, a mixed-income community, is an example of an infill development targeted to a range of incomes. Greenfield development could be used to describe new urbanist communities built in an area at the perimeter of a community. Laguna West outside of Sacramento is an example of this kind of development.

Eventually, working our way to the other coast, we have examples of new urbanism such as that in Mukilteo, Washington.[121] The Mukilteo Village Center, finished in 2002, provides a new urbanist mixed use of residential and commercial space and won a Vision 2020 award from the Puget Sound Regional Council in 2003. Reminiscent of European towns, the streets are narrow, and there is a public plaza where outdoor dining occurs in addition to green spaces with public benches. New urbanism, though certainly more popular along the East Coast than anywhere else, has more than a toehold on urban planning in America. It does not appear to be a fad. If anything, its popularity is growing given its benefits on health.

In North America, the largest developments prepared with new urbanist principles are in Markham, Ontario, where approximately 150,000 people will be accommodated in these new greenfield developments. Conveniently, from the standpoint of a comparison, the new urbanist developments in Markham are essentially across the street from conventional suburban developments.[122] The results of a study of these contrasting approaches to development in Markham indicated that in terms of units per acre (UPA) the new urbanist development had "76% higher gross residential density (7.9 vs. 4.5 upa) and almost 70% higher population density."[123] These data address some of the criticism of new urbanism as just another form of sprawl or an approach that ignores the preference for single-family detached homes (see, e.g., the work of Gordon and Richardson discussed later in this chapter).

NEW URBANISM AND HEALTH

Before moving on to critical comments about new urbanism, one more benefit should be offered: health. Although walkability was a founding principle

---

[121] Puget Sound Regional Council Vision 2020 2003 award winners. http://www.psrc.org/projects/awards/winners2003.htm.

[122] Gordon, D., & Vipond, S. (2005). Gross density and new urbanism: Comparing conventional and new urbanist suburbs in Markham, Ontario. *Journal of the American Planning Association, 71*(1), 41–54.

[123] Ibid., p. 46.

of new urbanism, the benefits of walking have taken on new meaning since the new urbanism movement began. Yes, walkability cuts down on energy use from automobiles and other sources of transportation using fossil fuels; walking also burns calories. The importance of that benefit of new urbanism has become much stronger given the increasing attention on Americans' battle with obesity. In an article headed "Less sprawl, less fat, less frenzy" reprinted in *The New London Day*, we are told that obesity is not our fault. Experts state, "It's the result of urban sprawl, a frenetic lifestyle and global food policy."[124] In addition to better eating habits, including that triple threat of fruits, vegetables, and fish, the physical environment is cited as playing a role in health. The by-now-familiar concept of walkability is highlighted in the article. The author makes a case that the Smart Growth (new urbanism) movement will be aided by the overwhelming problem of obesity in the United States.

This same association is made in another article, "Link between health and sprawl makes 'smart' growth look smarter."[125] At the same time, Smart Growth is presented as a "difficult sell" in many communities due to zoning restrictions and the reluctance of developers to take on projects involving a prolonged process of gaining variances. Also a source of resistance is the NIMBY (not in my backyard) reaction of community members to the idea of apartments and commercial establishments nestled within neighborhoods of single-family dwellings. We may be reaching the tipping point (no pun intended) in this country in terms of the health crisis we face, and as a number of articles suggest, new urbanism may be one of the beneficiaries of the need to change the way we live. But it is not clear whether less affluent homebuyers will be willing to pay more, up to 10 percent to 15 percent, to cover the cost of the additional sidewalks, streets, alleyways, and landscaping typically needed in places such as Southern Village, in Chapel Hill, North Carolina, featured in the article.[126] If federal funds were diverted from roadways to public spaces, private property owners would not need to cover so much of the additional cost to create environments that support healthy living.

Planners are becoming more interested in the potential relationship between obesity and land use. In San Francisco, researchers looked at use

---

[124] Creager, E. (2003, June 2). Less sprawl, less fat, less frenzy. *The New London Day*, pp. C1–C2, p. C1.

[125] Macaluso, N. (2003, June 10). Link between health and sprawl makes "smart" growth look smarter. *The New London Day*, p. C1.

[126] Ibid.

of the automobile, body mass index (BMI), and land use.[127] BMI is typically calculated by taking one's weight in pounds, dividing by one's height in inches (squared), and multiplying that quotient by 703. In this study, four areas were identified that were similar in population density, racial makeup, and median household income. In the summer of 2005, residents of these four areas were randomly selected to be interviewed in public places (although in all fairness the authors point out that the sample was not truly random). Typically research has shown that as density decreases, use of the auto increases, and the expectation is that BMI will increase. The researchers used a four-destination scale (how often respondents drove their autos to the grocery store, another shopping area, work or school, or a friend's house). Controlling for a variety of variables, the results indicated that auto use and population were inversely correlated. Further, those with higher levels of auto use indeed reported higher BMIs.

CRITICISMS OF NEW URBANIST COMMUNITIES

Not everyone agrees with the new urbanist approach, of course, even with the added emphasis on health benefits and energy conservation. Criticism has included the affluence of many who purchase residences in new urbanist communities, failure to reduce sprawl and increase urban densities, an overly optimistic vision of the ability to change how we use the automobile in this country, and even a misunderstanding of what sense of community means.[128]

Traditional academic authorities writing in peer-reviewed publications have debated the issue of sprawl. For example, Gordon and Richardson[129] have made what Ewing (in the same issue of the same journal) calls a "cottage industry"[130] in challenging the benefits of compact development. Ewing argues that a major difference between his point of view and the view of Gordon and Richardson relates to the way compact development is defined. Ewing states that his view is more inclusive, bringing together some of each of the following: concentration of employment, clustering of housing, and mixing of land uses, but rejecting the notion that compact development must involve high density and be monocentric (e.g., a single

[127] Pendola, R., & Gen, S. (2007). BMI, auto use, and the urban environment in San Francisco. *Health & Place, 13,* 551–556.

[128] Beauregard, R. A. (2002). New urbanism: Ambiguous certainties. *Journal of Architectural and Planning Research, 19*(3), 181–194.

[129] Gordon, P., & Richardson, H. W. (1997). Are compact cities a desirable planning goal? *Journal of the American Planning Association, 63*(1), 95–106.

[130] Ewing, R. (1997). Is Los Angeles-style sprawl desirable? *Journal of the American Planning Association, 63*(1), 107–126.

center such as a downtown). Ewing argues that it is not spatial patterns of sprawl that are undesirable, but the impact of those patterns, and he notes that Gordon and Richardson (i.e., those representing the counterargument) do not address the psychological and social impact of sprawl. With regard to compact developments, Gordon and Richardson oppose the idea of zoning regulations that require such patterns. Ewing acknowledges the validity of one of Gordon and Richardson's major points, that the American public prefers the detached single-family dwelling as a housing type. At the same time, he notes that although the public may prefer single-family dwellings, the public does not prefer the suburbs, the typical setting in which single-family housing occurs. Gordon and Richardson and those in favor of low-density spatial patterns see suburbanization as an effective approach to lowering congestion. This debate between spatial patterns of varying densities is important to continue. At the very least, Americans deserve choices from one end of the density spectrum to the other.

Beyond criticisms about spatial patterns leveled by Gordon and Richardson, other criticisms point to the idea that new urbanists have a certain naïveté, because "the small towns we idealize never really existed."[131] In other words, new urbanists are naïve to think that small-town America was wholesome and wonderful and that recreating the physical plan of those communities can somehow produce these elusive values and responses. In that article, Barbara Flanagan goes on to say, "Other new town critics include celebrated architects who decry their stylistic conservatism, and some developers, like one in Reston, Virginia, who assails the Kentlands project for not investing enough to attract retailers."[132] And there are critics such as Tim Padgett, writing in *Time*, questioning the ways in which we are trying to save suburbia. Seaside is criticized as being a "cute little instant town" too far from job centers.[133] Padgett goes on to discuss the growth of neotraditional (new urbanist) neighborhoods and how many have been constructed and are in the planning stages. Citing the results of housing surveys conducted by developers, he comments that having community space, as a kind of renewal of the concept, is the attraction of such new urbanist communities. As one indication of such attraction, a developer had expected about 200 people to show up when a new neotraditional community was opened, "a New England-style traditional neighborhood development near Indianapolis, Indiana called Centennial," but 2000 came – "ready to buy into the new small town of their dreams."[134] Rather than harshly criticizing

---

[131] Flanagan (1992), p. 111.   [132] Ibid.

[133] Padgett, T. (1999, August 16). Saving suburbia: Families that seek a sense of community are moving to new suburbs designed to resemble small towns. *Time*, pp. 50–51, p. 50.

[134] Ibid., p. 51.

new urbanism, Padgett identifies its existence as a movement for the readers of *Time*. But his description of these new urbanist communities as "cute little instant towns near major cities"[135] reveals shadings of his perspective.

In any review or analysis, negative or positive, it is important to consider the source of the review. For example, a negative review of Laguna West, designed by Peter Calthorpe, was published in *Demographia*, which is described as "pro-choice" with regard to urban development.[136] The article claims that Laguna West violates many new urbanist principles by having wide streets and cul-de-sacs, claiming that the community substantially fails to achieve neotraditional ideals. The pictures that accompany this article do in fact show wide streets, cul-de-sacs, and garages in front of houses. Of course the description using Calthorpe's own materials is different: "The streets are narrowed, tree-lined, and connected to the town center, as well as to the arterial. At least 50 percent of the houses have front porches with garages in the rear; some are on the alleyways."[137] Naturally the pictures shown in the Calthorpe materials illustrate the Town Hall facing a civic plaza and single-family homes with parking in the rear.

In June 2007 I visited Laguna West, about 10 miles outside of Sacramento. Truthfully, the residential parts of the community I saw by driving around the town hall, public parks, and small retail center were more like the *Demographia* analysis than Calthorpe's presentation. By driving around major roads and the center of the community I somehow missed the clear "new urbanist" sections. I did notice with some humor that many streets are named after individuals who figure prominently in the history of urban planning and design including Buckminster Fuller, Walter Gropius, and Lewis Mumford (East and West Mumford Court)!

RESEARCH ON NEW URBANIST COMMUNITIES

OK. Is new urbanism's impact on American design a lot of smoke and mirrors? We have taken a look at the principles and a number of examples, but what about evidence? What do we "know" about these communities, the people who live there, and their reactions?

Social Science Research: A Slippery Slope

Unlike most laboratory animals, humans are incredibly complex, have diverse learning histories, and are rarely, if ever, *randomly assigned to*

[135] Ibid., p. 50.
[136] http://www.demographia.com/db-nu-calgw.htm.
[137] http://calthorpe.com/Project%20Sheets/Laguna%20West.pdf, para. 3.

condition. The hallmark of an experiment is that you randomly assign your participants, and then you differentially manipulate some aspect of their experience. In the simplest form of an experiment, one group receives the treatment, such as a new drug, and is called the experimental group, and the other group receives a placebo (e.g., a pill that has no drug component) and is called the "control" group. If you can keep tight control of your experimental conditions, it is possible to make some *causal* statements about the effect of your drug. Real life, as we know, is not constrained in this manner. In research reviewed here, people are not randomly assigned to condition and there is no tight control over their lives. For those reasons, no one can legitimately make causal statements about the relationship between physical design and behavior. What we are entitled to say is that such-and-such an outcome (e.g., greater sense of community) *is more likely* to be associated with such-and-such a circumstance (e.g., new urbanism) than with some other circumstance. But why this is true we cannot say.

With regard to the issue of random assignment to condition (which would be like picking a name at random from a phone book and also picking at random where that person lives), it just doesn't happen. People generally choose where they will live, and we call this self-selection. Self-selection is a problematic component of social science research. Within a set of possibilities, people *choose* where they want to live for many reasons (ranging from income and schools to race to life cycle to . . . and on and on and on). We cannot control any of those variables, nor can we completely match people on the factors that shape their lives. So, remember the caveat that the research in this chapter (and this book) is about more or less likely associations of variables, not cause and effect.

Studies of New Urbanist Communities

More than 30 years ago, the late Donald Appleyard, professor of urban design at Berkeley, and the late Mark Lintell, an environmental planner, wrote a seminal article in *The Journal of the American Institute of Planners*. Entitled "The environmental quality of city streets: The residents' viewpoint,"[138] the research documented the kind of neighboring that took place in San Francisco on three city blocks described as having streets with light, moderate, or heavy traffic. This article showed that neighboring activities were much more likely to occur on the light street than on the heavy street. In a sense, this empirical article is one of the early indicators of the role physical design plays in the relationships between the street and neighboring.

[138] Appleyard & Lintell (1972).

In forming their opinions of new residential environments, most Americans rely on sound bites and limited coverage in newspapers and popular magazines. In many cases these snippets suggest causal relationships with the use of verbs such as "influence" and "affect." To understand the potential impact of new urbanist developments, we need to look at what we hope are well-designed empirical studies.

One of the few published studies on the psychological impact of new urbanist communities is based on a University of Michigan doctoral dissertation by Joongsub Kim, coauthored with Rachel Kaplan, a member of his dissertation committee.[139] In this study Kim examined the claim that sense of community is promoted in new urbanist communities, and he took as his target the new urbanist community The Kentlands, planned by the design team of Duany and Plater-Zyberk. As a comparison community, Kim took nearby "Orchard Village," the pseudonym given to this more traditional suburb.

The study looked at the differences in how people felt about sense of community, particularly in terms of the physical qualities of the environment that might contribute to those feelings of community. The authors looked at the role of pedestrianism (the degree to which the layout promoted walking), community identity (the degree to which people thought the community as a whole had an identity, a sense of uniqueness, and significance), community attachment (the degree to which people felt committed and connected to their community), and social interaction (how much contact they had with other members of the community, casual neighboring, and encounters).

Both communities, The Kentlands and Orchard Village, are located in Gaithersburg, Maryland, about a half-hour outside of Washington, D.C. The Kentlands, a 352-acre development, was designed in 1988. As previously discussed in this chapter, what makes The Kentlands different from typical suburban developments and characterizes it as a new urbanist community is narrower streets, greater density, wider diversity of housing types, and a more obvious town center. Cars are parked in back in the network of alleys, houses are on small lots and are set close to the street. There is an emphasis on walking, with many sidewalks and footpaths. Almost a third of the acreage of the development is devoted to open space. Density for The Kentlands is 7.2 units per acre, whereas at Orchard Village it is 2.8 units/acre.[140]

---

[139] Kim & Kaplan (2004).   [140] Ibid.

Orchard Village, on the other hand, would be recognized as a more typical suburban development with wider streets incorporating many cul-de-sacs. There is much less variety in the types of houses; they are set farther back on the lot and the lots themselves are bigger (average lot size is 8050 sq. ft. vs. 5300 sq. ft. for The Kentlands).[141] There are fewer sidewalks, cars are parked in driveways that face the street or on the street itself, and the setback of the houses from the sidewalk is greater. The study reports the average home price for a single-family dwelling was $360,000 for The Kentlands and $340,000 for Orchard Village. Figures for condominiums were $200,000 for The Kentlands and $150,000 for Orchard Village.

Of course we want to know whether there are differences in sense of community between the two developments that can be causally attributed to design. The underlying problem with this and other similar studies is that the residents self-select their community. The authors addressed this by asking questions regarding motivation for people's residential choices and then controlled for differences in how sense of community was valued as people made their housing decision. Even when such initial differences were controlled, respondents from The Kentlands reported a higher sense of community than did respondents from Orchard Village.

Are there any drawbacks to living in The Kentlands? Some, it appears. Among them, the authors point to residents' comments about the impact of higher density, including the narrow separation between single-family homes and lack of privacy. Sometimes there can be too much neighboring, with associated politics and infighting.

Another of our classic new urbanist communities, Seaside, has also been studied. Jeanne Plas and Susan Lewis from Vanderbilt took as their focus the premise that Seaside was a place "where the environment and architecture would compel sense of community."[142] The authors comment that Seaside's urban code contributes to the visual coherence of the community and in turn may be associated with the formation of a cohesive social unit. "The fences, diverse cottages with common architectural elements, wide porches, footpaths and streets leading to common public areas all are visual reminders that Seaside's major raison d'être is the development of the spirit of community within residents and visitors alike."[143]

Although the Census of homeowners exceeded 1000 when the article was published in 1996, fewer than 25 families lived at Seaside full time. So

---

[141] Ibid.

[142] Plas, J. M., & Lewis, S. E. (1996). Environmental factors and sense of community in a planned town. *American Journal of Community Psychology, 24,* 109–143, p. 111.

[143] Ibid., p. 116.

this study is more about annual visitors who rent cottages than about the perception of year-round homeowners. As discussed earlier in this chapter, Seaside is also an expensive place to own a house, and Plas and Lewis state that property values have increased by as much as 25 percent each year over the preceding decade. Seaside's popularity as a community has put it out of reach as the kind of residential environment with a diversity of income levels, and the authors argue that Seaside would not be affordable for the vast majority of Americans. Limitation of diversity by cost is a drawback to many new urbanist communities that have received attention in the press.

One might also want to question how representative this population is of those who agree with new urbanist principles, and of the U.S. population in general. The authors comment that Seasiders, both owners and renters, are essentially more liberal than not, more "green" than not in terms of subscribing to ecological principles, and more wealthy than not.

To assess sense of community, interviews were conducted with owners, renters, and workers. However, of the 125 interviewed, only 14 were owner residents. Interviewees were asked one main question, which was to talk about the strengths and weaknesses of Seaside. Almost all responses were categorized as positive rather than negative.[144] Among the comments shared in the article were, "Why aren't all towns designed like this – in a way that makes you feel like you belong and gets you making friends again?"[145] Further, "[m]ore than 70% of the people in this sample who work, reside, and visit in Seaside directly or indirectly cited sense-of-community variables as the most important reasons why they were drawn to this particular Gulf of Mexico town."[146]

Although it may be appropriate to take these comments at face value, it is possible that the publicity surrounding Seaside in part shaped people's perceptions of what Seaside offers its residents. In this way, it is more likely people would respond with comments related to sense of community, rather than to some other aspect, if an image involving sense of community is the image of Seaside familiar to them.

It is important to see if we can move beyond the research of Plas and Lewis on Seaside to a better-designed study with a less lopsided sample (because so many of the respondents in the study of Seaside were renters). Such a study is offered in the research of Barbara Brown and Vivian Cropper[147] of the

[144] Ibid., p. 134.   [145] Ibid., p. 137.

[146] Ibid., p. 137.

[147] Brown, B. B., & Cropper, V. L. (2001). New urban and standard suburban sub divisions: Evaluating psychological and social goals. *Journal of the American Planning Association*, *67*, 402–419.

University of Utah, who examined whether greater sense of community exists in new urbanist communities than in typical subdivisions. The researchers asked whether more informal interactions occur and whether more use is made of public spaces and recreation areas in new urbanist subdivisions than in traditional subdivisions, which they call standard sub-urban subdivisions. Is mixed use (and its impact on site design) a concept embraced by residents of new urbanist subdivisions?

To answer these questions, the researchers compared comparable new urbanist subdivisions and standard suburban subdivisions (identified by Realtors) in Salt Lake City. The subdivisions were comparable in terms of time frame of construction (1994–1996), sale prices, and square footages. The average home sale price in the new urbanist subdivisions was $194,122, whereas that for homes in standard suburban subdivisions was $196,534, and the initial selling prices when the subdivisions were opened were similar (≈$140,000). Consistent with new urbanist principles, the new urbanist subdivision homes were more likely to have front porches, shallow front yards, no cul-de-sac streets, back alleys, and narrower (50 foot) streets. In the standard suburban subdivision homes, garages were more likely to face the street and figure prominently in the house's façade, houses were likely to be on cul-de-sacs, and the streets were 60 foot. It should be noted that lot sizes were substantially larger in the traditional subdivisions (47 percent larger) than in the new urbanist subdivisions: ≈.24 versus .16 acre.

Findings indicated there were marked differences between residents of the two communities on five of the seven topics in the study's questionnaire. However, scores on a measure of sense of community were not significantly different. Residents of the new urbanist subdivisions did report a greater number of neighboring behaviors, possibly related to greater use of outdoor space. "The fact that NUS residents can live on much smaller lots without experiencing an erosion of community or other problems counters implied claims made by critics of New Urbanism that civility requires large buffers of space between houses. Good fences may make good neighbors, but large lawns do not necessarily make better ones."[148]

Although a generally positive picture of the new urbanist community emerges, residents feel the design creates certain challenges. Yes, those in the new urbanist development reported more social contacts, took part in more outdoor activities, and thought it was important to have accessory apartments (separate apartments over the garage) as well as back alleys (to a greater extent than was true for those in the standard subdivision). Yet,

---

[148] Ibid., p. 413.

the density in the new urbanist community created problems with cars (too many in the alleys). As the authors point out, new urbanism ironically has not solved the challenge of the automobile, especially because most families have at least two cars, and often one of these is a large SUV (as might be needed in the winter in a place like Salt Lake City).

In this study set in Salt Lake City, Brown and Cropper reported the widespread use of front porches, following earlier research where Brown and her colleagues asked whether front porches are just about nostalgic sentimentalism.[149] Their earlier research was set in Utah and Georgia and involved interviewees from two samples: the 1920s sample (anyone who recalled porch use between 1920–1955) and the 1986 and later sample (anyone who recalled porch use in the post-1986 time period). To get memories from that earlier time period (1920–1955), often touted as a design ideal by new urbanist practitioners, students who did the interviewing were required to interview at least one "older" person. Front porches, in any kind of housing, were the target because these design features play a significant role in new urbanism residences where porches are often set close to the edge or front yard. For example, in Seaside many such porches are just 16 feet back of the picket fence in front.

The results of the Brown et al. study indicate that porches were not just there for "looks"; they were used. The communities involved were not based on new urbanist designs. The authors suggest that new urbanists may have missed or at least underestimated the wide range of benefits, both social and psychological, of the front porch. Porches support a wide range of activities from those of a solitary nature (e.g., reading) to those of a communal nature. Porches provide a place for household members to interact and a place for family, friends, and neighbors to interact. Their research also highlights the flexible use of the porch; it can be used for many things (e.g., to talk, watch passers-by, read, eat, date, play games, sleep, and do arts and crafts), not just one activity. Although the authors write about the decline of the porch in the more recent (post-1986) sample, they nevertheless note the endurance of the role of the front porch. They suggest perhaps the new urbanists could focus on the use of these porches as opposed to the greater emphasis some new urbanists place on civic spaces and public places.

Until there are more new urbanism communities to study, researcher Hollie Lund at California State Polytechnic University in Pomona suggests substituting traditional neighborhoods built at the beginning of the

---

[149] Brown, B. B., Burton, J. R., & Sweaney, A. L. (1998). Neighbors, households, and front porches: New urbanist community tool or mere nostalgia? *Environment and Behavior, 30,* 579–600.

20th century. Her research focused on pedestrian behavior and the social benefits that accrue when people walk.[150] She compared a traditional neighborhood, built before 1945, with an automobile-oriented neighborhood (i.e., suburb), which she called a modern suburban neighborhood, built between 1950–1985. Both neighborhoods were in Portland, Oregon.

This was a relatively small study, with 57 respondents from the traditional neighborhood and 49 from the modern suburban neighborhood. Lund's findings indicate a higher sense of community in the traditional neighborhood than in the modern suburban neighborhood, as measured by a sense of community scale.[151] The most influential of the subjective variables was people's view of walking in the neighborhood. Further, scores on the sense of community scale were positively correlated with more than half the items in the perceptions of walking scale. But we again face the chicken or the egg problem. Do residents select the neighborhood *because* they perceive that it provides a particular kind of physical environment? But Lund also collected attitudinal responses involving pro-transit, pro-environment, and pro-automobile outlooks. These attitudinal responses show no neighborhood differences, so a self-selection bias with regard to these factors cannot account for the difference in the higher sense of community in the traditional neighborhood than in the modern suburban neighborhood.

Research on Cost and Trade-offs

Beyond the physical aspect of design, another theme in the literature, usually associated with those critical of new urbanism, is that such communities cost more than traditional subdivisions. Given that issue, one can reasonably raise questions about what costs people are willing to pay for these kinds of communities and/or what they might be willing to give up to have such communities. Ivonne Audirac of Florida State University addresses this issue of trade-offs in an important study.[152] She asks whether people really subscribe to the sense of community defined in new urbanism by the concept of physical space. Will people give up their big yards for proximity to amenities like parks and shopping plazas, destinations that are supposed to underlie the promotion of sense of community?

[150] Lund, H. (2002). Pedestrian environments and sense of community. *Journal of Planning Education and Research, 21,* 301–312.

[151] Nasar, J., & Julian, D. A. (1995). The psychological sense of community in the neighborhood. *Journal of the American Planning Association, 61*(2), 178–184.

[152] Audirac, I. (1999). Stated preference for pedestrian proximity: An assessment of new urbanist sense of community. *Journal of Planning Education and Research, 19,* 53–66, p. 53.

As part of a larger survey dealing with consumer attitudes in Florida, in 1991 questions were included to assess perceptions of neighborhood and environmental preference. Essentially the questions sought to find out what would attract people to the new urbanist environment, and in particular what they would be willing to give up (in terms of lot size) to acquire these residential physical characteristics. Here is what respondents were asked:

"If you were to move into a new residence, how likely would you be to live on a smaller lot if you could live within walking distance of...,"[153] and then that lead-in was repeated for five neighborhood destinations. These were:

1. open space and parks
2. shopping, such as pharmacies, convenience stores, or cleaners
3. jobs or employment
4. entertainment, such as pubs, cafes, theaters, or restaurants
5. community centers, such as post offices or churches.

What did the results show? The study attempted to identify how much pull the new urbanist way of living has for different kinds of residential groups, for example, single-family dwellers, apartment renters, those of different marital statuses, those of different ages, and so forth.

The results are numerous and complex, but the big picture indicates that about two-thirds of the respondents would not move to a smaller lot to be within walking distance of *any* of the five destinations. Respondents were least persuaded by the entertainment option and most persuaded by the options that involved (1) parks and open space and (2) community facilities such as post offices and religious facilities. Still, about one-third of consumers could be persuaded. What are the demographic characteristics of the people who could be persuaded?

Those persuaded are more likely to be downtown residents than either suburban or exurban (defined as semirural within commuting distance of a city or town *or* on a ranch or farm in the country); they are more likely to be apartment or condominium dwellers (the author notes that apartment or condo dwellers would not be giving up much because they don't have much land to start). In terms of lot sizes, those with the most land, greater than 2 acres, are less likely to give up lot size for the listed amenities.

In terms of demographic characteristics, it is younger people, those who have never married and those who have been divorced, and *not* the elderly or married women, who are more persuaded to give up lot size for the

[153] Ibid., p. 57.

new urbanist amenities. Further, income shows an inverse relationship to attraction, as those earning above $45,000 are less attracted, whereas those under $15,000 are likely to be more attracted.

Although the findings are complex, like most social science evidence with so many factors to consider, the author concludes these findings are in line with other surveys about new urbanism. Audirac states, "There is a core group attracted to the full new urbanist package but . . . those not buying in neotraditional developments do not want to give up their large yards, privacy, and automobility."[154]

Depending on your perspective, you may or may not think the one-third willing to trade lot size for amenities is encouraging. The author argues that what is encouraging is the particular amenities that *do* attract people. These are the amenities focused on parks and open space or those involving community destinations: " . . . proximity to gathering places such as civic or religious centers seems to evoke the 'sense of community' most cherished by new urbanism proponents."[155]

CHALLENGES TO NEW URBANISM

A picture emerges that we must do more to make new urbanism affordable, as many who indicate interest are those in single households with relatively low incomes. They are the people for whom being within walking distance of destinations such as pharmacies, dry cleaners, and other retail spaces has particular appeal. Although he is not in a low-income group, my older brother, who teaches at a college in Manhattan and lives on the Upper West Side, is hardly wealthy by Manhattan standards. Over the 30+ years he has lived in the city, I have heard him lament the loss of neighborhood amenities like the tailor, cobbler, and dry cleaner. High-rise co-op buildings have been built on the sites of these former service establishments. Although living in an apartment means my brother really has no lot size to trade, the loss of walkable destinations is a loss to many income groups in the city. Can new urbanism meet the needs of a variety of people? Emily Talen, professor in the School of Geographical Sciences and Urban Planning at Arizona State University, gathered data on more than 150 new urbanist developments, specifically those at market rate that were large. For a given locality, using as a criterion the average salary of a schoolteacher, she reports that only 10 percent would be affordable for that wage-earner classification.[156]

---

[154] Ibid., p. 63.   [155] Ibid.
[156] http://geoplan.asu.edu/talen.

Cost is one criticism of new urbanism that can be partly addressed. New urbanist projects receiving the bulk of the media coverage arguably are Seaside, The Kentlands, and Celebration. The popularity of these developments has put them financially out of reach many Americans, particularly in the case of Seaside, as discussed earlier in this chapter. But there have been some attempts to apply new urbanism principles to affordable housing ventures. One such program is HOPE VI, which began awarding grants in 1993 under the Clinton administration. Also known as Housing Opportunities for People Everywhere, the focus of the HOPE VI program was to deal with distressed public housing with the goal of eradicating this housing and transforming these projects into mixed-use and mixed-income communities.[157] By 2004, some 140,000 units of public housing had been demolished under this program.[158] Yet a cautionary note is in order. The extent to which the affordability of new urbanist developments is promoted by governmental initiatives such as HOPE VI cannot be underestimated. Research on developers that included affordable units in their new urbanist developments pointed to the role of support from government programs for more than 70 percent of those who included such units. Yet such support programs are decreasing, according to the authors of this research.[159]

New urbanist principles have played a role because the Department of Housing and Urban Development (HUD) has aligned itself with design guidelines for these new projects proposed by the Congress for the New Urbanism (CNU).[160] One such development influenced by new urbanist principles is Atlanta's Capitol Gateway, with 873 mixed-income dwellings, 160 apartments, a significant amount of commercial space (45,000 sq. ft.), and child development centers.[161] The proposed project is located within walking distance of two regional rail transit stations, the Georgia State University campus, and downtown. Townhouses are the primary building form. Urban Design Associates of Pittsburgh, the firm of Ray Gindroz widely known for its new urbanism work, has also been involved in HOPE VI projects, among them the redevelopment of the Arthur Blumeyer Housing Development in St. Louis.

---

[157] http://www.hud.gov/offices/pih/programs/ph/hope6.

[158] Elliott, J. R., Gotham, K. F., & Milligan, M. J. (2004). Framing the urban: Struggles over HOPE VI and new urbanism in a historic city. *City & Community*, 3(4), 373–394.

[159] Johnson, J. S., & Talen, E. (2008). Affordable housing in new urbanist communities: A survey of developers. *Housing Policy Debate*, 19(4), 583–613.

[160] Congress for the New Urbanism and U.S. Department of Housing and Urban Development (2000). *Principles for Inner-City Neighborhood Design: Creating Communities of Opportunity*. Washington, D.C.: U.S. Department of Housing and Urban Development.

[161] http://www.newurbannews.com/hopeVI.html.

It should be noted that there is some criticism of these HOPE VI projects, particularly in terms of their ability to adequately address the needs of public housing residents who have been displaced through the demolition of public housing projects. An evaluation of one of the more successful HOPE VI sites, Park DuValle Revitalization Project in Louisville, Kentucky, which has been favorably reviewed by the Congress for the New Urbanism, points to problems when the needs of the public housing tenants who were displaced are inadequately addressed. Some 80 percent of the residents of Park DuValle are non–public housing tenants. The authors suggest that a better use of program funds would be for scattered site housing in residential areas of the middle class.[162]

When high-rise units are demolished and replaced by new urbanist developments, there may be a net loss in housing units; at least that scenario is drawn by some critics. If insufficient replacement housing is provided, new urbanism may become "just another form of displacement of poor people."[163] Although new urbanist principles are being applied to a wider variety of income levels than those highlighted by media attention, criticism addresses the issue of cost and making such housing opportunities available to a broad spectrum of possible tenants.

Although the expense of amenities is cited as one factor driving up the cost of new urbanist housing, a basic problem is simply the success of some of the most well-known developments, such as Seaside. Some housing planned for Seaside in its center was envisioned as affordable for people of modest means, originally designed to be an inexpensive beachfront vacation community.[164] The development's popularity has certainly put it out of reach for middle-income Americans. Certainly one problem, then, is an insufficient number of units of affordable new urbanist housing (demand far outstripping supply). This point of insufficient numbers is also made by those mourning the loss of units of public housing for the HOPE VI replacement projects. There are an insufficient number of units there as well.

A final criticism is something in my experience only time can address, and that is the criticism of the "perfection" of developments that look overly planned with a restricted design vocabulary that some find unsettling. The Levittown developments were targets of such criticism in their early years.

---

[162] Brazley, M., & Gilderbloom, J. I. (2007). HOPE VI housing program: Was it effective? *American Journal of Economics and Sociology, 66*(2), 433–442.

[163] http://www.plannersnetwork.org/publications/2002_152_spring.smith.htm, para. 5.

[164] Katz (1994), p. 4.

Yet in the fall of 2007, some 60 years after the construction of Levittown on Long Island, articles pointed to the visual diversity that emerged in those developments over time. In fact, the remodeling of the original Levittown homes was sufficiently extensive that an original model could not be found to put in the Smithsonian.[165] Although the Levittown lots were small, people added new wings and porches, in addition to finishing the originally unfinished second floor. Ironically foreshadowing the emphasis on bigness to be discussed in this chapter, the "bigger is better" mentality also emerged in Levittown. Quoted in an article about the 60th anniversary of Levittown on Long Island, the president of the Levittown Historical Society commented, "Everyone thinks bigger is better and decides to renovate, and so the unique character of Levittown is all but gone."[166]

I think the future of new urbanist ideas rests with the ability of developers to translate the ideas across income groups in sufficient numbers to help popularize the concepts. But there are certainly those who remain pessimistic, among them Audirac:

> Whether new urbanist developments will just offer a wider choice of suburban and exurban neighborhoodscapes or truly contribute to urban containment will require, among other things, an energy crisis and another 50 years of community building. But whether new urbanism can effectively contribute to the alleviation of a social pathology remains, despite its seductive appeal, a hypothetical proposition.[167]

This quotation by Audirac seems like a fitting place to draw to a close our discussion of new urbanism. When we look back at Seaside, Celebration, and The Kentlands and further integrate the research findings on new urbanist communities and standard suburban subdivisions, a consistent picture emerges. Although planning goals for these communities included "mixed income," that goal has not yet been realized in any substantial way, and arguably not at all in Seaside. Even at The Kentlands the average home price was $360,000 at the time the Kim and Kaplan article was written,[168] and the average condominium price was $200,000.

In a sense there seems to be a bifurcated picture. If you consider the findings of Audirac, the people who would give up lot size for new urbanist amenities are those who do not own land and arguably could not afford a

---

[165] Everitt, D. (2007, February 27). Pivotal development. In the Region. *The New York Times.* http://www.nytimes.con/2007/02/05/yregion/nyregionspecial2/25liarts.html.

[166] Kilgannon, C. (2007, October 13). Change blurs memories in a famous suburb. *New York Times*, p. B1. http://www.nytimes.com/2007/10/13/nyregion/13suburb.html, para. 6.

[167] Audirac (1999), p. 64.   [168] Kim & Kaplan (2004).

home in the suburbs. On the other hand, it seems that new urbanism in its most public and publicized form is the domain of Americans who are well off.

What is it going to take for these housing options to trickle into the middle and lower middle classes, to say nothing of the lower class? I support new urbanist principles, but I recently faced a reality check when I visited my childhood home in Ann Arbor, Michigan. In August 2007 my childhood home at 1718 Shadford Road was on the market for $575,000. This brick home, built in 1939, fits in with the new urbanist paradigm. It is in a traditional neighborhood with sidewalks where the houses are close together. The assessor reports the house to be 1839 sq. ft., on a lot that is 60 × 128. The house is desirable for a number of reasons, including the fact that the school system is good and it is in a neighborhood called Burns Park where many academics from the University of Michigan live.

On that visit to Ann Arbor two summers ago, I attended an open house held by the realtor and could not get over how small the house seemed. Some of that impression is the difference in perception and memory of someone who had lived there as a child versus someone now in the over-50 category. But I don't think all of my impression can be attributed to that contrast effect. The house has 3 bedrooms (it used to have 4), $2\frac{1}{2}$ baths (it used to have $1\frac{1}{2}$), separate living and dining rooms, and a kitchen, enclosed porch, and full basement with a laundry room and furnace area. It also has a one-car garage that never held a car in my childhood because it was full of bicycles and wagons. There were five children in my family. Here is the new urbanist ideal, in close walking distance of schools, some stores, and a wonderful park, but I'm not sure I would buy the house if I had five children (even if I could afford it) because of its size. I have no interest in living in a very large house, but 1718 Shadford Road seemed pretty small.

It will take a crisis and certainly a change in the culture of how we view how we live to offer substantial alternatives to suburban growth in America. Whether that crisis comes in the form of global warming, obesity, or astronomical energy costs remains to be seen. Perhaps it will take gas at $20 a gallon, if a recent book is correct.[169] The book predicts that by $20 a gallon, we will have abandoned suburbia for downtowns and walkable neighborhoods, train travel will have replaced airline travel, big box stores will have disappeared, and telecommuting will have expanded dramatically. Remember the useful phrase, "You get what you reward"? For the spatial

---

[169] Steiner, C. (2009). *$20 per gallon: How the inevitable rise in the price of gasoline will change our lives for the better.* New York: Grand Central Publishing.

pattern of residential communities to change, it may take a change not only in the price of oil, but in what the federal government funds, which may be related.

MCMANSIONS: BIGGER? BETTER?

This section on McMansions, or large developer homes, will have a different flavor than the section on new urbanism, because most of what has been written about McMansions comes from the popular press, and most facts about "large houses" come from the U.S. Census. When I entered the search term "McMansion" as a keyword into PsycInfo, a popular database for psychology and psychology-related social science journals, I found no "hits" on July 16, 2007. On the other hand, when I used LexisNexis, a database that covers American newspapers and magazines, I found almost 300 references that same day. McMansions are not the darlings of planning departments, and much less attention is lavished on them in research journals in contrast to the attention given to the new urbanist movement in such periodicals. Yet very large houses on fairly small (and not-so-small) lots dominate residential suburban America in a way significantly more pervasive and profound than new urbanism.

Large houses are often defined as having nine or more rooms (excluding bathrooms, utility rooms, or unfinished basements) as mentioned in an article by Blaine Harden.[170] When talking earlier about new urbanism, we distinguished between infill developments that occur in cities in areas where previous structures had been built, and greenfield developments, which occur at the edge of the city. We can make a parallel distinction between McMansions wedged into existing neighborhoods (infill) and those that occur in entirely new developments, called plats. The house sizes may be the same in these two types of developments, but the impact is different. Infill McMansions often result in complaints by neighbors and the NIMBY (not in my backyard) reaction. Plat McMansions are more commonly associated with typical suburban problems, most notably sprawl and congestion, but also the infrastructure needed to support them. One advantage for infill McMansions may be the tax dollars generated through this construction. Further, if you live on the block where the McMansion is erected, your property value may increase by association with the larger structures.

---

[170] Harden, B. (2002, June 20). Big, bigger, biggest: The supersize suburb. http://www.nytimes.com/2002/06/20/garden/big-bigger-biggest-the-supersize-suburb.html.

In this article by Harden entitled "Big, bigger, biggest: The supersize suburb," we learn that according to the 2000 Census, half of the nation's 10 top "big house" communities are in the Washington suburbs. These are Travilah, Darnestown, Chevy Chase, Wolf Trap, and Great Falls. Rounding out the 10 are suburbs near Philadelphia, Chicago, Minneapolis, Denver, and Salt Lake City. "Local planning officials in the Potomac region say that 'many owners request fewer trees and less vegetation so prospective admirers passing on the street can get the full effect.'"[171] This arrangement has the intended effect of making the houses look even larger than they are. In many of the stories about such large houses the same remark is made that very little of the total space is used, just the kitchen, family room, and the bedrooms, and that the bigger is better mentality dominates residents' thinking.

What is the difference between a large house and a McMansion? A *Slate* article from January 4, 2006, by Witold Rybczynski entitled "Supersize my house!" quotes the *Oxford English Dictionary* in defining a McMansion as "a modern house built on a large and imposing scale, but regarded as ostentatious and lacking architectural integrity."[172] The primary focus of the *Slate* article is to criticize the lack of knowledge of architectural style exhibited in McMansions. The article contrasts some "everyday" McMansions with architecturally designed large homes that "work" because they have a sense of scale and use architectural elements to create a sense of coherence and consistent style.

Friends of ours in their early 50s recently bought what could fairly be described as a McMansion. They are a financially successful dual-earner couple and have no children. The layout and amenities of their home are exactly what Cathleen McGuigan, writing for *Newsweek*, described in a piece entitled "The McMansion next door: Why the American house needs a makeover."[173] The home has a huge foyer with a chandelier, it has the open plan of the expanded kitchen leading into the family room, there is an enormous master suite with its associated bathroom, and there is a 3+ car garage. Their entry foyer with the chandelier is known as a lawyer foyer. In a section of the Wikipedia entry on McMansions dealing with associated terminology, we learn that the phrase "lawyer foyer" refers to "the two-story entry space typically found on many McMansions which is meant to be visually overwhelming but which contributes little to the useful space of

---

[171] Ibid., para. 8.
[172] Rybczynski, W. (2006, January 4). Supersize my house! http://www.slate.com/id/2133029/, p. 3.
[173] McGuigan, C. (2003, October 27). The McMansion next door. Why the American house needs a makeover. *Newsweek*. http://www.msnbc.msn.com/id/3225775.

the house."[174] Some 20 years ago, writing in the *New York Times* Magazine section about homes "clustered for leisure," Carol Vogel[175] made a case that the labels we use to describe our housing are crucial. A living room is not a living room, it is a "great room." I have the feeling that people who live in large homes would be much more comfortable with the notion of having a great room than a lawyer foyer!

Visiting this couple in their McMansion for a small get-together a few years ago, I was amazed at the vast square footage, a square footage that was "there" but that you knew might never be used. What is the appeal of such a house? McGuigan points out that such developer houses, across a variety of price ranges, are strikingly similar across America. In a sense the description reminds me of Calvin Trillin's[176] critique of The Rouse Company's malls up and down the East Coast in an article in *The New Yorker*. The similarity of such houses obscures a sense of place. If you've seen one, you've seen them all, and you could be in Atlanta, Albuquerque, or Anchorage. McGuigan's critique is: "But, as the epithet McMansion suggests, they're just too big – for their lots, for their neighborhoods and for the number of people who actually live in them. And why do they keep getting bigger, when families are getting smaller? In 1970, the average new single-family house was 1,400 square feet; today it's 2,300."[177]

A similar negative view about McMansions comes from an essay entitled "McMansion: Over a billion served," posted on a Web site dealing with popular culture. On that Web site Thomas Goff writes about McMansions: "It is a disease that is spreading across America. It is infecting the landscape and polluting your neighborhood. And you can't stop it. . . . "[178] He goes on: "The MCMANSION is here. You can call it what you will – McMansion, Monster Mansion, Frankenhouse, Hummer House, Starter Castle, Plywood Palazzo, Parachute Home – it doesn't matter. That which we call a Mc-Mansion by any other name would be as evil, ugly, and disgraceful to society. At first the disease infects one or two houses: a small, nice house is knocked down and obliterated. Next, the site is cleared of all trees and all life. A new foundation is extended out to cover 75 percent of the site. And then . . . it rises."[179]

---

[174] http://en.wikipedia.org/wiki/McMansion, p. 10.
[175] Vogel, C. (1987, June 28). Clustered for leisure: The changing home. *The New York Times Magazine*, pp. 12–17, 38, 44–46, 64.
[176] Trillin (1977).   [177] McGuigan (2003), para. 5.
[178] Goff, T. (2006, Fall). McMansion: Over a billion sold. http://web.mit.edu/cultureshock/fa2006/www/essays/mcmansion.html, para. 1.
[179] Ibid., para. 2.

FIGURE 1.3. McMansion

In this critique, Goff says these poorly designed and constructed and devoid of variety houses sell so well because they appeal to the nouveau riche. He also criticizes the lack of appreciation of context in the construction of these homes, which he explains is the reason they are given the label "parachute homes" – the homes can be dropped in anywhere. In my view, McMansions may not be poorly constructed, the issue of poor "design" is certainly subjective, and not everyone is troubled by lack of variety.

But the criticism of size is one that needs to be addressed (see Figure 1.3). In a National Public Radio piece under the category "Your Money," Margot Adler[180] talks about the growth in the size of the average American home, from the 1950s to the present. Quoting figures from the National Association of Home Builders from March 2006, we see a chart of the average single-family home in 1950 as 983 sq. ft., and as 2349 sq. ft. in 2004. And we know that Americans are not having as many children as they did 50 years ago. A number of possibilities are offered for this disconnection beyond a simple display of wealth. A real estate agent states that the high price of land forces developers to build large houses to make a profit. An architect suggests that the threat of terrorism makes people think about their safety, with large houses representing a refuge. A Bridgehampton, Long Island,

---

[180] Adler, M. (2006, July 4). Behind the ever-expanding American dream house. http://www .npr.org/templates/story/story.php?storyID=5525283.

Town Planning member is quoted as saying, "If you have people coming out from the city, where they are bombarded by people, the tendency is to isolate themselves. Their house is their community. It is not the community's community, it is their community."[181]

A management professor from Cornell offers the idea of context, and the idea that so many people in the United States have a great deal of money that our reference for what is appropriate or normal has shifted. Although the article is slanted to present the views of people who dislike the big houses, even some of them recognize that construction of such homes fuels the local economy. Answering why people want big houses, a public relations executive, formerly a White House correspondent for the *Wall Street Journal* who lives in an 11,000-sq.-ft. house, says: "I think everybody has their individual wants. This is my dream. And let's face it: In America, in this day and age, many of us have gotten to the point where we can do this."[182]

Regarding what people attracted to such large homes may be missing, another point of view comes from Sarah Susanka. In such books as *The Not So Big House: A Blueprint for the Way We Really Live*,[183] Susanka, an architect, urges people to include the spaces that they really use, the functional spaces.[184] People who adopt her point of view, she says, have been disappointed with the soullessness of larger homes. Among the characteristics she champions is multiple uses of rooms. Not surprisingly, she uses Japanese design, known for its multiple use of space, as one source of inspiration. She argues that one explanation for the growth of American houses is that people consider separate spaces for each activity. Susanka is also a devotee of architect Christopher Alexander's pattern language, and she believes that architectural spaces, such as alcoves that communicate intimacy and safety, have a psychological foundation. Susanka is appealing to our souls as well as our sense of practicality.[185]

But another point of view about McMansions comes from a real estate perspective. I spoke with a local Realtor who has been in the business more than a decade (personal communication, July 19, 2007) about the attraction of McMansions. She commented that many upper management people move regularly and seek housing with which they are familiar (and ironically

[181] Ibid., para. 13.   [182] Ibid., para. 33.

[183] Susanka, S. (1998). *The not so big house: A blueprint for the way we really live.* Newtown, CT: The Taunton Press, Inc.

[184] Herbert, W. (1998/1999, December 28/January 4). Sarah Susanka: Homes for the way people really live. *U.S. News & World Report*, p. 61.

[185] Ibid., p. 61.

that also fits their large furniture). They are familiar with McMansion-type developments and feel secure, knowing what they are getting when they move from the Midwest to the East Coast, for example. In a sense, what they seek is a familiar brand, and the McMansion as a brand meets that need. They are also comfortable with the fact that the homes next door look somewhat similar. That aspect, too, is part of the security of familiarity. When I asked her about historic homes, and the audience she sees for those purchases, she said that the demographic was much smaller, and that people who were interested in the walkable community concept were more likely to be older as opposed to families with young children.

My, How We Have Grown

In the United States, some astonishing things have happened to the size of the average new one-family house over the last 30 years. In 1973, the number of average square feet in these new houses was 1660. By 2005, that number was 2434, with the biggest increases taking place in the Northeast (from 1595 to 2556).[186] One of the interesting tables in Census data from 2002 to 2005 relates to outdoor features in new one-family houses. The outdoor features listed are patio, porch, and deck. Although we don't know the exact location of the porch, let's assume that porches, in general, contribute to sense of community by bringing residents into contact, or at least view, of other neighborhood residents. The bottom line is that houses completed in 2005 have more porches than was true in 1992. In 1992, the percentage with porches was 42 percent, and the percentage without was 58 percent. In 2005, the percentage with porches had moved up to 53 percent, whereas the percentage without had decreased to 47 percent.[187]

I suppose the next question is whether there is simply more of other features, too. The answer is "no." The percentage with decks declined from 37 percent to 27 percent, but the percentage with patios increased from 37 percent to 46 percent. The numbers reveal this pattern of increases and decreases across geographical areas (Northeast, Midwest, South, West).

What about the number of stories? As you might guess, the number has increased.

More than 30 years ago in 1973 the number of one-story homes in the category of new one-family houses completed was 67 percent. Of new one-family houses completed, 23 percent had two or more stories (the category

---

[186] http://www.census.gov/const/C25Ann/soldmedavgsf.pdf.
[187] http://www.census.gov/const/C25Ann/sftotaloutdoorfeatures.pdf.

includes $1\frac{1}{2}$, $2\frac{1}{2}$, and 3 stories), and 10 percent were split level. In 2005, 44 percent had 1 story, 55 percent had 2 or more stories, and split levels were definitely out of favor, at less than 0.5 percent. One reason the split level has probably declined in popularity relates to building costs; you can squeeze much more usable space on a foundation that is a box (e.g., colonial design) as opposed to a split box (split level).[188]

Although the movement has been toward multistory houses, the demographics of our population might suggest a reexamination of the benefits of one-story homes. Two important concepts here are universal design and visitability. Universal design has replaced such concepts as accessible design and barrier-free design. It refers to the concept of creating structures that are usable by everyone, whatever the physical or cognitive challenges of the users. Visitability is a term that emerged in Europe but has been embraced here, primarily through the efforts of a group in Atlanta called Concrete Change. The group's focus is to effect change in the construction industry so that new homes offer a number of features to accommodate those with mobility impairments, as residents or visitors. These features are (1) at least one entrance that has no (zero) steps, (2) doors for wide passage, and (3) a minimum of a half bath/powder room on the main level.[189] When my father was 94 he moved from his home to an assisted living facility. In his home, although the study on the ground level had been transformed into a bedroom with a bathroom nearby, stairs confronted him at the front door and the garage entry into the house. These stairs were part of his undoing. Had his home met the definition of visitability with at least one functional entrance with zero steps, he might have been able to remain "home" longer. As we continue to build large homes, we might consider how these structures will meet our needs as we age.

Houses are getting larger in terms of the number of stories, even if they do not meet the nine-room definition. My brother Robert calls these smaller (but still large homes) McHouses. In a sense, we may see a kind of trickle-down effect of this visual emphasis on the size of homes. Just as we have seen couture design filter down to Target (Isaac Mizrahi) and H&M (Karl Lagerfeld, Stella McCartney), we have essentially seen this desire for larger houses in the United States move down relative income levels.

More than 30 years ago, psychologist Florence Ladd[190] wrote an article about how 60 Black youths in the Roxbury-North Dorchester section of

---

[188] http://www.census.gov/const/C25Ann/sftotalstories.pdf.

[189] Visitability. http://www.concretechange.org/visitability_defined.aspx.

[190] Ladd, F. C. (1972). Black youths view their environment: Some views of housing. *Journal of the American Institute of Planners, 38*, 108–115.

Boston viewed their housing. There were a number of telling findings about how these teenagers viewed the exteriors and interiors of their housing. Germane to the present discussion of house size, however, was their view of what kind of housing they would like in the future. These kids wanted single-family houses painted white, with big back yards and fences surrounding the yard. They wanted enough bedrooms so that each person had his/her own, and large rooms overall. What the article reinforced for me is that we operate in a powerful social context, and we are heavily influenced by what we see around us. There was an enormous gap between their existing housing and their desires for their future housing, perhaps a reflection of the trickle-down effect at that time. Today we surely see a trickle-down effect in our desire for "more house," as indicated by the statistics from the National Home Builders Association. Nationally we want more bedrooms, walk-in pantries, and home offices as a start.[191]

THE BACKLASH

However, there appears to be some backlash in Americans' love affair with large-scale houses. Austin, Texas, for example, passed an ordinance in June 2006 that limited the size of homes that can be constructed in certain parts of the city, although a bill has been filed in the Texas legislature to try to overturn the Austin ordinance.[192] And near the southern tip of Staten Island, recent changes in regulations guard against continued construction of large houses on too-small lots.[193] The Coral Gables, Florida, City Commission has also proposed an ordinance to essentially protect older neighborhoods constructed in the 1940s and 1950s from being razed and replaced with McMansions. One of the residents supporting the ordinance was quoted as saying, "Good design takes context into account and neighbors into account. They're taking away our light and giving back to us a blank wall. That's not very neighborly."[194] Other communities involved in regulations or petitions against large houses and overdevelopment include Chevy Chase, Maryland, Bayside, Queens, the Sunland-Tujunga area of Los

---

[191] Christie, L. (2005). "Die, die monster home! Die." http://money.cnn.com/2005/08/18/real_estate/monster_home_backlash/index.htm.

[192] http://crosslandteam.com/blog/2007/02/28/austin-mcmansion-ordinance-may-be-undone-by-tx-leg/.

[193] Wilson, C. (2007, April 29). If it stayed the same, that would be different. *New York Times*, Real Estate section, p. 9.

[194] Archbold, C. (2006, June 8). McMansions to go: New zoning code to prevent giant homes in single-family district. http:miamisunpost.com/archives/2006/06-08-06/seventhstoryfrontpage.htm.

Angeles, New Canaan, Greenwich, and Westport, Connecticut, the Bay Area of San Francisco, Boston, and the suburbs of Chicago.[195] However, the backlash is not universal. Recent research indicates that a substantial number of cities with oversized houses, either infill or greenfield plat, have not adopted regulations to constrain such houses.[196] There appears to be some concern among residents that regulations may reduce property values. The authors of this research on the regulation of "super-sized" houses suggest a proactive approach. They argue that if planners put regulations in place for areas likely to attract large houses (i.e., before applications are received), controls of such construction are more likely to be adopted than after the first such house is built. Recent research[197] contributes to our understanding of the likelihood that neighbors will judge large infill houses as too big and out of scale for their surroundings. Rather than absolute size, it is size relative to its surroundings that seems to matter for larger houses (twice the size of neighboring houses), and of the size dimensions, height has a greater impact than width. Further, compatibility of the style of the house appears to be even more important than relative size in this research using color simulations of an infill house inserted into a block of existing houses, totaling five in number. These findings are important because they give planning officials tools to construct regulations and to use during an evaluation of proposals. Such principles may help foster compatibility and constrain backlash.

Although some communities may be fighting the "large house" phenomenon, statistics show many Americans still want "more." As the size of homes increased, and as the number of family dwellers in them decreased, the lot size decreased from about 9000 sq. ft. to 8000 sq. ft. The result is "bigger houses on smaller lots with fewer people living in them."[198] According to data from the National Home Builders Association cited in an article about the McMansion backlash, "Some 87 percent prefer three or more bedrooms with 44 percent wanting at least four.... About 85 percent of Americans want walk-in pantries.... Seventy-seven percent desire separate shower stalls, 95 percent want laundry rooms and 64 percent home offices. More than a third crave media rooms. Then there are exercise rooms, sun rooms, and dens."[199] Some argue that if McMansions are properly sited, in a community of such homes or by themselves on sufficient acreage, no one complains. What people detest is houses that dwarf the building lot. People tear down bungalows in existing neighborhoods and erect McMansions.

---

[195] Christie (2005).   [196] Nasar et al. (2007), p. 354.
[197] Nasar, J. L., & Stamps, A. E. (2009). Infill McMansions: Style and the psychophysics of style. *Journal of Environmental Psychology, 29,* 110–123.
[198] Christie (2005), para. 13.   [199] Ibid., para. 14–15.

FIGURE 1.4. Villa at The Preserve

Although people may not complain if there is sufficient acreage, it is still possible to be bowled over by the size and style of houses built. I recently took a tour of the area around Dexter, Michigan, outside Ann Arbor. The area I toured was called The Preserve, which had been developed on the site of a former gravel pit.[200] My brother, a real estate agent, showed me one home in The Preserve that had been on a house tour when it was constructed. I can only describe it as a Roman villa (see Figure 1.4). How in the world this home fits in its context, even if there is sufficient acreage, is for me an unanswerable question.

A telling anecdote in our neighborhood involves former neighbors in a house diagonally across the street. The new owners of this large house, with a grandfathered apartment on the top floor reached by an exterior circular staircase, wanted to construct both a garage and a carport at two different lot lines (east and south).

Although there was a driveway, no garage existed on the lot. To build these new structures, which would have been right on the lot lines, required

---

[200] http://preserveofdexter.com.

variances. Construction of these "appendages" would have required a variance to the statute limiting the percentage of the lot that was buildable. A number of neighbors, myself included, went to the Planning and Zoning Committee hearing to speak against granting the variance. The variance was not granted. The neighbors moved.

When "zoning hounds" are released, according to Christopher Solomon in an article entitled "The swelling McMansion backlash," communities can take a number of steps to curb McMansion growth.[201] In his view, the backlash is occurring in areas of growth that are affluent: "You see it in areas like Santa Fe and Los Angeles and San Francisco and some parts of Atlanta – you probably don't see it in Detroit."[202] But I would add that you probably see it in nearby Grosse Pointe, Michigan. He tells the story of the backlash in DeKalb County, Georgia, after someone constructed a replica of the White House. It is not just the issue of the houses being out of character with the community (as would be the case if a replica of the White House went up in *your* neighborhood), but that such building causes an increase in property values, which in turn forces out longtime residents who often represent a wider range of ethnic and economic diversity. In the borough of Stonington, Connecticut, where the issue is not really McMansions but gentrification more generally, the Portuguese fishermen have been forced out by wealthy home buyers from Hartford and Fairfield County, Connecticut, and New York City, who have purchased and then impeccably and expensively restored or completely rebuilt from the ground up each clapboard home, typically for use as second homes.

Solomon suggests that the McMansionization of America may show some signs of slowing; between 2001 and 2004 the size of the average American home increased just 25 sq. ft. Somehow I doubt the continuation of this downward trend. In fact, a recent article titled "Smaller families want bigger homes: Trend toward larger homes shows no signs of stopping" gives no indication that downsizing is on the horizon.[203] Facts cited in the article are that at least 20 percent of American houses had four or more bedrooms in 2005. The vice president of economic research at the National Association of Home Builders quoted in the article claims you cannot sell a house with only $1\frac{1}{2}$ bathrooms, you must have at least $2\frac{1}{2}$ even if only two people reside in the house. In my childhood home on Shadford Road in Ann Arbor, Michigan, my older brother's bedroom is now part of a master bathroom,

[201] Solomon, C. (2006, March 26). The swelling McMansion backlash. http://realestate .msn.com/buying/Articlenewhome.aspx?cp-documentid=418653, para. 1.
[202] Ibid., para. 8.
[203] Ohlemacher, S., & Foy, P. (2007, May 23). Smaller families want bigger houses: Trend toward larger homes shows no signs of stopping. *The New London Day*, p. A10.

renovated to increase the number of bathrooms in the house from $1\frac{1}{2}$ to $2\frac{1}{2}$. Homes in many European countries are half the size of those in the United States, with Luxembourg the only country approaching our average home size, at 75 percent of our square footage, according to the Solomon article. This same research VP at the National Association of Home Builders claims that what Americans are buying is a lifestyle, rather than meeting the needs of a large family.

Yet results of a design trends survey of 500 residential architects for the first 3 months of 2007 show some indication of downsizing. This survey is sponsored by the American Institute of Architects and compares the 2007 figures with results from 2006.[204] Whereas 26 percent of residential architects claim home sizes are decreasing, 21 percent reported increasing home sizes. An important trend is the increased emphasis on clients' interest in accessibility. This trend may be related to the aging of the baby boomer generation, according to Kermit Baker, chief economist for the American Institute of Architects, commenting in the article. However, we must remember that the terms architect and developer are not synonymous, and the trends and patterns in architect-designed homes may not be reflected in those constructed by developers. Even if tempered by the recent economic downturn (in 2008, house sizes decreased by 11 percent[205]), I think the bigger home trend is far from over.

Teardowns and Pop-ups

A phenomenon related to McMansions is the teardown. Many American homes start on the site of torn down homes, and in 1999 about 10 percent of the single-family home starts in America ($\approx$1.3 million) were on lots where homes had already existed.[206] Mark Calabria, an economist for the National Association of Realtors, is quoted as saying, "No one tears down to downsize."[207] People want more garages, more bathrooms, master suites, and the list goes on. Whether those who oppose such growth will succeed in their efforts to rein it in remains to be seen.[208]

Related to the concept of a teardown is what is called a "pop-up." In nearby New London, Connecticut, we have an ongoing dispute involving

---

[204] Homes becoming more humble? (2007, May 11). http://archive.theday.com/re_print.aspx?re=6c812a7c-8057-4732-9054-ca0b8387038f.

[205] Riccardi, N. (2009, June 26). New houses getting smaller. *The New London Day*, Home Source, p. 31.

[206] Adamson, L. (2000, April 9). Salient facts: Tear-downs. Scraping by. *New York Times Magazine*, p. 46.

[207] Ibid.   [208] Ibid., p. 46.

FIGURE 1.5. New London pop-up house

such a pop-up house (see Figure 1.5). In the article, the author describes a pop-up and some related concepts: "A small house, perhaps a 1950s ranch or bungalow, is demolished ('scraped off') to make way for an oversized home ('McMansion'). Alternatively, a modest 1200-foot, one-story house may be expanded to a three-story, 5200-sq.-ft. home. This is a 'pop-up,' and can be seen everywhere in less desirable seacoast towns."[209] The author, a member of the New London Historic District Commission, then discusses the lawsuit involving a "pop-up" house in New London, Connecticut, on Glenwood Avenue. "The problems on Glenwood are the same as those faced by thousands of suburban communities across the nation that in the recent real-estate boom have undergone massive 'scrape-offs,' 'pop-ups' and 'monster additions.'"[210] The author describes how it works nationally, stating that the motive is typically views and profit. "Unfortunately, this kind of building undermines whatever character the neighborhood may have and ends up depressing property values.... Neighbors often complain about these large home additions that gobble up yards, block air and sunlight, and create eyesores."[211] To achieve aesthetic control, the author argues that homeowners may have to vote in a historic district. My house in Mystic is

[209] Baker, M. B. (2007, April 11). Glenwood flap is an issue of law. *The New London Day*, p. A7.
[210] Ibid.   [211] Ibid.

part of such a historic district. But even with such a historic district, it is still possible to have an eyesore, as would have been the case had my neighbors and I skipped the zoning variance hearing.

CLOSING COMMENTS

Perhaps a good place to end this chapter is with the August 2007 issue of *Money*, which features articles on where and how we live in America. In introducing the article "Best places to live" the reporters talk about the criteria they used to select the top 10 communities: "But there's a big difference between a gated McMansion subdivision and a town where you can put down roots and participate in a community that has a broader list of concerns than the height of the hedges. The latter are the kinds of places *MONEY* looks for in naming America's Best Places to Live."[212]

This statement has a familiar ring, doesn't it? In all fairness, the authors state that the focus that year was on smaller places, those between 7,500 and 50,000 in population. At the same time, the issue features an article "Where we'll live tomorrow."[213] Reviewing the migration pattern away from expensive cities like Boston, San Francisco, and Los Angeles, author Joel Kotkin makes a case that the baby boomers who retire as well as new professionals will be pulled to more affordable housing markets like Phoenix, Atlanta, Dallas, Charlotte, and the suburbs that surround those cities. He argues these are better places for kids, and that the suburbs are hardly sterile or dull. "Greater Portland, considered an earthly paradise by many new urbanists, may be a magnet for educated workers, but that doesn't mean most live in the hip urban core."[214] The article reports data from demographer Wendell Cox that "more than 95% of greater Portland's population growth"[215] since 2000 has occurred outside the limits of the city. Kotkin's conclusion, based on the data, is that those over 30 are seeking a somewhat less urban experience than the city core: "a bit less edgy and a lot less crowded, more family-friendly and usually more affordable as well."[216]

We in America face real problems on the home front. How do you persuade people that the 11,000-sq.-ft. American dream should not be pursued, nor by extension the 4,000-sq.-ft. dream or even the 3,000-sq.-ft. dream? The country cannot afford very large houses in terms of energy, upkeep,

---

[212] Ashford, K., Fitch, A., Gandel, S., Hyatt, J., Max, S., Merritt, J., & Rosato, D. (2007, August). Best places to live. *Money*, pp. 84–94, p. 85.
[213] Kotkin, J. (2007, August). Where we'll live tomorrow. *Money*, pp. 104–105.
[214] Ibid., p. 105.   [215] Ibid.
[216] Ibid.

or arguably quality of life. Getting to know your neighbors is not such a bad thing, and building a sense of community may help Americans recover some meaningfulness in life that so many say they have lost. Americans survived because they banded together to solve problems. Rather than isolate ourselves in large homes, we are more likely to solve problems when we share sidewalks.

Where does this look at new urbanism and McMansions leave us? Is some convergence possible, as it is unlikely that the American dream of bigger-is-better will completely fall out of favor? One could envision downsizing McMansions and at the same time building communities with amenities within walking distance. As a model, something like an affordable Kentlands comes to mind. To bring about this convergence will require continued pressure on energy conservation and sustainability. It will require continued media attention to the problems of global warming and obesity (strange bedfellows, but bedfellows nevertheless). And it will undoubtedly require federal support ("reinforcement") for these new residential and associated transportation initiatives. When 5 of the top 10 large house communities in the nation are outside Washington, D.C., we have some cause for concern. But at the very least, the fact that new urbanist communities are being built across the nation provides Americans with choice and some modicum of hope.

2

The Landscape of Health Care:
High Tech and Humanistic

PERSONAL REFLECTIONS

I come from a family of health care providers (what we used to call doctors and nurses). My father is a retired thoracic surgeon; his father was a general surgeon in West Virginia. My mother was a surgical nurse, and her mother was a nurse and her father a doctor in Ohio. I also spent time in college working in a hospital. Given that lineage one might imagine that I have a certain comfort level in health care settings. That may have been true at some point in my life, but no longer. And given my education as an environmental psychologist, I am particularly sensitive to the quality of the physical surroundings in which health care occurs.

Two anecdotes will suggest the role of the physical setting in my attitude toward health care. When my daughter was in college, she needed her wisdom teeth extracted. Her dentist recommended an oral surgeon, and we made an appointment for a consultation (consultation first visit; extraction second visit). The office was in a somewhat secluded and run-down commercial area near a number of gas stations and a roller rink. As we approached the office building, we went over railroad tracks and down an incline. At that point my daughter said to me, "This does not inspire confidence." As it turned out, she felt so negatively about the entire experience that day that we asked her dentist for a second referral and ultimately went elsewhere (see Figure 2.1). The second office was in a modern medical building. The waiting area was light and spacious, with an aquarium, television, plenty of magazines, and beverages and snacks for waiting relatives. This office provided "positive distractions," that is, outlets to take your mind off the impending procedure.

My own experience relates to needing what I called a "good detective" for a condition no one seemed able to diagnose. Ultimately I had major

FIGURE 2.1. Office building of second oral surgeon

surgery to address this condition, but that is a story for another book. I was referred to a specialist about my condition, and when I arrived at his office I was a bit underwhelmed. The building was small, somewhat out of date and unimposing, and the waiting room had wood paneling, which dampened my spirits. This physician missed the diagnosis of my condition. And although correlation is not causation, I was not impressed with the physical surroundings of his office, or with him.

My own research on health care settings points to the dilemma we as patients face when we select environments for health care (to the extent we are able to select them at all). On one hand, we want the best, which we often associate with new, large, and expensive medical facilities. On the other hand, we often find such facilities overwhelming and imposing, which is stressful and frightening. One might ask how we have arrived at what I call our current healthscape, that is, the buildings, landscaping, and locations in which health care is provided. How have our health care facilities arrived at their current configurations, and to what extent do these facilities shape the care we receive in them? Given our current concern with extending health care benefits to all citizens, it is easy to overlook the facilities in which care is delivered, but the facilities and care are part of the entire health care delivery system.

As we consider the evolution of health care facilities over the last 100 years, certain themes emerge that we will explore in this chapter. These include the impact of science and technology, including beliefs and theories about disease, incentives and barriers erected by the federal government, the rise of consumerism and patient-centered care, and the emergence of evidence-based design, that is, design based on outcomes, particularly objective outcomes.

HISTORY OF HOSPITAL DESIGN

In their comprehensive volume *The Hospital: A Social and Architectural History*,[1] John Thompson and Grace Goldin trace the history of inpatient units in hospitals with structures dating from the 5th century B.C. They start with the Greek stoa (porches) or Asklepieia (the god of dreams), essentially partial enclosures for patients whose dreams, after being reported to the priests, constituted information that directed the patients' medical therapies. What is interesting to me is that although enclosed on three sides, the Asklepieion of Epidauros, illustrated in their book, was open on the south side, providing an important source of light, with the temple itself visible from patients' beds through the open portico. Here in the 5th century B.C. a powerful aesthetic vista played a role in the patient's well-being. As we shall see, hospital architecture in the United States over the last 100 years has been more concerned with function than with the potential power of the environment itself to help in the healing process. But today in some quarters there is a return to a number of the values present in the early asklepieia.

To illustrate what hospitals were like in the United States more than 100 years ago, I have chosen The Johns Hopkins Hospital in Baltimore, Maryland. I selected Hopkins for a number of reasons. First, it provides a good example of the kind of hospital, albeit a university hospital, built in the United States in the latter part of the 19th century. Second, I have a personal connection to Hopkins. My parents met there, when my father was a resident and my mother was a surgical nurse. My older brother was born there.

I will also make references to the general hospital at the University of Michigan, where my younger siblings and I were born, where I worked in college, and where my father was a surgeon. Michigan's was the first hospital operated by a university in the United States, in 1869.[2] Replacing

---

[1] Thompson, J., & Goldin, G. (1975). *The hospital: A social and architectural history*. New Haven, CT: Yale University Press.

[2] http://www.umich.edu/pres/history/markers/firsthosp.html.

an earlier hospital, the specific building known as Old Main, designed by noted architect Albert Kahn, was opened in 1925 with 2 miles of corridors and nine levels, three below ground. The administration building, at the front of the hospital, was connected by a corridor to the large patient building, with the surgical wing behind that. Old Main was replaced by a new main medical building in 1986 and demolished in 1989.[3] I have a T-shirt with the logo "Remember Old Main" created to pay homage to this massive old teaching hospital. The occasion of the design of the replacement hospital offered the opportunity for considerable research about the ideal shape and function of the hospital of the 21st century, reflected in the principles of a book entitled *Design That Cares: Planning Health Facilities for Patients and Visitors.*[4] Hopkins and Michigan represent great traditions in medical care and arguably set a high standard for others to follow.

Almost until the end of the 19th century, hospitals were not really treatment facilities, and they were not places where people expected to improve; people in hospitals were chronically ill or went to the hospital to die. Where hospitals existed, the target population was poor; those who had the financial means were either treated at home or in private facilities. Writing eloquently about hospitals in his masterful book *The Care of Strangers: The Rise of America's Hospital System,* Charles Rosenberg states about hospitals in the period 1850–1920, "In architecture as well as in terms of their social organization, America's early hospitals differed little from any large home or welfare institution."[5] Rosenberg's book documents the proliferation of hospitals in this country to the point that by the early 1920s the number of hospitals approached 5000, contrasted with fewer than 200 in 1873.[6] A central tenet of his book is that the hospital reflects the larger society in which it has been shaped, and he argues that the bureaucracy characteristic of the hospital is seen in many facets of American life.[7]

Hopkins

As an illustration of early hospitals, Hopkins is remarkable for a number of reasons. From the very beginning, Hopkins placed great emphasis on

---

[3] http://www.umich.edu/pres/history/markers/oldmain.html.

[4] Carpman, J. R., Grant, M. A., & Simmons, D. A. (1986). *Design that cares: Planning health facilities for patients and visitors.* Chicago: American Hospital Publishing, Inc.

[5] Rosenberg, C. (1987). *The care of strangers: The rise of America's hospital system.* New York: Basic Books, pp. 339–340.

[6] Ibid., p. 341.

[7] Ibid., p. 349.

medical education and strove to be in the forefront of medicine, arguably a status it holds to this day, where it is usually in the top tier of research-based hospitals in the *U.S. News and World Report* rankings.[8] With this emphasis on being at the forefront in every aspect, the Building Committee for Hopkins considered the design of the hospital thoroughly, sending out a request for information to physicians in other parts of the United States about the advantages and disadvantages of different hospital configurations. The Building Committee seemed particularly concerned with the trade-off between the pavilion approach, consisting of detached and permanent components, typically two or more stories in height, and the barrack system, distinguished by its temporary purpose, replaceable on site and typically one story in height.[9]

Of particular concern in selecting Hopkins's layout was what we today call HVAC (heating, ventilation, and air-conditioning); in the late 1800s heating and ventilation garnered attention, and in turn their implications for sanitation and disease. Of those who responded to the Building Committee's request for information, John Shaw Billings, an assistant surgeon in the U.S. Army and known as an expert on construction issues in hospitals, caught the eye of the committee. Importantly in terms of the Building Committee, Billings stressed the importance of sanitation. In his response to the request for information, Billings "elaborated at length upon the causes of 'hospitalism,' or the 'hurtful influence of hospitals,' by which he meant the increased incidence of infectious diseases in hospitals, and emphasized the need of proper provision for preventing the spread of such diseases within the Hospital."[10] Billings, who championed the pavilion approach, although it was more expensive than the barracks approach, was appointed to be chief adviser to the hospital on construction. The final design of The Johns Hopkins Hospital was 400 beds, with 12 common wards of 27 beds each (324 beds); 2 isolation wards of 20 beds each (40 beds); 2 pay wards of 13 beds each (26 beds); and 10 beds to be placed in tents. The tents were reserved for what were described as the most dangerous cases, that is, those with contagious diseases.[11]

---

[8] http://grad-schools.usnews.rankingsandreviews.com/usnews/edu/grad/rankings/med/brief/mdrrank_brief.php.

[9] Chesney, A. M. (1943). *The Johns Hopkins Hospital and the Johns Hopkins University School of Medicine: A chronicle. Volume I: Early years, 1867–1893.* Baltimore: The Johns Hopkins University Press, p. 21.

[10] Ibid, pp. 23–24.   [11] Ibid., p. 33.

In terms of principles that are important in health care facilities today, a number stipulated for Hopkins strike me as prescient. These principles from the Building Committee are

> 2. That a special feature of the Hospital shall be a large, open central space, ornamented with trees, flowers, a fountain, etc.

> 5. That the south ends of all wards shall be clear of rooms or buildings, and be fully exposed to air and light.[12]

Thus early on the role of nature and vistas appeared among important considerations.

What is interesting to me is that the hospital plan resembles the components of what was called the matchbox-and-muffin hospital design scheme of the mid-20th century. The matchbox-and-muffin design was a configuration in which you have patient towers atop clinical functions (so the muffins or towers are put on top of the matchboxes or clinical functions).[13,14] In the Hopkins configuration, in the absence of elevators you have the components, the surgical and clinical buildings (matchboxes) and the patient pavilions (muffins), spread over the site as a campus but ready to be stacked in the future as would be the norm.

The reason to create separate pavilion wards had to do with beliefs about disease; in particular, separation worked to contain the air, that is, to keep the air on one ward from "infecting" the air of other wards. To connect these buildings, a walkway called the bridge was built,[15] and chairs and divans were placed along this path so patients could benefit from being in the fresh air. The pavilions themselves were 100 feet in length and just under 30 feet in height, culminating in a bay window, with windows along the exterior to provide light for 24 beds.[16]

When the hospital was dedicated in 1889, a number of addresses were given; among them was an address by Billings. In something of an irony from our perspective today, Billings talked about the fact that the hospital was to provide care for the wealthy, and not just the poor. The care of the wealthy had most commonly been carried out in their own homes. Further, he notes that with advances in medicine, there were treatments provided in the hospital with its technology (however simple at that point) that could not be undertaken in private homes. Although Billings might have hoped

[12] Ibid., pp. 28–29.
[13] McLaughlin, H. (1976). The monumental headache: Overtly monumental and systematic hospitals are usually functional disasters. *Architectural Record, 160*, 118.
[14] Thompson & Goldin (1975), p. 201.   [15] Chesney (1943), p. 62.
[16] Ibid., p. 63.

that the same standard of medical treatment would be available to everyone, most of us would agree that this goal has never fully been realized. Arguably differential treatment based on social class and wealth has always existed, in whatever facet of our lives we examine.

In his address Billings referred to the wishes of the donor, Johns Hopkins. Although Hopkins prescribed no precise plans, he was concerned about the aesthetic impact the hospital would have on the city of Baltimore. Hopkins had made reference to the importance of landscaping to provide comfort to the sick, and the importance of the sun, by leaving the south end of the buildings laid out in a way to provide a lot of exposure.[17,18]

Among the addresses given at the opening, the first president of The Johns Hopkins University, Daniel Gilman, talked about opportunities the hospital could provide for interchanges among professionals.[19] Beyond their relevance to the hospital setting, Gilman's comments foreshadowed the notion of workspaces that promote communication, a topic presented in Chapter 4 (e.g., Pfizer, Corning Glass).

Also foreshadowing a major force in health care delivery were the hospital's expenses. A report from the Committee on Revenue and Expenses in December 1898, 9 years after the opening of the hospital, indicated that the hospital was in the red, with an expected deficit of about $12,000.[20] To remedy the financial situation, a number of fee changes were proposed. Among them was that private patients, at that time paying $25 per week, would pay a reduced rate but be placed in rooms with more than one patient. The issue of the appropriateness of private versus shared spaces (two-, four-, and six-bedroom) has been at the forefront of hospital care for at least 100 years and is a topic addressed later in this chapter.

FLORENCE NIGHTINGALE

In this discussion of hospital design, and in particular of the distribution of patients across wards, Florence Nightingale merits attention. She had a substantial impact on health care delivery as we know it today. In particular, she emphasized the role of a number of factors in the ambient environment: ventilation and warming, noise, light, and cleanliness.[21] Nightingale's insights

---

[17] Ibid., p. 245.   [18] Ibid., p. 246.

[19] Ibid., p. 262.

[20] Chesney, A. M. (1958). *The Johns Hopkins Hospital and The Johns Hopkins University School of Medicine: A Chronicle. Volume II, 1893–1905*. Baltimore: The Johns Hopkins University Press, p. 214.

[21] Nightingale, F. (1992). *Notes on nursing: What it is, and what it is not. Commemorative edition*. Philadelphia: J. B. Lippincott Company.

into nursing care and the environment in which it occurred were substantially shaped by her work during the Crimean War, where she went with 38 nurses to provide care to British soldiers at the army hospital in Scutari. Nightingale's comments about the origin of disease and the conditions under which care is provided reflect an early concern with the environment's role. She said disease may be the absence of things such as fresh air, light, warmth, quiet, and cleanliness, and further that disease is in fact a restorative process, nature's way to fix what is awry.[22] She further commented that "bad sanitary, bad architectural, and bad administrative arrangements often make it impossible to nurse."[23] Her first canon has to do with air. She urges that the air in the hospital should be the same degree of purity as the air outside, but that in doing so the patient should not be chilled.[24]

Another of Nightingale's insights had to do with her understanding of how important it is for people, especially those who feel they have lost control of their bodies, as is often the case for patients, to have a semblance of control over some aspects of the environment around them. As a psychologist, I find it ironic that Nightingale's comments 150 years ago were spot on in terms of understanding the issues of control in the environment. It is often the unpredictability of a stimulus that causes more harm than does a constant source, and intermittent noise is the real culprit.[25] She comments that unnecessary noise is the "most cruel absence of care" that those who are ill *or* well can experience.[26]

Variety is also important to the health care environment, a theme that emerges in research today. Nightingale points out the sterility of the hospital environment, one that actually harms the patients. Although she does not use the term stimulus deprivation, she talks about a situation where harm is caused by the lack of change in the environment,[27] and she appreciates the role aesthetics can play: "The effect in sickness of beautiful objects, of variety of objects, and especially of brilliancy of colour is hardly at all appreciated."[28] Using her situation as an illustration, she claims that when she received flowers during an illness, the speed of her recovery accelerated. She also notes the kind of suffering patients can experience when they cannot see out of a window.

Environmental psychologists and those interested in the architecture of health care benefit from familiarity with Nightingale's views: "People say the effect is only on the mind. It is no such thing. The effect is on the body,

[22] Ibid., p. 5.
[24] Ibid., p. 8.
[26] Ibid., p. 27.
[28] Ibid.

[23] Ibid., p. 6.
[25] Ibid., p. 25.
[27] Ibid., p. 33.

too. Little as we know about the way in which we are affected by form, by colour, and light, we do know this, that they have an actual physical effect.... Variety of form and brilliancy of colour in the objects presented to patients are actual means of recovery."[29] She has her own advice for the rate of change of variety, however, and suggests that it occur slowly, changing by the day or week or month instead of all at once.

Nightingale also stresses the importance of light; in her view its level of importance is close to that of the quality of air provided to the patient. In a poetic sentence she says it is sunlight rather than simply light that is important: "The sun is not only a painter but a sculptor.... The cheerfulness of a room, the usefulness of light in treating disease is all-important."[30] Nightingale comments that planners may not recognize the difference between those who are well and *sleep* in bedrooms and for whom the view is of little importance because they *are* asleep versus those who are sick and spend their time in sickrooms where the view can make a difference. She says that in positioning the beds in sickrooms the patients should be able to see the sky and sunlight without effort, that is, without having to lift or turn their heads.

Other aspects of care that she advocated ring true today, including pet therapy, which she recommended especially for the chronically ill. Regarding pets, she especially endorsed caged birds, and whatever the pet, she advocated that the patient try to care for the creature, feeding it and cleaning it.[31] This advice foreshadowed the important work of Ellen Langer and Judith Rodin, who demonstrated that elderly patients in a nursing home made more progress toward recovery when they selected a plant to tend and did that tending themselves than when a staff member selected and looked after the plant.[32]

HOSPITALS EVOLVE: SHAPE, STYLE, AND THE IMPACT OF THE ELEVATOR

During Nightingale's era and into the 1900s, hospitals had a horizontal rather than vertical configuration; elevators had yet to make an impact despite being known in the middle 1800s. The origins of disease were not fully appreciated at the end of the 1800s, and the emphasis on separating patients continued to dominate the design of the hospital complex. But

[29] Ibid., p. 34. [30] Ibid., pp. 47–48.
[31] Ibid., p. 58.
[32] Langer, E., & Rodin, J. (1976). The effects of choice and enhanced personal responsibility for the aged: A field experiment in an institutional setting. *Journal of Personality and Social Psychology, 34,* 191–198.

advances in building construction, including the use of steel, coupled with the availability of the elevator and the pressures of building hospitals in cities, where land was scarce and valuable, precipitated a change from horizontal to vertical.[33]

What emerged as a building template was the composition of a high rise with patient towers rising above a foundation of support services. This form dominated our healthscape for most of the 20th century, perhaps culminating in the 1970s with patient towers arising from underlying supporting services, which has also been called the matchbox-and-muffin scheme I mentioned earlier.[34] But this particular hospital paradigm was criticized because it could not rapidly respond to changes in technology that were becoming overwhelming.

THE GOVERNMENT, THE WARD, AND THE ROOM

Before moving on to other design solutions that emerged due to pressures of technology and cost, it is important to discuss a number of issues related to the general hospital that also apply to other health care facility types as these types emerged. These issues relate both to the sheer number of hospitals in the United States and to their internal configuration. In terms of the sheer number of hospitals, the role of the federal government in offering incentives to expand the number of hospitals in the United States must be addressed. In terms of the internal configuration of hospitals, inpatient issues are the shape of the hospital ward or unit and the number of people accommodated in patient rooms.

Although the exterior configuration of the hospital was relatively familiar over the course of the 20th century (some form of stacking; more vertical than horizontal), debates ensued about the interior of the hospital. Two of the issues over which there was a difference of opinion were (1) the configuration of the hospital floor itself; the relationship of corridors to patient rooms and the distance that staff, especially nursing staff, had to travel to deliver care, and (2) the number of people in a patient room, one versus two or more.

The impact of the federal government has affected the design of health care facilities, beginning in the 1900s and continuing today. As we see in other chapters, especially the chapter on housing, the federal government has the power to significantly shape important aspects of our lives. Health care is no exception. At its core, the federal government represents the idea

---

[33] Thompson & Goldin (1975), pp. 189–203.   [34] McLaughlin (1976).

of some kind of control over our lives, and for that reason there was resistance, especially in the medical community, to a role extending beyond typical public health functions (something like the Centers for Disease Control [CDC] now) until after World War II.[35] The first major government involvement and expenditure came in the form of construction monies, which was viewed as a less intrusive role than policy.[36]

The role of the federal government has been two-pronged; it has influenced what is built (structures and construction) and how health care is delivered (policy). In 1946, the Hospital Survey and Construction Act of 1946, or the Hill-Burton Act (P.L. 79–725), was passed. The legislation was known for its sponsors, Senators Lister Hill of Alabama and Harold Burton of Ohio. For almost half a century this act shaped the construction of health care facilities in the United States (general hospitals, health centers, and long-term care facilities) and provided funding for more than 9000 hospitals,[37] with funds provided until 1997.[38] In the period from July 1947 to June 1971, our government spent more than $3.7 billion on such health facilities.[39]

Initially the role of the federal government focused on the construction of hospital facilities, in terms of financing their construction, especially in areas where few hospital beds existed. The major impact of Hill-Burton seems to have been a redistribution of hospital beds to reduce the unevenness in the rich state/poor state division. Some thought physicians might be redistributed as well, but that outcome does not seem to have occurred.[40] With the advent of Medicare and Medicaid in the 1960s, programs received more attention as the emphasis on construction waned.

SHAPE OF WARDS

When Thompson and Goldin published their seminal book in 1975, they wrote: "Square, round, rectangular, and hexagonal wards have been

---

[35] Walsh, J. (1978, May 26). Federal health spending passes the $50-billion mark. *Science, 200*, 886–887.

[36] Ibid., p. 886.

[37] Lipscomb, C. E. (2002). Lister Hill and his influence. *Journal of the Medical Library Association, 90*(1), 109–110.

[38] Hill-Burton free and reduced cost health care. http://www.hrsa.gov/hillburton/default.htm.

[39] Clark, L. J., Field, M. J., Koontz, T. L., & Koontz, V. L. (1980). The impact of Hill-Burton: An analysis of hospital bed and physician distribution in the United States, 1950–1970. *Medical Care, 18*(5), 532–550.

[40] Clark et al. (1980).

proposed, built, debated, and defended in recent years and we are still in the throes of the argument."[41] In trying to determine which spatial configuration best served the needs of the health care community, the emphasis was largely on staff efficiency. In 1958 at Yale New Haven Hospital, a study was conducted on four units to determine the efficiency of different corridor arrangements in terms of staff "trips" (to and from a destination). Of the wards studied, each had one unit with 30 beds, the other with 48 beds. More than 20,000 trips were analyzed, of which just more than 70 percent involved the nursing staff. From this initial research the authors developed what is known as the Yale Traffic Index, which allows administrators (and others) to look at the functional efficiency of different corridor designs. Using a sample of 30 plans, the researchers examined a critical element called the traffic link – how many different ways particular destinations are reachable.[42] The idea is to try to identify the layout or floor plan that is the most efficient, meaning the one that minimizes the distance traveled to perform functions over a 24-hour period.[43] The research did not yield one specific design with maximum efficiency. Rather, when looking at corridor length and arrangement, the research suggested that of the two categories of corridor design specified, simple (with only one path from A to B) or compound (with alternate paths from A to B), the compound or redundant design is likely to yield greater efficiency, and this advantage is even more pronounced when the ward has more than 30 beds.[44] So, as the researchers note, there was no significant correlation between efficiency on the units and their size; further, efficiency did not correlate with privacy. What really mattered in efficiency was the configuration of the floor plan, and layouts with multiple routes were superior to those with just one route between origin and destination.

There were a number of different floor plans that provided route choice and other important qualities, like the ability of caregivers to see patients and the privacy available to patients. Starting in the 1960s, the radial corridor arrangement was popular because it provided more opportunities to observe patients and reduced the distance staff had to travel to deliver care.[45] Over time, other configurations, in particular the triangular and saw-tooth, surpassed the radial design because the designs offered more privacy for

---

[41] Thompson & Goldin (1975), p. 201.   [42] Ibid., p. 287.
[43] Ibid., p. 289.   [44] Ibid., p. 294.
[45] Trites, D. K., Galbraith, F. D., Jr., Sturdavant, M., & Leckwart, J. F. (1970). Influence of nursing-unit design on the activities and subjective feelings of nursing personnel. *Environment and Behavior, 2*, 303–334. Also, Verderber, S., & Fine, D. J. (2000). *Healthcare architecture in an era of radical transformation.* New Haven, CT: Yale University Press.

patients and fewer irregular spaces. The ward designed in the shape of a triangle was in fact justified by the Yale Index. Although the triangular design was not perfect (there were sometimes difficulties with the relative placements of the bed, patient window, closet, and washroom), this spatial configuration emerged as more popular than radial design.[46]

PRIVACY AND THE PATIENT ROOM: ROOM FOR ONE OR MORE?

Another critical issue over the course of the 20th century that continues today is whether patients are better served in single- versus multiple-occupancy rooms. I have an opinion on this matter, and there is also considerable literature to support my experience. Both times I have been hospitalized, one to give birth, the other to have major surgery, I have had a roommate. I don't remember much of my roommate during my hospital stay after my daughter's birth. I do remember being in a unit without air-conditioning, and in the first room on the right after entering the unit through double doors. I was also in the inboard (next to the hallway) bed. My most vivid memory of what I might call the ecology of this room was the heat and the noise. I don't know who said it, but the notion that you can't get any rest when you go to the hospital has some validity in my opinion. After my major surgery, not only did I have a view of a brick wall and a roof exhaust system, but I also had a roommate in terrible pain. She was ultimately transferred, but not for 3 days. As in my earlier experience, there was no rest in this double-occupancy room in 1998.

The debate about the number of people who should occupy a patient room was an issue early on; it was an issue at Johns Hopkins where wealthier patients housed in multiple-occupancy rooms could help balance the budget, and it was often discussed in the context of finances and not simply in terms of what might benefit the patient. Some authors have argued that the American character, and in particular our independence, has shaped our view that patient rooms should be singles, and further that privacy has been a theme that has expanded in all aspects of our lives over the course of the 20th century.[47] One need only think of the expansion of the suburb to see this emphasis on separation in American life.

Looking at the history of the single room in American health care, there were two fundamental reasons it was proposed. One was related to health itself (e.g., for contagious diseases); the other was related to social class. Among the opponents of the single room was Florence Nightingale,

---

[46] Verderber & Fine (2000), p. 42.   [47] Thompson & Goldin (1975), p. 207.

who, although British, had an impact on American health care. From the standpoint of delivering nursing care, she preferred an open ward where all patients were visible. The efficiency of nursing was more important to her than the provision of patient privacy.[48] But as early as 1908, there was a hospital in the United States comprised only of private rooms.[49]

Over the course of the debate on private versus shared rooms, finances have consistently played a role. That was certainly the case when the Depression occurred: "Some hospitals closed down whole floors, others remodeled private as semiprivate accommodations, and still others whisked two beds into every private room where there was space for them."[50] Thompson and Goldin argue that the move to semiprivate rooms was substantially influenced by Blue Cross because its reimbursement levels were greater for multiple-occupancy than for single bedrooms. They point out that the impact of single versus multiple occupancy on care was profound. It determined whether you would see the house doctor (for ward patients), whether there was the choice of a private physician (for a fee) if you were in a semiprivate room, or whether you could be treated by a private physician in a private room at significantly greater cost.[51]

What are the benefits of the private room? The semiprivate room? Certainly if you have a contagious disease or need peace and quiet for recovery, the private room meets those needs better than a shared room. Most evidence favors the benefits of the private room, but there is evidence that those who have shared rooms in their lives and are familiar with that arrangement may feel more comfort in the company of others in a semiprivate room or ward than in a single room.

Thompson and Goldin report on an important series of studies they conducted, primarily at Yale–New Haven Hospital, in the late 1950s. Their work showed that the patient's social class was linked to a preference for privacy; the higher the social class, the more the patient preferred privacy (a private room).[52] Among their scales, these studies employed what is known as the Hollingshead-Redlich Index of Social Class, which categorizes social class into five levels. In their research, the authors report that 80 percent of patients categorized in Classes IV and V (at the lower end of the scale) on the index preferred sharing a hospital room, that is, they were less comfortable with the idea of a private room. Again, familiarity seems to best explain this outcome. If you are used to sharing rooms, you may prefer

[48] Ibid., p. 207.

[50] Ibid., p. 216.

[52] Ibid., p. 224.

[49] Ibid., p. 211.

[51] Ibid.

a roommate because the familiarity of the arrangement is comforting.[53] If a patient feels isolated and craves social interaction, a multiple bedroom better meets those needs than a single bedroom. Also, some patients feel that if they need help, having a roommate will facilitate alerting the medical staff. Further, critically ill patients require more monitoring and greater staffing in single-patient rooms. In research in England, almost 90 percent of patients recovering from a stroke preferred a multiple-occupancy ward rather than a private room.[54]

DESIGN GUIDELINES ON ROOM OCCUPANCY

The 2006 Guidelines for Design and Construction of Health Care Facilities from the American Institute of Architects (AIA) set single-bed rooms as the minimum standard in general hospitals for units housing medical/surgical patients and units housing postpartum nursing patients.[55] The new AIA standards also include sections for urgent care facilities, office surgical facilities, gastrointestinal endoscopy facilities, renal dialysis centers, and psychiatric outpatient centers, underscoring the proliferation of facilities outside of the general hospital.[56] I mention these other facilities because their presence highlights the pervasiveness of ambulatory care, that is, care provided in facilities that have been "unbundled" from the core hospital, a phenomenon discussed in a later section.

As a component of formalizing these new guidelines, a comprehensive review of the costs and benefits of single- versus multiple-occupancy rooms was sponsored by the AIA Facilities Guidelines Institute and conducted by researchers at Simon Fraser University.[57] It says something about the state of hard evidence in the health care architecture domain that most research located and consulted for this review was based on self-report as opposed to measurable behavioral outcomes. Of the studies consulted for the Simon Fraser review, the vast majority were in the category Design and Therapeutic Impacts; of these 158 articles, 108 were nonempirical. In the category Disease Control and Falls Prevention, there were 31 articles, of which 22 were empirical. It is undoubtedly easier to document and count falls than

---

[53] Ibid., p. 224.
[54] Sharma, A. K., & Monaghan, J. (2004). Enhancing privacy and dignity on rehabilitation wards: New NS estate regulations do not equate patients' preferences. http://www.basp.ac .uk/MONAGHAN.HTM.
[55] http://www.aia.org/aah_gd_hospcons.   [56] Ibid.
[57] Executive summary (2003, November). Single- and multiple-occupancy patient room study. http://www.aia.org/aah_gd_hospcons.

to evaluate the impact of design. Relatively speaking, research evaluating the impact of single- versus multiple-occupancy rooms has been nonbehavioral. A comprehensive review of the advantages and disadvantages of the single-occupancy room, in contrast to the multiple-occupancy room, appeared in 2005. This article is essentially the published version of the work by researchers at Simon Fraser University.[58]

If you asked the person on the street about the cost of single- versus multiple-occupancy rooms, I think most people would probably respond by saying that single rooms are more expensive. Surprisingly, the costs of building single-bed rooms are recouped relatively soon in the life of the facility. The financial advantages associated with single-bed rooms include cost reductions due to transfer reductions (moving patients less often), higher occupancy rates, shorter patient stays, and reduction in costs associated with medication errors. These financial advantages more than offset higher costs associated with construction, staff labor, maintenance, furniture, and energy.

In the research by Simon Fraser University, interviews were conducted with nursing staff and administrators at four hospitals in the northwest United States. It should be noted that the sample size was small (73 nursing staff and 4 administrative staff). Single rooms were decisively favored by nursing staff for the following reasons: they offer flexibility in meeting the family's needs; privacy is offered when patients need to be examined; patient comfort level is improved, patient recovery level is accelerated, and there is less chance that errors in medication or diet (meals delivered to the wrong patients) will occur. Among nursing staff, privacy was the most frequently cited reason for patient transfer, followed by patient behavior issues, and then infection control.[59]

Beyond single rooms, there is also a trend toward what is known as the universal room or the acuity adaptable room. Essentially these universal rooms can be changed to accommodate any level of care needed for a given patient. These rooms are single bed and usually larger than the standard hospital room. Procedures are typically performed in the room itself, reducing the need for patient transfers. Bathrooms that accommodate the

---

[58] Chaudhury, H., Mahmood, A., & Valente, M. (2005). Advantages and disadvantages of single- versus multiple-occupancy rooms in acute care environments: A review and analysis of the literature. *Environment and Behavior, 37,* 760–786.

[59] Chaudhury, H., Mahmood, A., & Valente, M. (2003, November 20). *The use of single patient rooms vs. multiple occupancy rooms in acute care environments: Pilot study on comparative assessment of patient care issues in single and multiple occupancy environments.* Unpublished manuscript. Simon Fraser University.

disabled usually accompany these adaptable rooms, further extending their flexibility. The rooms also typically accommodate family members, who can help in patient care.

A 2007 review of the literature by researchers from the Netherlands[60] regarding the impact of single rooms on patients mirrors evidence in other areas of health care research. Specifically, the research tends to be more subjective than objective, focusing on issues like satisfaction with care and experience of dignity and privacy. Fewer studies have been done on objective outcomes like infection rates, accident rates, and more pointedly, recovery rates. Although 36 years (1970–2006) were included in the database searches and 103 articles were initially examined, only 25 articles were ultimately included because they truly focused on the effects of single rooms for patients. What is eye-opening is that the authors report only four randomized controlled studies. One explanation given for the small number of studies is the difficulty moving through the Institutional Review Board (IRB) process that protects human subjects (who are typically patients) within medical facilities.[61]

The largest number of studies that involved data gathering (as opposed to expert opinion) dealt with patient satisfaction and showed that patients are more satisfied with private than with shared rooms. All 12 articles representing expert opinion favored single rooms. In single rooms, privacy and quality of sleep increase, coupled with a decrease in noise. Although the experts argue that staying in a single room will speed recovery rates, no controlled studies to that effect were found. The authors note that problems with experimental control restrict the ability to attribute effects to the single room. The authors are not ready to state whether patients benefit from single rooms. In their view, the data are still out. In calling for more research, they echo an important theme. We need more high-quality research (randomized controlled studies) if we are to pinpoint real effects of design on patient and staff behavior.

Although the recommendations about providing single rooms are persuasive, they are based on research that tends to be correlational rather than causal and that tends to emphasize self-report. We know less than we should about the effects of single rooms on patient outcomes, primarily I think because of the difficulty in doing the kind of research that could

---

[60] Van de Glind, I., de Roode, S., & Goossensen, A. (2007). Do patients in hospitals benefit from single rooms? A literature review. *Health Policy, 84*, 153–161.

[61] Robert Sloan, UEM Consultant to Trinity Health System (personal communication, June 6, 2008).

actually isolate the role of the single room in contrast to the myriad other variables that might have an effect. Mardelle Shepley has been a leader in research in health care environments who has worked to provide guidelines to improve the health care environment based on research.[62] Among other research projects, she has recently examined the effect of single-family rooms (SFRs) in neonatal intensive care units (also known as NICUs). In that study, in addition to the three authors, she gives credit to 11 other members of the research team. I think that number of participants only hints at the intricacy of doing this kind of research in complex health care environments.

With regard to SFRs, she argues that HIPAA, the Health Insurance Portability and Accountability Act, which we all remember signing at the doctors' and dentists' offices we frequent to ensure the safety of our health care data, is partly responsible for the increase in the number of SFRs to provide patient privacy. Comparing two hospital units, one entirely SFR and the other combining both open bays and SFRs, the outcomes were quite clear. Nurses in the unit comprised solely of SFRs reported greater job satisfaction and lower stress than those in the combination unit.[63] Other articles in addition to those mentioned earlier have cited similar advantages and disadvantages to single rooms.[64]

As previously discussed in this section, in the United States the standards from the 2006 Facilities Guidelines for Design and Construction of Health Care Facilities from the American Institute of Architects call for single-patient rooms in most new hospital construction, as a minimum requirement.[65] These guidelines are followed by more than 40 state governments. In an article in the *Wall Street Journal* discussing this mandate, estimates of new construction, either through teardowns or new sites, are predicted to pass $30 billion by 2009, up from just under $20 billion in 2005. Although competition to attract patients with amenities and comfort, coupled with the fact that affluent baby boomers could pay for them was, for some time, the argument for providing single rooms, the article argues that the rationale now has shifted to better care and economics.

[62] Shepley, M. M. (2004). Evidence-based design for infants and staff in the neonatal intensive care unit. *Clinics in Perinatology, 31*, 299–311.

[63] Shepley, M. M., Harris, D. D., & White, R. (2008). Open-bay and single-family room neonatal intensive care units: Caregiver satisfaction and stress. *Environment and Behavior, 40*(2), 249–268.

[64] Jolley, S. (2005). Single rooms and patient choice. *Nursing Standard, 20*(9), 41–48, p. 42.

[65] Landro, L. (2006, March 22). New standards for hospitals call for patients to get private rooms. *The Wall Street Journal*, p. A1.

FIGURE 2.2. Bronson Hospital

One hospital that has received a substantial amount of attention for its single rooms and other examples of patient-centered care is Bronson Methodist Hospital in Kalamazoo, Michigan (see Figure 2.2). In 2000, the hospital was built with all private rooms. Bronson participates in what is known as the Pebble Project, an initiative to conduct research to provide evidence for design decisions. The big piece of news out of this hospital and this research was the drop in infection rates, by 11 percent, from rates in the old hospital with semiprivate rooms. Although the construction costs may be 10 percent to 30 percent higher than with single-occupancy-only rooms,[66] cost savings are projected to arise from fewer patient transfers, shorter hospital stays, fewer medication errors, and better patient outcomes.

UNBUNDLED SERVICES AND AMBULATORY FACILITIES

Unit design and room occupancy continue to be issues grappled with today, although for the time being it appears that the debate about single rooms has quieted. What began to change toward the end of the 20th century and continues today is the concept of the singular hospital structure. The

---

[66] Romano, M. (2005, August 1). Personal space. *Modern Healthcare, 35*(31), 20.

paradigm of the large general hospital is waning, replaced by an approach that emphasizes smaller facilities as health care struggles to respond to pressures of technology and cost. As authors comment in a book about the delivery of medical services in malls, "changes in the location of healthcare facilities alter perceptions in medicine, which in turn reinforce the other institutional shifts occurring in healthcare"; and it is argued that ambulatory care will become the dominant facility type during the 21st century.[67] The emphasis on cost containment appears as well in the new pavilion at The University of Chicago Medical Center, in which the 10-story medical structure has been designed with a modular interior to facilitate change and flexibility without the typical disruption of operation that occurs when spaces are reconfigured.[68]

What paradigms emerged as the hospital responded to these pressures of technology and cost? In 2000 an important volume entitled *Healthcare Architecture in an Era of Radical Transformation*[69] was published. Essentially a sequel to Thompson and Goldin, this book by Verderber and Fine explained the evolution in health care architecture during the latter part of the 20th century. The radical transformation referred to in the book's title reflects a number of tensions that the authors identified. These are bigness versus smallness; compactness versus linearity; low-rise versus mid- or high-rise design; and centralized versus decentralized approaches. Another point they make is that vernacular forms such as the single-family detached home, the roadside hotel, and the suburban shopping mall have made an impact on health care architecture.

A number of authors have discussed how the form of the medical building changed as priorities in health care changed; the 1970s and 1980s in particular were decades when technology and growth were paramount, whereas by the mid-1980s and moving into the 1990s, there was some emphasis on the need to create a welcoming environment for the patient.[70] An argument has also been made that the strictness of the regulations for acute care hospitals created more opportunities for ambulatory care facilities, subject to less restrictive guidelines, to be developed.

[67] Sloane, D. C., & Sloane, B. C. (2003). *Medicine moves to the mall.* Baltimore: The Johns Hopkins University Press, pp. 165, 138.

[68] Buildings & grounds: Hospital pavilion at U. Chicago will have modular design. http://chronicle.com/blogs/architecture/2180/hospital-pavilion-at-u-of-chicago-will-have-modular-des.

[69] Verderber & Fine (2000).

[70] Nesmith, E. L. (1995). *Health care architecture: Designs for the future.* Washington, D.C.: The American Institute of Architects Press.

I think these smaller visual prototypes (i.e., the roadside hotel, the detached single-family dwelling, the suburban shopping mall) had a positive influence on the direction of health care design, and decentralization in its own way replaced centralization. Verderber and Fine suggest that health care functional deconstruction means teasing apart the internal components (i.e., the various functions) and placing them in different locations within the health care campus or elsewhere altogether.[71]

But there is always a risk that the fundamental relationship of patient and care provider will be jeopardized with the "commercialization" of health care in terms of its physical presentation with the ubiquitous presence of the hotel and mall.[72] One of the primary vernacular forms is in fact the shopping mall. In their book *Medicine Moves to the Mall*, Sloane and Sloane explain why the mall, though an unlikely choice, emerged as the template for hospital services. They link it to the development of suburbia, with parking, signage, and recognizability. In a word, malls are familiar.[73]

Facilities in small shopping centers and along commercial streets often bring the health care building into contact with what might be considered questionable surroundings, such as tattoo parlors, nail salons, and palm readers, and also into contact with approaches characterized as alternative medicine, such as acupuncture. The medical facility in the mall or the medical minimall may provide much-needed accessibility, but some authors have argued that such accessibility is provided at the cost of stability (leases may not be renewed; health care providers move), and at the cost of the prestige of the profession: "In a perverse irony, America's most prestigious profession utilized one of the culture's least exalted built forms to reorder its relationship with its clientele."[74] I am reminded of a picture from Macau, an island west of Hong Kong, in which the English words " Medicine No Fakes" and the red cross symbol appear on a sign beneath the Chinese characters for medicine, government registered, and authentic merchandise. I think the concept of "fakes" often crosses one's mind in judging the quality of services based on context. What do we think of a doc-in-a-box?[75]

When I moved to southeastern Connecticut in 1973, Lawrence and Memorial Hospital, the community hospital in New London, Connecticut, had no ambulatory care or other ancillary facilities. In an ad on May 14, 2008, the hospital boasted seven different facilities. There was the main hospital and two ambulatory care facilities, one east of New London, the

---

[71] Verderber & Fine (2000), p. 135.   [72] Sloane & Sloane (2003), pp. 88–89.
[73] Ibid., p. 92.   [74] Ibid., p. 167.
[75] Ibid., p. 138.

other west of New London. In addition, the hospital advertised an occupational health center, a lab for drawing blood, a diabetes center, and a medical
office building in a community about 20 minutes away with rehabilitation
services, therapeutic fitness and sports medicine, education and wellness
programs, and a variety of diagnostic services.[76]

EXPERT OPINION

In writing this chapter, I interviewed two professionals who work in the
health care industry. One was Robert Sloan (March 15, 2008), UEM consultant to Trinity Health System, which had 43 hospitals and 379 outpatient
facilities with revenues of $6.1 billion in 2007. The other was Jennifer Gal-
lagher (April 24, 2008), co-CEO of Med-Options, a health care personnel-
sourcing service. I asked them about the state of health care in the United
States, the challenges they see, and the role of architecture and design in
that future.

Sloan was pragmatic, arguing that hospitals compete for physicians
because physicians admit patients. Competition for physicians, according to
Sloan, is the "real deal" because physicians are the source of income; physicians get patients through the door. Asked what role he thought the designed
environment played in the competition for physicians, he responded that
hospitals with modern, up-to-date facilities will attract doctors. Patients
defer to their physicians in their hospital of choice. The top medical staff
will be attracted to places with the nicest amenities and the most advanced
technology.

In terms of the kind of research being advocated in this chapter, his
view is that it is very hard to do sound research because you can't keep all
other variables static as you examine a particular factor. He thought that
bigger hospitals generally do a better job at patient care because expertise
accumulates at larger institutions. With 180 inpatient provider facilities in
Michigan, the 9 largest hospitals discharge 20 percent of the patients.

In the interview, Sloan referred to the relationship between the core
facility and ambulatory services as hub and spokes. In his view, the cost
incentives to develop ambulatory centers are great because you do not
have to replicate every step of the treatment process, ancillary services,
information systems, and so on, as a backup as you do in the main hospital.
Sloan commented that many ambulatory facilities provide limited types

---

[76] Lawrence and Memorial Hospital (May 14, 2008). We've got your care covered; with a
variety of convenient facilities and affiliates, L&M is caring for our community. *The New
London Day*, MGM Grand at Foxwoods supplement, p. 3.

of care, focusing on eye surgery, arthroscopic surgery, or MRIs, and the operational costs associated with carving out those lucrative markets are substantial (e.g., central sterile supply needs to prepare only one type of operating room instrument tray for one type of procedure for a group of five physicians vs. a main hospital with hundreds of surgeries and hundreds of physicians). The procedures where you *do* need a backup are performed in the critical care main facility.

Sloan also talked about the sense of entitlement people in the United States have about health care and felt that some citizens need to take more responsibility for their health. He pointed out that we stress the extension of life for life's sake, rather than for the quality of that life, which may lead to high health care expenses. Any number of surveys and indicators show that our health care system is inefficient in the sense that relative to other countries, we spend more money on health care with arguably poorer outcomes in terms of such measures as life expectancy. As an indication of health care performance in the United States, Sloan recommends comparing GDP (gross domestic product) with life expectancy rather then using per capita expenditures on health care with life expectancy. GDP data point to the ability to spend rather than sole consideration of expenditures. For the time period 2000–2005, total health expenditures as a percentage of GDP show the United States second only to the Marshall Islands among more than 190 countries.[77] A similar picture emerges in data for 2007 in a comparison of 30 countries, where the United States leads the way at 16.0 percent.[78] At the same time, our life expectancy at birth (78.11 years) places us 50th in the list of some 224 countries.[79] How can we improve? If the value of our health care is defined as the quality divided by the cost, the attributes that characterize such value have been identified by some advocates of a better health care system in this country as a patient-centered orientation, leadership exhibited by physicians, and a not-for-profit approach.[80]

Jennifer Gallagher made points similar to Sloan, particularly around cost as a driver. In her view, everything in health care is driven by how people are paid. When the government started paying/reimbursing more for

[77] Total Health Expenditures as % of GDP, 2000–2005 – Country Rankings. http://www .photius.com/rankings/total_health_expenditure_as_percent_of_gdp_2000_ to_2005.html.

[78] Health expenditure. Total expenditure on health, % gross domestic product. *OECD Health Data 2009-version: June 2009*. http://www.oecd.org/document/16/0,2340,en_2649_34631_ 2085200_1_1_1_1, 00.html.

[79] Country comparison: Life expectancy at birth. *CIA – The World Factbook*. https://www.cia .gov/library/publications/the-world-factbook/rankorder/2102rank.html.

[80] Cortese, D. A., & Korsmo, J. O. (2009, September 23). Putting U.S. health care on the right track. http://healthcarereform.nejm.org/?p=1890.

outpatient than inpatient services; when diagnosis-related groups (DRGS), which categorize illnesses into groups that are then reimbursable at a capped level, were implemented; and when surgeons were paid more money if the patient was admitted for only a day (the concept of "same-day surgery"), the emphasis shifted from the core hospital to ambulatory care facilities. Further, as physicians became tired of being tied to Medicare, they diversified, leading to the rise of the medical mall, with "one-stop shopping." Taking a service out of the primary facility is more effective for the hospital. Gallagher said that decisions around the construction of facilities are probably 70 percent driven by reimbursement and 30 percent by the consumer. Consumers certainly like to have conveniently located facilities, and rather than renovation, new buildings are replacing older buildings; this approach saves money with the added benefit that technology can be more easily accommodated. This emphasis on satellite facilities has happened even at prestigious institutions like Yale, which has outposts in Old Saybrook and Flanders, Connecticut, close to territory staked out by Lawrence and Memorial Hospital.

Gallagher predicts we will have a two-tier medical system in this country involving the concept of concierge medicine. Those who can afford it will avoid the hassles of waiting in the doctor's office. They will pay for the convenience and personal attention of having a doctor on call. It could be argued that we already have a two-tiered system in this country, given the differences in income that predict when women will be diagnosed with breast cancer, for example.[81]

With regard to physical design, she talked about the impact of Certificate of Need (CON) provisions for the 36 states that currently have some form of them, such as Connecticut. The CON program sets the standards for facility construction (dollar per construction), requiring the provider to build within the capital amount. Coupled with the public health code, these laws govern how facilities are constructed and in Gallagher's view lead to a cookie-cutter approach, severely hampering creativity in the design process. Only in places where there is significant choice in where your health care is provided will the role of facility design become greater through the process of competition. She thinks design may have an impact in more competitive health care markets, such as Boston and New York, where there is consumer choice. It is less likely in communities without such competition. On the other side of the CON argument, it is possible that having such

[81] Wells, B. L., & Horm, J. W. (1992). Stage at diagnosis in breast cancer: Race and socioeconomic factors. *American Journal of Public Health, 82*(10), 1383–1385.

provisions guarantees a certain standard, without which facilities would be less adequate.

Like Sloan, Gallagher thinks health care providers will market to doctors and will provide the best facilities to lure the best doctors. They will pay attention to facilities to increase their market share; also, marketing to wealthy individuals allows them to obtain money directly, and she sees more facilities adopting that approach. In other words, health care will reflect who we are as a culture; it will reflect the demographic that uses it. If you live in an area with a third-tier mall that carries fewer goods at high price points, watch out for your health care!

THE PATIENT AS CONSUMER: COMPETITION AND PREFERENCE

What about the patient as a consumer, and the patient's preferences? There has been a shift in the data used to measure patients' experience in the hospital and in the ability to compare experience. We are now reaching the stage where it is possible to compare apples to apples. Measurement of consumer satisfaction has been the primary way in which to assess patients' and visitors' responses to the hospital. How many of us have returned from a hospital procedure and shortly thereafter received a questionnaire in the mail to ask us to evaluate our hospital stay? Such evaluations have existed for many years. More recently, there has been a movement to standardize the questions to permit comparisons across hospitals.

The Hospital Consumer Assessment of Healthcare Providers and Systems (HCAHPS) was developed in 2002, and voluntary collecting of these data for use by the public started in October 2006, with the first comparability data available to the public in 2008. The survey has 27 questions, many of which have to do with communication (e.g., "During this hospital stay, how often did nurses *listen carefully to you*?"). There are two questions under the heading "The Hospital Environment" that I would categorize as directly having to do with the physical environment: (1) "During this hospital stay, how often were your room and bathroom kept clean?" and (2) "During this hospital stay, how often was the area around your room quiet at night?" Certainly other questions may indirectly have to do with the physical environment (e.g., a question dealing with frequency of communication may be related to the layout of the physical environment and the distance it takes to get from a nursing station to a patient room).

Admittedly, it is important to know about cleanliness and quiet, but these two questions do not tap into many other aspects of the physical environment that may be related to health care outcomes. In research today, health care outcomes are being defined in three different ways. There are the direct clinical outcomes like level of analgesic medication and blood pressure, there are the patient and staff reactions assessed by HCAHPS and other self-report documents, and then there are financial outcomes (e.g., the cost of beds; monies spent related to staff turnover).[82]

PATIENT DISSATISFACTION

From my own research experience, people are more willing to complain when they are dissatisfied than to tell you when they are satisfied, as long as they do not feel in a vulnerable position (i.e., potential loss of benefits) when they complain. An anonymous survey provides a good opportunity to complain, especially with regard to aspects of your life that really matter, such as health care. The federal government has made it easier for all of us to make our degrees of satisfaction and dissatisfaction known with a national uniform survey,[83] and we can all go online and check out the performance of our local hospitals at http://www.hospitalcompare.hhs.gov. Frequently reported problems include being treated with less respect than patients would have liked, poor communication, and less than adequate comprehension of discharge orders. As in other aspects of our lives, the consumer model is part of health care. We purchase an education, and we seem to purchase health care as well. And because we purchase health care, we have the right to complain about the delivery of service.

In the data reported in 2008, the nationwide average for definitely recommending the facility where they received treatment to a friend was 67 percent, and on a scale of 0 to 10, 63 percent of patients rated their institution either a 9 or 10. This is not faint praise; on the other hand, there is room for improvement.

New York Times readers responded to an article about this uniform survey with a barrage of comments. Selected comments include the following:

- "My concern: Hospitals fail to police their own employees."
- "Know-it-all-doctors."
- "There was no opportunity to tell them how bad things were."
- "High prices."

[82] Ulrich, R., & Gilpin, L. (2003). Healing arts: Nutrition for the soul. In S. B. Frampton, L. Gilpin, & P. A. Charmel (Eds.), *Putting patients first: Designing and practicing patient-centered care* (pp. 117–146). San Francisco: Jossey-Bass.

[83] Pear, R. (2008, March 29). Study finds many patients dissatisfied with hospitals. http://www.nytimes.com/2008/03/29/washington/29hospital.html?_r=1&oref=slogin.

- "Until Hospitals recognize that patient satisfaction is directly linked to nurse patient ratios they will continue to see dissatisfaction."
- "The routine daily care: the belligerent, neglectful nurses' aides; most of the nurses themselves; the unresponsiveness; the food; the inability to see the sky or the outdoors if not by window; the constant noise at night; the smell; in short, EVERYTHING."
- "The nighttime care: Utterly frightening." (Parenthetically, I might add that some hospitals, recognizing increased risks from lower staffing levels during night shifts, have begun to address that problem by having "nocturnists" who work only the night shifts.)[84]
- "Hospitals certainly are lacking in what is expected in today[']s consumer conscious America.... As a nurse I am also a consumer and hospitals are some of the dirtiest places you never want to enter. I would never want to be a patient."

But to be fair, one astute reader reminded us, "The article should have been titled 'Most Patients Satisfied with Hospital Care,'" pointing out that 67 percent are very satisfied. Another pointed out that hospitals are pretty good for acute procedures. "We do have Star Wars-like technology for emergencies which other countries may not have access to."[85]

Others talk about patients' desire for more empathy from their health care providers; to that need, CarePages.com, a Web site offering online support groups, has developed.[86] We still want a special, magical relationship with our physician, and this may run counter to the notion of evidence-based medicine, essentially that we should treat the person based on statistics from the group. In the process we miss the person. Some experts who work with patient satisfaction data argue that gross errors that negatively impact verifiable outcomes have nowhere near as frequent or as big an impact as personal slights and that you can reduce almost all patient dissatisfaction to one construct: I have to know how much you care before I care how much you know.[87]

In a "hospital meets-the-mall" form of technology, some larger hospitals are installing Internet connections to links for health care education and the purchase of medical products to aid during recuperation at home.

---

[84] Landro, L. (2008, May 28). Hospitals move to reduce risk of night shift. *The Wall Street Journal*, pp. D1, D2.

[85] http://community.nytimes.com/article/comments/2008/03/29/washington/29hospital.html.

[86] More empathy, doc. (2007, December 16). Biztalk. *The New London Day*, p. F1.

[87] Robert Sloan, UEM Consultant to Trinity Health System (personal communication, June 6, 2008).

At Northwestern Memorial Hospital in Chicago, for example, the home page links to four choices: television, the Web, medical education, and hospital information.[88] This arrangement provides information about patient illnesses, with links to more than 1000 pages. "By offering Internet access to patients on big-screen TVs, though, hospitals are providing a 'wow' factor that... helps them compete against other facilities nearby."[89] But as this article indicates, perhaps it is the visitors rather than the ill patients who are using the Web to inform themselves about the patient.

In addition to using the Web for medical information, the Internet provides the opportunity for patients who share a disease to compare notes. PatientsLikeMe is a Web site with data; the participants create a "rich database of disease treatment and patient experience" that is quantified and available for comparison. More than 100 million adults are getting some kind of health information from an Internet source.[90]

The use of the Internet by health care consumers is also having a trickle-down effect on health care design. At a recent conference I heard about collaboration between a division of Steelcase and the Mayo Clinic.[91] In designing the workspace for a clinical examination room, the shape of the table/desk was a major concern. A semicircular table was constructed to provide more space for patients to view their clinical records (in conjunction with their physician) on a plasma monitor on the table. One comment made by the conference presenters is that patients are increasingly bringing their own information with them (gathered from the Internet) and need a work surface to spread out their documents. In the research trial, the semicircular table was warmly endorsed by both physicians and patients, which had not been expected in terms of the physicians' response. The six physicians in this study were willing to share space at a table that essentially put them at the same status level, at least in terms of the workspace, as their patients.

THE APPEALING SETTING EFFECT: HOW IT LOOKS MATTERS!

There is no reason to believe that competition for patients and doctors will abate, and it makes sense for health care designers to understand what both

[88] Tedeschi, B. (2008, March 17). Even if you're ill, you can still stay connected. *The New York Times*, p. C6.

[89] Ibid., p. C6.

[90] Goetz, T. (2008, March 23). Practicing patients. *The New York Times Magazine*, pp. 32–37, p. 34.

[91] Almquist, J., Kelly, C., & Bromberg, J. (2008, May). *The relationship between workspace, activity and hierarchy in a clinical exam room: An innovative design in practice*. Presentation at the 39th annual conference of the Environmental Design Research Association, Veracruz, Mexico.

patients and providers want. To that end, a number of researchers, including me, have looked at perceptions of facilities, waiting rooms, and credentials as indications of competence. An underlying question in much research is how a health care setting looks; the idea of an appealing setting is related to any of a number of outcomes, including patient satisfaction. Essentially the appealing setting effect is the idea that when we judge people in an aesthetically pleasing setting, they are viewed more positively than when the setting is not aesthetically pleasing. More than 50 years ago there was research on this topic[92] by Maslow and Mintz (Maslow is well known for his hierarchy of needs). In a more recent field study in a hospital, patients were matched on a number of characteristics (e.g., age, gender, insurance type, mix of services, pain control), and their reactions to either an "appealing room" or a typical room were compared.[93] Questions came from what is known as the Patient Report Card (PRC), which is used to have patients evaluate a recent hospital stay. Although patients rated physicians more favorably in appealing as opposed to typical rooms, there was no significant difference in the ratings of nurses across room types. Housekeeping, food service staff, and food service itself were rated more positively in appealing than in typical rooms. Moreover, the appealing rooms were rated more positively in terms of patients' intentions to use the hospital again, to rate it more favorably, and to recommend it to others.

The visually appealing rooms were in a facility called the Magnolia Pavilion, described as hotel-like with wood furniture, decorator art, carpeted floors, crown molding, and ceramic tile baths. The typical units were near the Magnolia Pavilion and contained typical metal hospital beds, inexpensive chairs where family members could sit, and no artwork. The typical rooms were slightly smaller and noise levels were higher than was true of rooms in the Magnolia Pavilion.[94] Certainly there were problems with the research, notably different response rates, the self-selection of patients for the appealing room, and the fact that these self-selected patients paid $40 more per day for that appealing room. One could also argue that the concept of appeal lacked a true operational definition. Until there are randomly controlled studies about the effects of such units, we have correlation and not causation.

---

[92] Maslow, A. H., & Mintz, N. L. (1956). Effects of esthetic surroundings: I. Initial effects of three esthetic conditions upon perceiving "energy" and "well-being" in faces. *Journal of Psychology, 41*, 247–254.

[93] Swan, J. E., Richardson, L. D., & Hutton, J. D. (2003). Do appealing hospital rooms increase patient evaluations of physicians, nurses, and hospital services? *Health Care Management Review, 28*(3), 254–264.

[94] Ibid., p. 255.

My own research has addressed a similar domain in terms of what appeals to patients (or potential patients). Over the past 5 years, I have conducted research on the impressions that health care facilities make: their exterior appearance; impact of the waiting room; and most recently the impact that displaying credentials makes on judgments about therapists. Here I will focus on the exterior view.

Often research in architecture takes the form of what is known as postoccupancy evaluation (POE). In a POE, the researcher looks closely at a single structure and tries to determine what worked well in the design and what could be improved. The postoccupancy aspect refers to the fact that the evaluation occurs after the building is occupied, that is, once users inhabit the structure. My own approach has been different. Rather than approaching the evaluation of health care facilities from the standpoint of POEs, I wanted to find out what people thought of a variety of buildings, not a single building, and to see what these buildings had in common from the standpoint of the people who rated them. By looking at building groupings, one might argue that themes in design would more clearly emerge than is true in the case of POEs, and the possibilities for generalization would be greater than is true for the evaluation of a single structure.

In this research on exteriors,[95] the facades of 34 medical facilities from Connecticut, Rhode Island, and Michigan were photographed, and then 188 college students were asked to rate these facilities in terms of two central dimensions: the quality of care they thought would be provided in these facilities and how comfortable they felt in these facilities. For each building, respondents were asked to indicate what about the building prompted their ratings. In addition they were asked how often they had visited a physician, what kinds of medical buildings they had visited, and a number of demographic variables (e.g., age, gender, parental income) to characterize the populations.

Respondents' ratings on these two different dimensions were grouped into clusters by a statistical technique. In terms of the quality of care ratings in this study, three clusters emerged, which I called Traditional House type, Brick Office type, and Large Medical type. Out of a score of 100, the buildings grouped under the Large Medical category received the highest average ratings for quality of care ($\approx$81), followed by the Traditional House

[95] Devlin, A. S. (2008). Judging a book by its cover: Medical building facades and judgments of care. *Environment and Behavior, 40,* 307–329.

category ($\approx$61), with the Brick Office category garnering the least support ($\approx$56). For the Large Medical facilities, typical comments to describe them were professional, impersonal, smart, sterile, intimidating, high-quality, modern, expensive, high-tech, and large. For the Traditional House-type, descriptions included quaint, homey, small, bright, shabby, clean, cheerful, cluttered, and residential. To respondents, the Brick Office-type facilities were brick, cold, dark, institutional-looking like a school, dirty, older, and uninviting.

When you look at how these same 34 buildings grouped together in terms of the degree of comfort people felt in these environments, a somewhat different story emerged. Overall, the ratings went down. Just because people think high-quality care is likely to be delivered in a setting does not guarantee that their comfort level is equally high. For comfort in the environment, in addition to the same three factors that had emerged in the quality of care ratings (Large Medical, $\approx$68; Traditional House, $\approx$62; Brick Office, $\approx$51), a fourth dimension emerged: Low Budget ($\approx$46). For the Low Budget buildings, comments that emerged were motel-like, rundown, and even strange and creepy (one begins to picture something like Norman Bates and the Bates Motel in the movie *Psycho*).

The biggest drop from quality of care to degree of comfort was in the Large Medical-type. This difference speaks to the idea that we may want the quality of care that we think accompanies impressive medical facilities, but these facilities are less comforting than they are impressive. For the Traditional House-type and the Brick Office-type, the difference between quality of care and comfort was relatively small.

Recent photographs of medical facilities with the highest and lowest ratings for quality of care appear in Figures 2.3 and 2.4 (rated as 88 vs. 34). The highest-rated building loaded onto the Large Medical-type factor, whereas the lowest-rated facility loaded as part of the Brick Office-type factor. Ironically, the medical building with the lowest rating contains the former office of my daughter's pediatrician. It is hard to reconcile the appearance of this office building with the practice of pediatrics.

The title of the article, "Judging a book by its cover: Medical facilities and judgments of care," reflects what I think is the case. The title is certainly communicated by the two anecdotes at the beginning of this chapter. We do judge each other by the physical characteristics we see; it is also the case that we judge a variety of aspects of our surroundings based on data we receive from our senses. How something looks, sounds, smells, tastes, and feels affects our judgment. In fact, the Planetree model of patient-centered

FIGURE 2.3. Facility with highest judged care ratings

FIGURE 2.4. Facility with lowest judged care ratings

care, discussed next in this chapter, is centered on the idea that we want to create health care environments that nourish our senses, rather than deplete them.

The Planetree model of patient-centered care has its roots in one woman's unpleasant encounter with the American health care system, and we should note that women are reported to make the majority of health care decisions for the family, up to 75 percent.[96] That woman was Angelica Thieriot. Her perception was that technology had overshadowed the ability of nurses and doctors to deliver care in a humanizing manner, and she set out to create an approach to health care to change that sterile model, to personalize it, putting the patient's understanding of his or her illness and the patient's comfort in the environment at the core of the concept of care. That model is Planetree, named after the tree under which Hippocrates sat in Greece to teach early medical students.[97] In this model, the patient is truly empowered and is a partner in his or her own health care. Founded in 1978,[98] patients in this multifaceted approach are encouraged to educate themselves about the medical predicaments they face. Others have pointed to Maslow's hierarchy of needs related to the idea of patient empowerment.[99] The first Planetree unit opened in San Francisco in 1985. The design of a hospital based on Planetree principles has numerous amenities that encourage patient empowerment and the active role of family members. These amenities include a library, open nursing stations that invite communication, alternative therapies such as massage and aromatherapy, and open kitchens on each unit where family members can prepare meals. A 24-hour visiting policy and sleeper sofas help create an environment where family members are welcomed. The architectural environment has been described as hotel-like, with carpet and artwork in the hallways and computer and cable hookups as well as artwork in patient rooms. Patients can order food, the equivalent of room service, and the smell of baking cookies

---

[96] Kobus, R. L. (2000). Perspective. In S. A. Kliment (Ed.), *Building type basics for healthcare facilities* (pp. 1–7). New York: John Wiley & Sons, Inc.

[97] http://www.planetree.org/about/ourfounder.htm.

[98] Martin, D. P., Hunt, J. F., Hughes-Stone, M., & Conrad, D. (1990). The Planetree Model Hospital Project: An example of the patient as partner. *Hospital & Health Services Administration, 35,* 591–601.

[99] Thompson & Golden (1975).

or other pleasant odors often permeate the units, as does music from the lobby.[100]

The mission of the organization is embodied in the following principles:

We believe:

- that we are human beings, caring for other human beings.
- we are all caregivers.
- caregiving is best achieved through kindness and compassion.
- safe, accessible, high-quality care is fundamental to patient-centered care.
- in a holistic approach to meeting people's needs of body, mind, and spirit.
- families, friends, and loved ones are vital to the healing process.
- access to understandable health information can empower individuals to participate in their health.
- the opportunity for individuals to make personal choices related to their care is essential.
- physical environments can enhance healing, health, and well-being.
- illness can be a transformational experience for patients, families, and caregivers.[101]

In February 2008, some 80 hospital or health care systems in the United States were listed as Planetree affiliates on their Web site, with eight international affiliates. Coincidentally, the organization's current home base is the hospital where I conducted research in the early 1990s.

My own research on the Planetree model[102] involved a hospital in Connecticut near New Haven that has the status of a Planetree affiliate, which means that the health care facility subscribes to the Planetree principles to create a healing environment. At the time of my research, there were 161 beds in the facility. My interest was in comparing two units that had been remodeled in a manner consistent with the Planetree philosophy with a unit that had not yet been renovated. I involved more than 100 patients, more than 30 members of the nursing staff, and more than 60 visitors in a survey of satisfaction of the three units. The participants were asked to evaluate the units on a variety of dimensions, including the mode of nursing, the sense

[100] http://www.achosp.org/Planetree.aspx.
[101] http://www.planetree.org/about/welcome.htm.
[102] Devlin, A. S. (1995). Staff, patients and visitors: Responses to hospital unit enhancements. In J. Nasar, P. Grannis, & K. Hanyu (Eds.), *26th Environmental Design Research Association conference proceedings* (pp. 113–117). Oklahoma City, OK: Environmental Design Research Association.

of well-being in the environment, the ability to choose in the environment, how you felt in the environment, the flow of information between patients and staff, whether people felt able to make changes in the environment, and how responsive the unit was to the individual's needs. In addition, members of the nursing staff filled out a stress inventory used with health professionals. Across units, nurses did not differ in the amount of stress they reported.

In general, the renovated units were viewed more positively than the unrenovated unit. From the standpoint of ruling out other factors that might explain these changes, there were no significant differences across units in the number of visits patients reported receiving or in the number of visits family members or visitors reported making. With regard to the issue of visits and visitors, it's important that no differences were reported because such variability might affect the patients' perceptions of quality of care and other affective reactions to the environment.

Importantly, 70 percent of the comments made by nurses on the unrenovated unit were about the need for improvement, whereas staff on the renovated Planetree units made no such comments about the need for improvement in the environment. Although all three units were arguably models of patient-focused care in terms of a nursing management philosophy, the environments differed considerably (see Figures 2.5 and 2.6). A similar trend appeared for patients. Just less than 50 percent of the comments patients made on the unrenovated unit involved the need for the environment to be improved, whereas comments about environmental improvement were 20 percent on one of the renovated units and 0 percent on the other.

What I noticed was a phenomenon consistent with what is called Herzberg's two-factor theory of work motivation.[103] To simplify, this theory says there are some factors called content or motivator variables in the work environment that are capable of producing satisfaction; others called context or hygiene variables are capable of producing dissatisfaction, but not of producing satisfaction. The nature of one's work (i.e., its content) is a motivator variable, whereas the environment is categorized as a hygiene or context variable. With regard to my study, there is some validity to Herzberg's ideas. We seem to be ready, willing, and able to criticize the environment when it falls below some acceptable level. But when it rises above that level, it does not seem worth writing home about, as it were.

---

[103] Herzberg, F., Mausner, B., & Snyderman, B. B. (1959). *The motivation to work*. New York: John Wiley & Sons, Inc.

FIGURE 2.5. Unrenovated unit

FIGURE 2.6. Planetree unit

That is, we often seem to take environmental *improvements* for granted, as if the environment should have been at that level all along. When chipped paint attracts our attention and clanking radiators distract us, it is easy to pass judgment about the inadequacy of the environment. If the walls are painted and the heating system is quiet, nothing out of the ordinary exists; we expect no less. As I stated about this research, "the environment emerges most significantly in openended questions when it is a liability; when it is an asset, it seems overlooked."[104]

A 2003 book *Putting Patients First: Designing and Practicing Patient-Centered Care*[105] describes a variety of approaches taken to improving patient health, beyond what might be termed normal allopathic or conventional care. These additional approaches typified in the Planetree model essentially focus on the patients' senses – what they see (art, design, and lighting), what they taste (home-baked goods), what they hear (soft music), what they feel (massage), and their spiritual needs. One of the most important chapters in this book is written by Patrick Charmel, president and CEO of Griffin Health Services Corporation, which oversees the Planetree organization and Griffin Hospital. In this article entitled "Building the business case for patient-centered care,"[106] he talks about the pressures that arose after Congress passed the Balanced Budget Amendment in 1997, which dramatically curtailed Medicare expenses, reducing hospitals' profits and leading hospitals to find ways to balance their budgets. Efficiency alone (reduction in staffing) did not accomplish this bottom line, and he argues that lengths of stay were reduced by bringing patients with similar diagnoses into alignment in terms of the number of days they were typically hospitalized. These practice guidelines, or care pathways as they have been called, shaped patient care.[107] He goes on to explain that these steps were not sufficient in balancing budgets, and hospitals turned to the revenue side of the ledger, figuring out how to enhance revenue. What has driven the growth of revenue is the idea of health care consumerism, with educated and mobile consumers willing to travel to find care they perceive to be high quality. Charmel talks about the approach of hospitals to build a brand identity based on product quality,

---

[104] Devlin (1995), p. 116.
[105] Frampton, S. B., Gilpin, L., Carmel, P. A. (Eds.) (2003). *Putting patients first: Designing and practicing patient-centered care.* San Francisco: Jossey-Bass.
[106] Charmel, P. A. (2003). Building the business case for patient-centered care. In S. B. Frampton, L. Gilpin, P. A. Carmel (Eds.), *Putting patients first: Designing and practicing patient-centered care* (pp. 193–204). San Francisco: Jossey-Bass.
[107] Ibid., p. 196.

reputation, and service. The Planetree model of care has nicely meshed with this idea; in a sense it is providing value-added qualities of health care, or perhaps even reestablishing what potential patients will consider minimum services and surroundings. "Currently, in health care, the patient equates customer service with quality. Therefore, valued providers are those that deliver an exceptional patient experience."[108]

NATURE, ARTWORK, AND PATIENT RECOVERY

Aesthetics play a role in the Planetree model to be sure, but perhaps an even more important element of the environment, and one that may not be so easy to provide, is the role of nature itself in well-being. A seminal study by Roger Ulrich in 1984,[109] published in the prestigious journal *Science*, used archival data to look at the recovery of a matched set of gallbladder patients. The view of one group was of what one might call everyday nature (out the hospital room window to a cluster of deciduous trees). The other group looked out the window at a brown brick wall. The group with the view to nature had shorter postoperative stays and took fewer doses of analgesics in the moderate or strong categories than did their matched compatriots. There were other more subjective differences among the nature viewers (fewer negative evaluative comments from nurses), but the shorter stay and less potent levels of pain medication constitute what may be one of the first examples of evidence-based design. In this case, the design has to do with a view provided to nature. A significant body of research from Stephen and Rachel Kaplan at the University of Michigan, among others, has documented the role nature plays in human well-being, and has argued for an evolutionary basis to the preference humans have for nature.[110] Even the infamous Hannibal Lecter (*Silence of the Lambs*), who has been incarcerated for 8 years when we first see him, says, "I know they will never, ever let me out while I'm alive. What I want is a view. I want a window where I can see a tree, or even water."[111]

Where a view to nature is not possible, as in areas of the hospital where scans are being done and radiation emitted, pictures of nature have often been substituted, largely because of the impact of the initial work by Ulrich.

[108] Ibid., p. 197.
[109] Ulrich, R. S. (1984, April 27). View through a window may enhance recovery from surgery. *Science, 224*, 420–421.
[110] Kaplan, R., & Kaplan, S. (1989). *The experience of nature: A psychological perspective*. New York: Cambridge University Press.
[111] http://www.imsdb.com/scripts/Silence-of-the-Lambs.html.

As examples of virtual nature, simulations of nature have been provided through the use of an electronic window of nature that simulates the diurnal cycle, created by Joey Fischer/Art Research Institute Limited and first used in the United States at Stanford.[112]

What difference might it make what specific "art" a patient sees? Although this question has not been answered definitively, there is evidence that the display of artwork on the walls of patients' rooms improves morale, but that not just any artwork helps. A substantial amount of research on this topic has been done by Roger Ulrich, author of the aforementioned study on the view of nature from a hospital bed. In Ulrich and his followers' research, people seem to prefer representational rather than abstract art. In fact, there is evidence that if you display abstract art, the effect may be more harmful than the display of no artwork at all.[113]

And it is important to ask patients in particular about their preferences, because students in the design professions (interior design; architecture and building science) make different judgments than patients.[114] The display of nature scenes has been linked to increasing pain tolerance, better pain control, and a reduction in fatigue and anxiety.

A recent study[115] has looked at the preference for art in hospitals in more depth. Popularly selling art images were paired with abstract and nonabstract versions of particular scenes, such as abstract and representational images of a kiss. Respondents were asked both about how the images made them feel and how likely they would be to hang this particular image in the hospital room. Hospital patients and university students in design departments participated in the study. Realistic nature-based art was preferred by patients, and what patients liked best was a photograph of a rocky waterfall. Nature trumped abstract and stylized images. Regarding what to hang in the room, interior design students tended to select well-known art images, such as Seurat's *Sunday Afternoon on the Island of La Grande Jatte* and Rabi Khan's *The Kiss*. University students in the study, from the interior design (primarily women) and building sciences/architecture majors (primarily men), were not as consistent in their preferences as were patients.

---

[112] Seligmann, J., & Buckley, L. (1990, March 26). A sickroom with a view. *Newsweek*, 61.

[113] Ulrich, R., & Gilpin, L. (2003). Healing arts: Nutrition for the soul. In S. B. Frampton, L. Gilpin, & P. A. Charmel (Eds.), *Putting patients first: Designing and practicing patient-centered care* (pp. 117–146).

[114] Nanda, U., Eisen, S. L., & Baladandayuthapani, V. (2008). Undertaking an art survey to compare patient versus student art preferences. *Environment and Behavior, 40*, 269–301.

[115] Ibid.

THE NEED FOR EVIDENCE-BASED DESIGN

A good deal of research on art in hospitals is compelling, but much of it focuses on patient satisfaction, preference, and other indices of self-report. In other words, the evidence is soft. For example, in terms of the early Planetree units in California discussed earlier in the chapter, research did not initially show any impact on what might be called hard outcomes. In a randomized trial design, patients assigned to Planetree versus other units differed in satisfaction with their stay, but there was no significant difference in the health behaviors of patients in different types of units.[116]

I think there has been a tendency for those involved in the work on improving the physical setting of health care environments to be viewed as people who are artists rather than scientists, more as interior designers than researchers. For the field of health care architecture to make a greater impact, a more hard-nosed approach has been needed. That approach now is being provided under the rubric of evidence-based design and helped by the Center for Health Design and its Pebble Project as well as the Robert Wood Johnson Foundation.

An influential step in providing evidence-based design has been the creation of The Center for Health Design (CHD), which has now absorbed another health care research initiative, the Coalition for Health Environments Research (CHER). With some funding from the Robert Wood Johnson Foundation, CHD promotes improvements in health care facility design through research (especially evidence-based research), education, and advocacy. The current initiative of CHD garnering a good deal of press is known as the Pebble Project,[117] started in 2000. Ripples are created when a pebble skims across the top of a pond. The Pebble Project incorporates this idea, hoping initial projects will lead to others. The goal is improving quality of care through facility design, as well as improving the financial health of the organization. Already the completed projects have indicated that the quality of care can be improved, more patients can be attracted, productivity and efficiency can be enhanced, and staff can be recruited and retained.[118]

Some 4 years after the start of the Pebble Project, an article appeared summarizing the business case for hospitals based on such evidence-based

[116] Martin, D. P., Diehr, P., Conrad, D. A., Davis, J. H., Leickly, R., & Perrin, E. B. (1998). Randomized trial of a patient-centered unit. *Patient Education and Counseling, 34*, 125–133.
[117] http://www.healthdesign.org/research/pebble/.
[118] Ibid.

design.[119] A fictitious hospital, Fable Hospital, is created from the principles of evidence-based design and a number of initial Pebble Projects. This hypothetical 300-bed hospital was estimated to cost $240 million, with $12 million dollars in expense above and beyond a typical hospital. The additional costs were for oversized single rooms, acuity adaptable rooms (standardized rooms of particular space, dimensions, and features to accommodate a range of patient needs), decentralized barrier-free nursing stations, artwork, noise-reducing features, patient education centers, and staff support facilities. The authors argue that by the end of the first year, additional capital essentially will be recouped through a series of behavioral outcomes that save money. These outcomes include a reduction in the number of patient falls, patient transfers, nosocomial infections, drug costs, and nursing turnover, and increased market share and philanthropy.[120] There seem to be distinct advantages to being a Pebble Partner, including research assistance to evaluate the impact of design decisions on patient, staff, and financial outcomes,[121] although it should be clear that the research support provider is not an uninterested third party.

Although not limited to health care, a new database project about research driving design is called InformeDesign[122] (where research informs design). The American Society of Interior Designers (ASID) and the University of Minnesota have launched this site to communicate research-based design criteria, understandable to an audience without a background in research.

Why did it take so long to build a solid and convincing database on health care facilities? One reason is the difficulty of doing research in the health care setting. A second is the culture of medicine that places physicians close to heaven, where their authority cannot be questioned. The expertise of physicians provided a cure; a cure could hardly come from the environment. Yet another reason a database has been long in coming is the unfamiliarity of the research process to health care professionals.

A former student and I reviewed the literature about the relationship between health care environments and patient outcomes to investigate the

---

[119] Berry, L. L., Parker, D., Coile, R. C., Jr., Hamilton, D. K., O'Neill, D. D., & Sadler, B. L. (2004, November). The business case for better buildings. *Healthcare Financial Management*, pp. 76–86.

[120] Ibid., pp. 82–83.

[121] Sandrick, K. (2003, September). A higher goal: Evidence-based design raises the bar for new construction. *Health Facilities Management*, pp. 16–21.

[122] http://www.informedesign.umn.edu/.

extent to which researchers had been able to establish causal relationships, or at the very least strong correlational patterns.[123] What we argued at that time was that although the environment has been increasingly important in the views of health care providers,[124] the database to establish causality (i.e., that the environment can make a difference in healing) just had not been built.

In showing the need for an empirically valid base of evidence, one article has provoked a considerable amount of discussion. This article is a review of the literature where some 38,000 articles were consulted about the role of the environment that in some way showed a relationship to patient outcomes. Of this large number of articles, fewer than 50 were judged to meet the criteria established, and the authors claim that fewer still were methodologically sound.[125] Even Ulrich's well-known study[126] showing that a view of nature from a hospital window can speed recovery from surgery more than was true of a view of a brick wall was questioned. In this study about the effects of the view of nature, patients recovering from gallbladder surgery might have benefited from the amount of light as much as the view itself.

But the antiresearch culture of the health care environment is changing. Beyond the Center for Health Design and the Pebble Project, another indication is that the entire issue of the March 2008 journal *Environment and Behavior* is devoted to "building the evidence base for evidence-based design." One article title suggests the potential for the environment to make a real difference: "Impact of emergency department built environment on timeliness of physician assessment of patients with chest pain." The article

---

[123] Devlin, A. S., & Arneill, A. B. (2003). Health care environments and patient outcomes: A review of the literature. *Environment and Behavior, 35,* 665–694.

[124] Devlin, A. S. (1995). Staff, patients, and visitors: Responses to hospital unit enhancement. In J. L. Nasar, P. Grannis, & K. Hanyu (Eds.), *Proceedings of the 26th annual conference of the Environmental Design Research Association* (pp. 113–117). Oklahoma City, OK: EDRA; Martin, D. P., Hunt, J. R., & Conrad, D. A. (1990). The Planetree model hospital project: An example of the patient as partner. *Hospital and Health Services Administration, 35,* 591–601; Ruga, W. (1989). Designing for the six senses. *Journal of Health Care Interior Design, 1,* 29–34; Ulrich, R. (1992). How design impacts wellness. *Healthcare Forum Journal, 35,* 20–25; Ulrich, R. (1995). Effects of healthcare interior design on wellness: theory and recent scientific research. In S. O. Marberry (Ed.), *Innovations in healthcare design: Selected presentations from the first five symposia on healthcare design* (pp. 88–104). New York: Van Nostrand Reinhold.

[125] Rubin, H. R., & Owens, A. J. (1996). *Progress report: An investigation to determine whether the built environment affects patients' medical outcomes.* Martinez, CA: The Center for Health Design.

[126] Ulrich (1984).

points to the importance of visibility (whether there is a solid door creating a visual barrier) and distance from the patient workstation as factors that increase the time to evaluate a patient.[127] Remarkable to me is that the article was authored by four physicians (from Northwestern University). This is the first time I can remember seeing an article in a journal devoted to environment and behavior that was authored solely by physicians. Another useful aspect of this study was that it used archival data from a departmental computerized database. More than 200,000 patient visits were considered during the time frame for the study ($\approx 2\frac{1}{2}$ years), with just more than 2,000 meeting the criteria for the study (e.g., chief complaint, age, time of day). Studies of this kind are much easier to do than surveys or interviews (in terms of the personnel required) and should provide a model to expand the number of studies done in health care settings.

To assist in the construction of a database of evidence-based design, there are a number of other signs that the communication between the research community and health care practitioners may be improving. The American Institute of Architects has a practice specialty in health care architecture, the Academy on Architecture for Health. In more than 30 years the group has grown from less than 100 members to as many as 4000. Another organization is the American College of Healthcare Architects, the governing body that credentials health care architects in the United States. There is also the Academy of Neuroscience for Architecture and the Academy of Architecture for Health Foundation. The challenge to designers is one where humanity must be combined with cutting-edge (no pun intended) technology. We seem to have moved beyond the attitude that health care architecture held little appeal for designers (and design schools) and was considered a kind of dead end specialty.[128] Now, health care architecture is seen by a good number of firms as providing at least some opportunities for creativity, and certainly for commissions.

WHAT DOES THE FUTURE HOLD?

In the spring of 2007, David Walker, who ran the Government Accounting Office (GAO) as comptroller general of the United States, made an appearance on the news show *60 Minutes* in which he talked about the impending bankruptcy of the United States. One of the biggest factors in

---

[127] Hall, K. K., Kyriacou, D. N., Handler, J. A., & Adams, J. G. (2008). Impact of emergency department built environment on timeliness of physician assessment of patients with chest pain. *Environment and Behavior, 40,* 233–248.

[128] Devlin & Arneill (2003).

our overspending, if not the biggest factor in his judgment, is health care.[129] In the interview he described the country's financial situation as suffering from a "fiscal cancer."[130]

When the first members of the baby boomer generation reach age 62 and become eligible for Social Security starting January 1, 2008, and for 2 decades thereafter, 78 million Americans will become part of a benefit package the country cannot afford, according to Walker. When they turn 65, members of this generation will be eligible for Medicare. In tables and charts, he demonstrates the fiscal condition we will be in by 2040 if policies do not change. By then, the budget will do little more "than pay interest on the mounting debt and some entitlement benefits. It won't have money left for anything else – national defense, homeland security, education, you name it."[131]

The biggest problem, he says, far bigger than Social Security, is health care. In terms of scale, he places Medicare as a problem five times larger than Social Security. The fact that we live longer and that medical costs are rising at twice the rate of inflation are the problems, he says. Walker points to expanded coverage, such as the prescription drug bill passed in late 2003, as adding to the problem. "The prescription drug bill was probably the most fiscally irresponsible piece of legislation since the 1960s" says Walker.[132] "With one stroke of the pen," Walker says, "the federal government increased existing Medicare obligations nearly 40 percent over the next 75 years."[133]

Walker's judgment is that the current health care system is overrated. "On cost we're number one in the world. We spend 50 percent more of our economy on health care than any nation on earth," he says. "We have the largest uninsured populations of any major industrialized nation. We have above average infant mortality, below average life expectancy, and much higher than average medical error rates for an industrialized nation."[134] Walker's message is that without fundamental reform, bankruptcy awaits us.

Given this bleak picture, what does the future of health care facility design hold? I think there will be less attention to what are considered the frills and more attention to what constitutes the bottom line, and in particular more attention to whether a particular procedure statistically predicts a positive outcome. Presumably there will be attempts to address the issues that worry Walker, and these steps may lead to less attention on environmental design,

---

[129] http://www.cbsnews.com/stories/2007/03/01/60minutes/main2528226.shtml.
[130] Ibid., para. 12.   [131] Ibid., para. 18.
[132] Ibid., para. 23.   [133] Ibid., para. 25.
[134] Ibid., paras. 31–32.

unless there is more evidence that attention to design features actually impact the *cost* of health care.

TECHNOLOGY, COMPLEMENTARY AND ALTERNATIVE MEDICINE, AND CONCIERGE MEDICINE

Certainly there are other issues, some related to cost concerns Walker identifies, that will continue to challenge us. These issues are technology, complementary and alternative medicine, and litigation and physician honesty. Competition abounds, and what facilities typically advertise is the latest technological advancement. For example, a hospital in New Haven, Connecticut, advertises in our local newspaper in southeastern Connecticut to recruit patients. The ad proclaims, "Tumors have nowhere to hide from CYBERKNIFE at the Hospital of Saint Raphael." In this ad the hospital's corporate message is "Leading experts. The latest technology."[135]

But technology often presents ethical dilemmas when we as family members face issues surrounding end of life care. I have personal experience with this issue, as my mother died of heart failure after battling lung cancer for 3 months. She had surgery, but the tumor was inoperable. She never recovered her stamina after that surgery. Twenty-four years earlier she had successfully battled breast cancer at a time when few people survived. With a husband who was a thoracic surgeon, there was no question she would have aggressive treatment for the lung cancer. One of my father's friends who was a thoracic surgeon in Great Britain said that had my mother been in Great Britain, they would not have treated her that aggressively. But it is easy to make that kind of judgment when it is not your loved one. And doctors are not trained to stop trying. Physicians and patients in this country need more help to understand end of life processes.[136] In terms of the physical environment, hospice facilities can be expected to play an ever more important role as the baby boomer generation ages.

Complementary and Alternative Care

Another dimension to the health care landscape that confronts us is complementary and alternative medicine (CAM), and it is no longer considered

---

[135] Hospital of Saint Raphael (May 14, 2008). Tumors have nowhere to hide from CYBERKNIFE. *The New London Day*, p. A5.

[136] Mithers, C. (2008, June 1). For the dying, less can be more. Special to the *Los Angeles Times*; reprinted in *The New London Day*, pp. E1, E4.

medicine on the outer fringe. In fact, alternative care has been and is being embraced in traditional, straightforward, empirical western medical centers. Some form of CAM is offered in 18 hospitals cited by *U.S. News & World Report* in its America's Best Hospitals List. Among the most endorsed and familiar forms of CAM are yoga and massage.[137] But there is considerable debate over the effectiveness of even recognized treatments such as acupuncture, and definitive empirical support has yet to be provided for the full range of types of CAM.

Concierge Medicine

I have a vague memory that during the O.J. Simpson trial, Simpson's Beverly Hills physician was asked to testify about Simpson's physical limitations. What I recall was not whether the physician thought Simpson could have physically committed the crime; rather, what I recall was that the physician was asked to reveal the fee he charged for the examination. Let's just say the fee was in excess of what Blue Cross/Blue Shield would authorize for a physical! For those who can pay, more personalized services are available. These services are sometimes referred to as concierge medicine, although those who practice this form of medicine object to the label.[138] Among the alternative labels are "retainer-based medicine" and "patient-driven health care."[139] Although patients want to be seen promptly, to avoid long waits, to personally hear back from the doctor about test results, and so on, not all patients can afford this kind of service. In 2004, what was then called the American Society of Concierge Physicians and is now called the Society for Innovative Medical Practice Design had a membership of about 30, with the number of physicians practicing what could be categorized as concierge medicine estimated at between 150–200.

Physician Honesty and Patient Care

With the bombardment of television advertising admonishing us to seek legal representation when confronted with medical error or a poor outcome, there has been some movement to encourage physicians to admit their

[137] Comarow, A. (2008, January 21). Embracing alternative care: Top hospitals put unorthodox therapies into practice. *U.S. News & World Report*, p. 32.
[138] Guadagnino, C. (2004, April). Forming a national society of concierge physicians. *Physician's News Digest.* http://www.physiciansnews.com/spotlight/404wp.html.
[139] Ibid., para. 2.

mistakes when they occur.[140] A dramatic decrease (more than 65 percent) in the number of malpractice claims and actions occurred after the University of Michigan Health System began a program of full disclosure. The chief risk officer at the medical center was quoted as saying, "Improving patient safety and patient communication is more likely to cure the malpractice crisis than defensiveness and denial."[141] Beyond helping to restore the faith of patients in the information they receive, another argument is that transparency in reporting medical errors will lead to "teaching moments," which may in turn reduce future errors.

CLOSING COMMENTS

With regard to the physical design of health care facilities, there may be more uniformity in architecture, partly as a result of the fact that hospitals are becoming parts of chains. Even as long ago as 1982, as many as 35 percent of hospital beds in the United States were part of multihospital systems.[142] As Jennifer Gallagher mentioned earlier in this chapter, regulations associated with health care construction, including certificate of need requirements and public health codes, have a significant effect on the configuration of health care facilities. It is hard to be creative.

On the other hand, though I am not enthusiastic about the concept of consumerism pervading our lives, I do think that pressure from patients and their families, through standardized feedback that the federal Department of Health and Human Services has created through the Hospital Compare project (http://www.hospitalcompare.hhs.gov/Hospital), can lead to improvements in the quality of our health care environments. Moreover, I am confident that the emphasis on evidence-based design will result in environments that are more supportive of outcomes for patients and their families.

[140] Sack, K. (2008, May 18). Doctors start to say "I'm sorry" long before "see you in court." *The New York Times*, p. A1, A17.

[141] Ibid., p. A17.

[142] Stevens, R. (1989). *In sickness and in wealth: American hospitals in the twentieth century.* New York: Basic Books, p. 304.

3

The Landscape of Schools: Big Schools, Small Schools

PERSONAL REFLECTIONS

I know my parents had good intentions regarding our schooling when they insisted on keeping all five of us (me, my sister, and three brothers) in the laboratory schools of the University of Michigan's Department of Education, rather than allowing us to attend public school. In retrospect, the freedom characteristic of these lab schools was probably a much better fit for some of my siblings than for others. These schools were University Elementary School (UES) and University High School (UHS).

These schools, especially the elementary school, were wonderful environments for learning, and the physical facilities played a role in creating a supportive environment. In addition to a typical gymnasium, the elementary school had what we called The Rhythm Room, constructed with wood planked flooring and an indoor slide for recess on rainy days and Michigan's cold winter months. The center hall of the elementary school was lined with Pewabic tile (see Figure 3.1) from the nationally known pottery founded in 1903 during the Arts and Crafts movement. The centerpiece of the hallway was a small fountain across from the main entrance to the school. The high school had a gymnasium, as well as a room for gymnastics and fencing. There was also a "shop" for woodworking and a separate house with a kitchen for home economics. The school had an art room for grades K–12 with a kiln, and the art room had a side area with cots used for naps for the youngest students. Although there was no swimming pool and the elementary school had just a small side yard with a jungle gym for outdoor recess, we never felt we had inadequate facilities.

By today's standards, some physical facilities and grounds in fact might seem inadequate. But I have to admit that we received a wonderful

FIGURE 3.1. Interior, University Elementary School

personalized education, which is probably why my parents selected the school and insisted that we stay there despite our more than infrequent protests.

Schools make a difference in children's and parents' lives, as I will argue in this chapter, and the school facility can play a role in children's experience. Unsolicited my daughter once said that her favorite school was the Children's School at Connecticut College. This was the place where she and her best friend Nick Baumann built the Emerald City (from *The Wizard of Oz*) that took up the entire block area and stayed for weeks. Her least favorite educational stretch was probably public elementary school, where a number of teachers who had stayed long past their teaching prime constrained and squeezed the joy out of what should have been the excitement of learning. Admittedly, that had nothing to do with the school building.

When she told me about the positives and negatives of her schooling, it reminded me that some of my most memorable school days were also early on, and what I remember was the *doing*. At the University Elementary School (UES) we made papier-mâché characters from the story *The Princess and the Goblin*, and I kept the princess I made in the basement of our house for many years. I remember the pinhole cameras we made out of shoeboxes, and the pumpkin seeds we roasted and ate in October in

Mrs. Tipton's class, and Mrs. Tejada's art class where we created mosaics and used the potter's wheel. One of my favorite memories was having Mrs. Stevenson, the librarian, read to us each week in a wonderful library with a fireplace and balconies. In the fourth grade, she read us Dickens's *A Tale of Two Cities*. What these memories say to me is that the teachers at UES created a special place. I would argue that such memories are more likely to be formed (although certainly not guaranteed) in a small school, which provides opportunities for active learning.

In recent years one of the most vivid "procedural" memories I have is the field trip my college environmental psychology class and I took to the Corrigan Maximum Security Prison in Montville, Connecticut, just up Route 32. We were going there to learn about prison designs and view what some called a "glamour slammer" – a description derived from the fact that we spend more money on the construction of prisons than new schools in this country.

We were in the car, listening to the radio, on the day the O.J. Simpson verdict was announced. The prison can be an intimidating place under normal circumstances. On one visit, for example, a student fainted and was tended to in the prison infirmary. When we went into the "pod" or living quarters the day the O.J. verdict was handed down, you could feel the tension between the correctional officers, who in general were angry about the verdict, and the inmates, who were decidedly less angry. People in my generation remember where they were when they learned that President Kennedy had been assassinated; my guess is that the people in my environmental psychology class will remember where they were when the O.J. verdict was announced.

As I think back to where I was when I heard that President Kennedy had been shot, what comes to mind is that it was a Friday, and my best friend and I were walking back from our class swimming lesson at the women's swimming pool at the University of Michigan. We stopped in at The Apothecary Shop on South University Avenue (known as South U) to get a candy bar on our way back to geometry class. Beyond the recall of the events of that horrific day, the fact that the two of us were meandering back to school by ourselves from an activity that was part of the school physical education program says something about how much schools have changed from a management and liability standpoint.

The anecdotes here reflect some of the principles that will be the focus of this chapter, in particular the interrelationships between school culture and school size, and the role of personalization.

FIGURE 3.2. Silfen Auditorium, Connecticut College

A WORD OR TWO ABOUT SCHOOL BUILDINGS
AND ARCHITECTURAL DETERMINISM

A colleague of mine said that she could teach on a rock, implying that the physical facilities made essentially no difference in her effectiveness. What I will argue here is that architecture and the configuration of space can make certain outcomes of interest more or less likely, more or less probable or possible. This question about the certainty of a particular outcome centers on issues of architectural determinism, architectural probabilism, and architectural possibilism.[1] Determinism suggests that the design creates the outcome; probabilism suggests that the design makes a certain outcome more likely, and possibilism suggests that an environment creates the opportunity for an outcome (i.e., the outcome is not ruled out).

Although I believe that architecture can influence behavior, I do not believe that architecture can determine behavior. It can set the stage. A classroom such as Silfen Auditorium at Connecticut College (see Figure 3.2), with its fixed seating, is essentially communicating the idea that the students will face forward toward the professor and that a lecture style of teaching will

[1] Bell, P. A., Greene, T. C., Fisher, J. D., & Baum, A. (2001). *Environmental psychology* (5th ed.). Belmont, CA: Wadsworth Thomson.

FIGURE 3.3. Charles Chu Reading Room in Shain Library

probably dominate. I agree with the eminent environmental psychologist Robert Sommer, who, when writing a chapter titled "Movable chairs, fixed beliefs, hard classrooms," said, "By itself no single change, including carpeting, decorations, portable chairs, reduced class size, or open-air surroundings is going to revolutionize American education, but without these changes no improvement is likely."[2] He made this statement in 1974. Sommer's view is one that I share and will emphasize in this chapter. The physical environment can make a difference, but the philosophy of students and teachers as interactive learners needs to be embraced.

Spaces Can Make a Difference

In my course in environmental psychology, I often talk about spaces of great character. In my view these are spaces that lift up one's spirits when one uses them. And I ask students to identify some spaces from their educational experience that fit this definition. Some students can identify no such spaces in their experience. At Connecticut College, some students mention the Charles Chu Reading Room in Shain Library (see Figure 3.3). I offer my own experiences studying in great rooms. One such space is in the University of

---

[2] Sommer, R. (1974). *Tight spaces: Hard architecture and how to humanize it.* Englewood Cliffs, NJ: Prentice Hall, p. 101.

FIGURE 3.4. University of Michigan Law Library

Michigan Law Library (see Figure 3.4), where I went to read despite the fact that I was not in law school.

Do such uplifting spaces make a difference? Spaces of great character have been talked about as places where there is a connection of people, place, and landscape.[3] When we began a master planning process at Connecticut College in the late 1990s, we did precisely what is recommended – we identified rooms, walks, places, vistas, and thresholds that faculty and students deemed memorable. We also were asked by the master planning team to identify what we considered our sacred spaces. For most people, the sacred space involved a vista from the top of the college's Tempel Green out to Fisher's Island Sound. The landscape itself can be an important resource in education and can lift one's spirits in a way that may be unrivaled by a space of bricks and mortar.

Architecture has been described as providing the setting for social relationships, communicating the values of the institution and providing the context for particular patterns of behavior, and many of us believe that architecture and design play a role in the educational process.[4] A similar sentiment was expressed by a writer blogging in the *Chronicle of Higher*

[3] Vaughn, T. W. (1991, July–August). Good teaching rooms: A campus resource. *Academe*, 77(4), 11–15.
[4] Dutton, T. A., & Grant, B. C. (1991, July–August). Campus design and critical pedagogy. *Academe*, 77(4), 37–43.

Education's section on buildings and grounds: "Great campuses, like great cities, should be agglomerations of all of the cultures and all of the times that make up their history. If everyone in every era builds well and builds authentically, the result is a rich record of the institution – and a perfect home for it to grow and thrive in.... I mean we should be making buildings that reflect the values, lifestyles, issues, and technologies of today."[5] Architecture serves as an archive for our institutional values.

With regard to spaces of great character, it is possible to think you are on the right track but to miss the boat, as it were. Mary Jo Olenick, an architect who was involved in Connecticut College's master plan of the early 1980s, is in charge of the higher education practice of the S/L/A/M collaborative, an architectural firm in Connecticut. She asks why spaces built to facilitate interdisciplinary exchanges may fail to inspire. "So why, when we walk into many of these shiny new buildings, do they feel so empty?"[6] In her experience, spaces need to address specific functions to work well and attract people, creating what she labels a "beehive effect."[7] Spaces generic in their function generally fail to entice people to use them.

SCHOOL SIZE: THE CONTRIBUTIONS OF ROGER BARKER AND PAUL GUMP

When I thought about writing this chapter and initially gave it the working title "Big school, small school," a reference to the pioneering work of Roger Barker and Paul Gump, I had no idea how central that theme would be to the challenge facing the design of our educational landscape today. We are struggling with big facilities that, according to the research that has been done, do not serve our students well in providing skills they need to compete in an increasingly fast-paced information culture where the key to surviving will be the ability to learn throughout adulthood. When employers and professors are asked about our high school graduates, they complain that students are deficient in basic skills (grammar and spelling; coherent writing; rudimentary math). Moreover, students are not perceived to have good work habits or high motivation. At the same time, students are rated as much more proficient in computer skills than in the three Rs.[8]

---

[5] Speck, L. (2008, June 2). Guest blogger: What does it mean to build a building of our time. *The Chronicle: Buildings & Grounds*, para. 5 & 6.

[6] Olenick, M. J. (2008, March 18). Can less space be more? *The Chronicle: Buildings & Grounds*, para. 2.

[7] Ibid., para. 6.

[8] Johnson, J., & Duffett, A. (2002, March 6). Reality check 2002. *Education Week*, 21(25).

Of course the curriculum and those who teach it are fundamental in shaping our educational outcomes. But those variables are not the whole story. As this chapter highlights, a majority of those who write about educational policy favor educational facilities that are smaller rather than larger, terms that will become more clearly defined in this chapter.

What makes the work of Gump and Barker important is their emphasis on what is called ecological psychology, of which they are often described as founders, and in particular the notion of a behavior setting, in which the parameters of a setting, its place in space and time, help shape the behavior that occurs there, rather than expecting personality to shape the entirety of behavior. In other words there is a relationship between the physical environment and behavior; one can expect *patterns* in behavior settings as opposed to random displays.

In the United States in the mid-20th century in the area of personality psychology, trait psychology was fairly dominant, providing a paradigm. In trait psychology, one's behavior is hypothesized to be influenced largely by the traits one possesses. Someone might be extraverted, or conscientious, or neurotic. These traits are thought to predict behaviors across environments or settings. Arguably psychology has gone through a number of paradigms, or worldviews, or at least a variety of theoretical approaches since its inception in the late 1800s. As explained in the influential work of Thomas Kuhn in his book *The Structure of Scientific Revolutions*,[9] a paradigm is a consistent way of looking at the work that shapes which phenomena are examined and how research questions are posed.

With the work of Gump and Barker in behavior setting theory, the explanation of behavior changed to include a sharper role of the environment. Following the work of Kurt Lewin, who proposed the formula $B = f(P\,E)$,[10] behavior was a function of the person *and* the environment as it was experienced. Writers after Lewin sometimes represented the formula as $B = f(P \times E)$,[11] but the important point is that in Lewin's model people constructed the environment they were perceiving or interpreting; Lewin was dealing with the concept of the psychological life space. The ecological psychology of Gump and Barker involves a different focus, naturally occurring phenomena outside of the person. With a focus outside of the person,

---

[9] Kuhn, T. (1962). *The structure of scientific revolutions.* Chicago: University of Chicago Press.

[10] Lewin, K. (1933). Environmental forces. In C. Murchison (Ed.), *A handbook of child psychology* (2nd ed. rev.) (pp. 590–625). Worcester, MA: Clark University Press.

[11] Emery, F. The social engagement of social science. Vol. 3, *The socio-ecological perspective.* http://moderntimesworkplace.com/archives/ericsess/sessvol3/sess3Intro/sess3Intro.html.

the environment takes on a role that essentially has little place in the trait theory of personality psychology, and the environment becomes an essential ingredient in predicting how an individual might behave; "the course of the life space can only be known within the ecological environment in which it is embedded."[12] Barker and Gump identify a number of components of the ecological environment, the most basic of which is its structure, which means there are parts that maintain their relationship to one another.

The environment can be studied empirically, it has an objective reality, and it occurs in bounded units, and although individual people may differ in their behavior within a given ecological environment, people considered together will "exhibit a characteristic overall extra-individual pattern of behavior; and the inhabitants of different ecological units will exhibit different overall extra-individual patterns of behavior."[13] Thus groups of people within a bounded setting might be expected to exhibit stable and characteristic patterns of behavior. These behavior settings often occur at a particular day and time and with a prescribed series of activities. As an example, I often teach a particular course in a particular room during a particular time slot, T, Th, 10:25–11:40 a.m.

A good deal of Gump and Barker's research has implications for school size and the creation of the school milieu in the lives of students and teachers. In their research, Gump and Barker often pose the dichotomy of an overmanned versus an undermanned environment; today using gender-neutral language, those terms have become overstaffed versus understaffed. An overstaffed environment is one in which there are more people than needed to carry out specific activities (e.g., to mount the school play or to field a soccer team). In an understaffed environment, there are fewer people than needed to carry out these same activities. In this lean situation, pressure exists for people to step up and be involved. Such involvement has the benefit of distributing more opportunities for responsibility and leadership than one would have in an overstaffed environment.

Although there are benefits to a large institution such as a large high school, for example, a greater diversity of course offerings, the research of Gump and Barker clearly indicates that the benefits of the small school are more numerous than those of the large school. In their research involving 13 schools ranging in enrollment from 35 to 2287 students, they talk about the illusion of school size. Yes, they say, the larger school is impressive in any number of ways: its sheer size, its facilities, its vitality. But the inside view,

---

[12] Barker, R., & Gump, P. V. (1964). *Big school, small school: High school size and student behavior.* Stanford, CA: Stanford University Press, p. 8.

[13] Ibid., p. 9.

they note, communicates a different story; the inside story shows distinct advantages of the small school, including the fact that a larger proportion of students at a small school have deeper involvement through positions of status and responsibility than is true of students at larger schools.

Consider the difference between a small high school with 60 students in the junior class and a larger high school with 600 in that class. With 60 students, almost everyone is needed for the class play – actors, stage managers, lighting technicians, costumers, scenery painters, after-party planners, and so on. The junior class play is used as a vehicle by Barker and Gump to explain the sources of satisfaction and opportunities for leadership that are more available at small than at large schools. But overstaffed environments have their advantages as well, particularly in terms of greater diversity and more choice of behavior settings, but of course less depth of involvement across individuals. A large high school might offer as many as eight languages, and a small school fewer. In today's environment, we would probably count the number of advanced placement courses offered as one way to distinguish the opportunities offered at a big school from those of a small school.

In the summary of their work, Barker and Gump clearly indicate that there is a negative relationship between size of the institution on one hand and participation of the individual on the other. In other words, if you want to be a "player," you are more likely to accomplish that goal at a small school. They say they cannot answer the question "How large should a school be?" and suggest that to some extent the answer depends on your focus. For example, for a range of experience, the small school is preferred; for specialization, the larger school is preferred. When enrollment expands, they suggest that rather than simply expanding the facility, either additional new smaller schools be built or a campus school approach be endorsed, in which most academic work is done in smaller units within a larger physical setting while still providing for extracurricular options on a school-wide basis.

As the chapter will show, their ideas, essentially suggesting a school within a school (SWAS), foreshadowed an approach taken today when communities want small school culture but are restricted to one high school, for example, because of limited funds. It is also worth remembering that the school is just one aspect of the educational process, and as Barker and Gump comment, "Good facilities provide good experiences only if they are used. The educational process is a subtle and delicate one about which we know little, but it surely thrives on participation, enthusiasm, and responsibility. . . . The data of this research and our own educational values tell us that a school should be sufficiently small that all of its students are needed for its enterprises. A school should be small enough that students are not redundant."[14]

THE LOGIC BEHIND LARGE HIGH SCHOOLS

In the second half of the 20th century, America embraced the concept of building large schools, particularly large high schools. When the United States moved in that direction, it was responding to the perception that we were falling behind in our influential role in the wider world. In particular, the successful launch of the Russian Sputnik in the late 1950s, and the unsuccessful launch of many American rockets during the same time period, was seen as evidence that we needed to bolster science and math education in our schools.

Educators writing about the issue of school size in this country frequently point to a book published in 1959, *The American High School Today: A First Report to Interested Citizens*,[15] written by James B. Conant, a chemistry professor who had been president of Harvard from 1933 to 1953. The book makes the case that America needed larger schools to affordably offer the depth of curriculum in science and math required to be competitive in the world (Sputnik was successfully launched in October 1957). The heading at the top of one page of Conant's book reads "Elimination of the Small High School – A Top Priority," and he goes on to say, "I am convinced small high schools can be satisfactory only at exorbitant expense."[16] In his view, course offerings in small schools were being restricted due to financial limitations, and the way to address the problem was through school consolidation.

Ironically, the minimum graduating class size he advocated, at least 100, might seem small today, but another recommendation of a ratio of 1 guidance counselor to at least 250 students seems overwhelming in terms of the kinds of personal attention we hope our children receive. For his assessment of American high schools, with a focus on mathematics, science, and to a lesser degree foreign language, Conant and his associates visited what he labeled 22 comprehensive high schools. What made a high school comprehensive was that many different subjects were taught to students with a range of abilities. In addition to his recommendations about school size, he voiced concern about the health of foreign language instruction and the small number of girls taking advanced courses in math and science.

[14] Ibid., p. 202.

[15] Conant, J. (1959). *The American high school today: A first report to interested citizens.* New York: McGraw-Hill.

[16] Ibid., p. 37.

It was also Conant's impression that students were not being sufficiently challenged, that is, they didn't work hard enough. Although there were more than 15 recommendations in his report, the one that has by far received the most attention involves school size.

There is no doubt that schools have been consolidated since the period following World War II, and school districts and schools themselves have become larger. For example, since 1940 there has been a 69 percent drop in the number of public schools in this country, but the number of students has risen by almost 70 percent. Similarly, in the time period 1930 to 2001, we went from 262,000 public schools to 91,000.[17] In addition to the impact of Conant's book on school consolidation and the increasing size of schools, another factor mentioned is the impact of legislation on school desegregation in the 1960s.[18]

GETTING TO SCHOOL

Along with the dramatic decrease in the number of public schools in this country over the last half century, we have also seen a change in the way students are transported to school. In 1969, if you lived within a mile of school and were between the ages of 5–15, there was a 90 percent chance you walked or biked to school. By 2001, for that same age group, only 1 percent biked and fewer than 15 percent walked.[19] The Environmental Protection Agency provides these data, so you could expect it to stress the importance of environmental quality in its recommendations for creating safer and higher quality walking and biking environments. And what is a poor walking environment? A poor walking environment is one with incomplete sidewalks, long blocks, little variety in the mix of land uses, and low densities. This last variable is important in my view because it relates to the idea of positive surveillance. If there are few houses on the route, then it is less likely people will watch out for each other's children. In a sense this issue is reminiscent of the perspective of Jane Jacobs, whose critical analysis about urban life in her book *The Death and Life of Great American*

[17] Lawrence, B. K., Bingler, S., Diamond, B. M., Hill, B., Hoffman, J. L., Howley, C. B., Mitchell, S., Rudolph, D., & Washor, E. (2002). *Dollars and sense: The cost effectiveness of small schools.* Cincinnati, OH: KnowledgeWorks Foundation.

[18] Smith, D. T., & DeYoung, A. T. (1988, Winter). Big school vs. small school: Conceptual, empirical, and political perspectives on the re-emerging debate. *Journal of Rural and Small Schools*, 2–11.

[19] United States Environmental Protection Agency (2003, October). *Travel and Environmental Implications of School Siting*, EPA 231-R-03-004, p. 1.

Cities[20] spoke to the need to have a sense of community in mixed-use neighborhoods. Although the kind of mixed use she envisioned may be far more difficult to achieve unless new urbanism principles are adopted (see Chapter 1), the notion of density itself is worth considering. If neighbors are to keep a watchful eye on each other's children, there have to be neighbors in close proximity to do that.

Prior to this research from the EPA that focused on Gainesville, Florida, little research had been done linking school distance to transportation choices, according to the authors, and they were forced to cast a wider net of variables. One of the factors that emerged was what they call the pedestrian-friendliness of the route. This variable was measured by the overall density of the route, the commercial floor area (FAR), the sidewalk coverage, the average sidewalk width, and the street network density. This constellation of variables accounted for 60 percent of the variance. The Gainesville survey included a total of 709 trips, of which 548 were by car, 105 by school bus, 32 by foot, and 24 by bicycle.

Having sidewalks and sidewalk coverage was a good predictor of the likelihood of walking, but the built environment as measured by the variables did not have a significant relationship to the choice of bicycling. Walking was most strongly related to the number of vehicles per capita (having fewer vehicles was related to greater likelihood of walking). And school size was not directly related to the choice of transportation mode. What does this mean? What it probably means is that your kids are more likely to walk to school if they live closer, you have fewer vehicles, and if the places where the kids walk have sidewalks in decent repair. Kids who bike probably bike in the streets as much as on the sidewalks, and the sidewalks therefore have less impact on them. And it is the distance and not the size of the school that makes sense to think about in terms of transportation mode. Whether large or small, if the school is closer, you're more likely to walk or bike there.

We have larger schools. Our children don't generally walk or bicycle to school. But those are really small potatoes in terms of the challenges we face.

TODAY'S SCHOOL CHALLENGES

Today we face challenges in education that are broader than Conant's concern about math, science, and foreign language instruction. In a recent article[21] bemoaning the fact that the 2008 presidential candidates had paid

[20] Jacobs, J. (1961). *The death and life of great American cities.* New York: Random House.
[21] Hawkins-Simons, D. (2008, May 19). Not a primary concern: In the background, the candidates make plans for America's schools. *U. S. News & World Report*, pp. 29–31.

almost no attention to educational initiatives in their platforms, some startling statistics are discussed. Parenthetically, in a telephone poll I was asked to take in August 2008 prior to the presidential election, there were probably 10 questions dealing with my approval/disapproval of a variety of different energy initiatives, and not a single question about educational initiatives.

The article criticizing the backburner approach to educational initiatives in the presidential campaign mentions the organization America's Promise, founded by Colin Powell, which had documented just how poorly we are faring with regard to graduating our students from high school. A report from America's Promise had documented that in 17 of our largest cities, the graduation rates in high school fell below 50 percent. In a word, "frightening." Moreover, "Seventy percent of eighth graders are not proficient in reading, over a million high schoolers drop out each year, and nearly one third of college freshmen must take remedial math or English courses."[22] The author goes on to talk about some of the fallout of the No Child Left Behind legislation, where schools and consequently children are penalized because a good number of schools that have been unable to meet the standards are trying to educate a high percentage of students that may have English as a second language and a high proportion of students who may have disabilities.

Not surprisingly, there are other views about the concept of standards, and a good number of educators in positions of authority favor enforcing standards because they see a relationship between countries that enforce high standards and student achievement. "In high-performing countries, there are clear, high standards on what will be taught, matching and fair assessments of student performance, curriculum frameworks that are aligned to the standards, and instructional materials that fit those frameworks." So says a former superintendent of instruction in the California public school system.[23]

In tracing educational initiatives, this former superintendent cites the Morrill Act of 1862, signed by Lincoln to establish the land-grant college system. World War II brought the GI Bill of Rights. The School Lunch Program of 1946 signed by Truman guaranteed that eligible children would not be hungry. And under the Eisenhower administration, the National Defense Education Act, signed at the time of Sputnik, promoted the education of students in the realms of science, engineering, and teaching. She argues that

---

[22] Ibid., p. 29.
[23] Eastin, D. (2008, June–July). Political report card. *Miller-McCune: Turning Research into Solutions, 1*(2), 20–25, p. 21.

one of our biggest failures is in science education. Certainly if we think back to one of the reasons Conant promoted the consolidation of schools, it was to address science education in the United States. We apparently have not succeeded in this quest. Another major effort for which she argues is universal preschool, which is overwhelmingly supported by research. "Educate them, or you will eventually have to incarcerate them."[24]

ALTERNATIVE PERSPECTIVES ON SCHOOL BUILDINGS

In 1972, 13 years after Conant published his book, Robert Propst, head of the Herman Miller Research Corporation (Herman Miller is well known for its office furnishings such as the Aeron Chair; discussed in Chapter 4), wrote about the challenges facing our schools and especially about the challenges related to the buildings themselves.[25] Since the publication of his book, little has changed about the buildings he critiqued. Propst was sympathetic to the idea of schools that foster a sense of community and the role of the school facility in supporting community. Others, too, point to the change in the nature of our schools, and the concomitant loss of sense of community as the schools have grown in size.[26] It has been argued that the school, often just one room, was the center of the community in the early part of the 20th century. It may have been viewed as the "center of daily community life."[27] The argument is that a quality education must fundamentally address the issue of sense of community. A provocative chart in one article shows the dramatic decline in the number of one-teacher schools in this country. In 1930, of 238,000 schools, 149,000, or 62.6 percent, were one-teacher schools. By 1980, we had 61,000 schools, of which 900, or 1.5 percent, were one-teacher schools. Over that time period we went from 128,000 school districts to 16,000.[28]

In the opening chapter of Propst's book, he posed the question, "Do we like our schools?" and answered it by saying that liking our schools has become much harder. The book looks closely at the role that the facility, the schoolhouse as he calls it, plays in the lives of students. In reviewing the history of schoolhouses in the United States, the book covers the English Lancastrian system introduced to America in 1806. The system involved what was called "batch-process education," with a group, or batch, of students

[24] Ibid., p. 25.
[25] Propst, R. (1972). *High school: The process and the place.* New York: Educational Facilities Laboratories.
[26] Smith & DeYoung (1988).
[27] Ibid., p. 8.   [28] Ibid., p. 3.

attached to a teacher in what was essentially a box for learning. The physical form in which this process occurs has essentially remained static; many school buildings look as they did more than 100 years ago. "Ask almost any child to draw a plan of a school and he will draw a large box around a series of smaller, equal-size boxes, set side by side."[29] The design of a building with spaces the same size meant that any group of students, typically 25–30, could be assigned to the space, often by grade or age. According to Propst, the typical physical arrangement, with the teacher in front, the children in rows listening, worked as long as children were docile and the curriculum was relatively constant. One need only think of that marvelous scene from the movie *Ferris Bueller's Day Off*,[30] where Ben Stein, in the role of the frustrated teacher, faces what one might politely call an uninvolved group of students arrayed in rows in front of him and the blackboard. After asking each question that goes unanswered, he laments, "Anyone?"

The class in a box formula, Propst argues, does not work with the explosion of knowledge that began after World War II and certainly continues at an even greater pace more than 35 years after the publication of his book. With altered social patterns and the exponential growth of information technologies, learning can hardly be viewed as static, he argues. What implications do these changes have for the physical environment in which learning occurs? How can the spaces themselves be responsive to change?[31]

Propst articulates the many failings of traditional school design, among them the lack of places for social interaction to occur; hallways and classrooms are not designed for social interaction. These facilities are typically dull, with little planned visual and acoustical variety, and the materials with which they are constructed do not wear gracefully. The reaction to an unresponsive environment is often vandalism, described as a way to say "this doesn't work." A 17-year-old student whose commentary is included in Propst's book says, "Vandalism is a way of forcibly stopping the educational machine."[32]

Many of the challenges in creating a responsive environment that Propst addresses parallel his comments in his book *The Office: A Facility Based on Change.*[33]

If the forces of change require physical movement, interaction, and community, as Propst argues, then the school building must accommodate those

---

[29] Propst (1972), p. 11.
[30] Hughes, J. (1986). *Ferris Bueller's Day Off.* Paramount Pictures.
[31] Propst (1972), p. 11.   [32] Ibid., p. 14.
[33] Propst, R. (1968). *The office: A facility based on change.* Ann Arbor, MI: Herman Miller Research Corporation.

factors. One design response is movable walls; another response is no walls at all. What emerged from the pressures that Propst discusses was the open plan school or the school without walls, which Propst says was "the first major change in the design of schoolhouses for more than a hundred years."[34] But although the open school of the 1960s was a positive development in his view and widely adopted, especially at the elementary school level, it was not universally successful.

One of the major issues presented in the open plan, says Propst, is the tension between enclosure and access, between intimacy and vista. We have the need for both, but the open plan was probably stronger on access than enclosure. The solution is a space sufficiently flexible to be sectioned into smaller units when necessary. These territorial spaces where visual and auditory privacy can be managed are discussed in *The Office* and are fundamentally a part of Oscar Newman's theory of defensible space.[35] Defensible space allows us to adopt a territorial prerogative over it, which is essential to our feelings of safety and security. Propst also makes the point that flexible design is not the same as flexible use, and that training in how spaces can be used to achieve particular ends needs to accompany the creation of the spaces themselves.

As he does in *The Office*, Propst talks about the many conflicts the schoolhouse (the facility) must address. Among the most pressing are privacy versus involvement, geometry versus humanism, and old culture or new culture. All of us feel the competing desires to be separate at times, but also to have moments when we are part of a group. A schoolhouse has to provide spaces for us to do solo work and group work. And more than was the case 35 years ago, there is a movement in education toward work in teams, because the world of work is interdisciplinary and the problems we are tying to solve increasingly involve multiple disciplines. The physical environment has a role to play in encouraging or discouraging interaction; it cannot cause such interaction, but it can make interaction more likely to occur.

Consider a number of design examples. In the Lokey Laboratory Chemistry building at Stanford, one of the labs run by professor Justin DuBois (the DuBois group) has labs that run almost the length of the building subdivided by pods open to one another (see Figure 3.5). Parenthetically, in something of an irony, the architect in charge of the renovation of classroom space in the building where I teach worked on the Lokey Laboratory

---

[34] Propst (1972), p. 23.

[35] Newman, O. (1972). *Defensible space: Crime prevention through urban design.* New York: Macmillan.

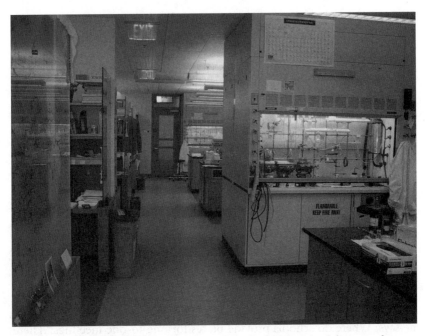

FIGURE 3.5. DuBois Lab, Lokey Laboratory, Stanford University (photograph courtesy of Abigail Sloan Devlin)

building as his first major project for Ellenzweig, an architectural firm in Cambridge, Massachusetts. The open arrangement of the labs in the Lokey building means that the graduate students can easily interact with one another so that consultation and conversation are promoted. Another example comes from the W. C. Decker Engineering Building, a research facility for Corning Glass Works in Corning, New York.[36] In this laboratory building, the corridors were designed with bow-windowed coffee lounges equipped with wall-sized tablets for writing. The intention was that engineers from different disciplines, meeting along the corridor, could stop, have a cup of coffee, and exchange ideas, supported by the physical environment. Although along an interior corridor, a similar coffee break-as-exchange-of-idea-space was designed in the Pfizer Central Research Facility in Groton, Connecticut.

Geometry versus humanism speaks to the principle that human communication is not linear, but moves in fits and starts, says Propst, and a rigid spatial order cannot accommodate the various ways in which humans

---

[36] Brenner, D. (1981, September). A meeting of the minds at Corning. *Architectural Record*, pp. 79–85.

communicate. I am reminded of a principle from Humphrey Osmond, who influenced the work of Robert Sommer (Sommer actually worked for Osmond on a research study at a large state hospital in Canada). Osmond[37] wrote about spaces that pull people apart, which he called sociofugal spaces, and spaces that pull people together, which he called sociopetal spaces. Places like narrow hallways where there are no real spaces designated for conversation tend to pull people apart; places where tables and chairs allow people to stop and sit at 90 degrees to each other (rather than side by side or across) tend to promote conversation. The research settings I have described at Corning Glass and Pfizer are more sociopetal than sociofugal, and that is their goal. I remember touring the adolescent ward of the Institute of Living, a psychiatric facility in Hartford, Connecticut, and being impressed by one of its "corridors," which was so wide that it accommodated a ping-pong table, which in turn promoted a great deal of social interaction.

Propst describes different arenas or venues that the school must provide. The first is the social arena. What must a space provide? The response is that it has to provide a place to practice – to practice social engagement, which involves places to meet, to talk, to listen, to disagree, to persuade, to explore, he says. Where do schools provide places for one-to-one meetings? There must be smaller spaces within larger ones, so our original schoolhouse of the 1800s cannot satisfy this requirement. The spaces have to vary.

A second arena is play and games. Especially today, among adolescents, where adults in educational settings truly feel at risk of losing control (and often have), it may be easier to think of counterexamples than models to endorse. It is hard to create places for play. Tone, Propst argues, is especially important, and the finishes and materials should not evoke what Sommer calls "the security mentality," which almost instinctively elicits from us a response to fight back. What *do* we want? From my perspective, the most important response Propst gives is an environment that is "human-scaled, welcoming, and approachable."[38] There needs to be a range of such spaces, for singles, for twosomes, for groups of 10–20, and for groups of 100 and larger.

The values he provides for planners are a series of questions they must answer (one hopes in the affirmative): "Will the schoolhouse be a humane place?" "Will it nurture the educative process?" "Can it accommodate the future?"[39] Remember that his comments were published in 1972, at a time

---

[37] Osmond, H. (1957). Function as a basis of psychiatric ward design. *Mental Hospitals, 8*, 23–39.

[38] Propst (1972), p. 45.   [39] Ibid., p. 117.

when America was moving ahead full throttle to build large schools. My purpose in emphasizing Propst's contributions is to show that the design philosophy that many educators embrace today has its roots in an earlier generation.

What do students think about how schools should be designed? In a design competition entitled "Redesign Your School" sponsored by the American Architectural Foundation and Target, a number of themes emerged.[40] Two hundred fifty students submitted projects from an initial online registration of more than 5000. The design principles from the American Architectural Foundation that were a guide to student designs were to support a variety of learning styles; enhance learning by integrating technology; support a small, neighborhood school culture; create schools as centers of community; engage the public in the planning process; make healthy, comfortable, and flexible learning spaces; and consider nontraditional options for school facilities and classrooms. Students' designs had to address at least one of these principles.

The student who won the grand prize with a design that emphasized light and nature said, "A great school design has the potential to make student performance better."[41] The students wanted daylight, not fluorescent lighting; they did not want their schools to resemble boxy prisons. They proposed schools that were integrated with the community, and they championed sustainable technology. One of the jurors reflected that the students emphasized places where they feel welcome, with personalized spaces and places to socialize. They seemed to be channeling Propst.

The analogy of the school as prison has emerged in a number of places, including in a 2006 online survey of more than 1000 British students who took part in a survey called "Make Your School Cool."[42] More than 60 percent said they did not like their classrooms, and the words used to describe school buildings were "old, dirty, and boring."[43] Moreover, these buildings exuded poor maintenance. What students thought would improve classrooms included brighter colors, more light, more space for personal storage, and spaces for socialization, and more than 70 percent said "no" responding to the question "Do you like the places where you can hang out

[40] Saffir, B. J. (2008, January 1). Competition yields insights; thoughtful "Redesign Your School" entries show what kids want in their schools. *Architectural Record, 196*(1), p. 521. http://archrecord.construction.com/schools/071213-SCH_AFF-1.asp.
[41] Ibid., para. 2.
[42] *Design for learning forum: School design and student learning in the 21st century: A report of findings.* Washington, D.C.: American Architectural Foundation.
[43] Ibid., p. 38.

at breaks?"[44] There is a lot of work to do to improve schools and students' evaluations of those facilities.

Thirty-five years after Propst's book and almost 50 years after Conant's book, what is the look of our educational landscape? Before talking more specifically about the benefits and drawbacks of schools with different sizes and configurations, it might help to understand how many children we are educating today and in what kinds of existing and planned facilities. One characteristic of our nation is that we gather data (think of the Census); we know a lot about who we are, at least "by the numbers." A useful service our government provides is the collection of data about school age children.

"In 2007 there were 73.9 million children in the United States, 1.5 million more than in 2000. This number is projected to increase to 80 million in 2020. In 2007, there were approximately equal numbers of children in each of these age groups: 0–5 (25 million), 6–11 (24 million), and 12–17 (25 million) years of age."[45] But after the peak of the baby boom, in 1964, children have been decreasing in terms of their *proportion* of the population. In 1964, children comprised 36 percent of the population; in 2007 they comprised 25 percent.

What that declining percentage means is that in the next decade there will be more people who are *not* children and may not hold an interest in supporting the needs of children, especially as those voters age. Still, at this point Americans have a reasonably high level of support for education. In 2007, we approved 62.1 percent of school construction bond issues.[46]

We have more children than when Conant wrote his treatise on American high schools, and our schools are older. The National Clearinghouse for Educational Facilities (NCEF) provides data about our school facilities from a variety of sources and consolidates those data for easy reading.[47] Citing a report published in 1999, the NCEF Web site in the summer of 2008 indicated that almost half of our public schools were built before 1969; 28 percent were built before 1950. Including public and private schools, we have about 126,000 elementary and secondary schools in the United States

[44] Ibid., p. 39.

[45] *America's children in brief: Key national indicators of well-being, 2008.* http://www.childstats.gov/americaschildren/demo.asp, para. 2.

[46] National Clearinghouse for Educational Facilities. http://www.edfacilities.org/ds/statistics.cfm#.

[47] http://www.edfacilities.org/ds/statistics.cfm#.

in the 2005–2006 data (of these, just under 29,000 were private schools). There were more than 300,000 portable classrooms in use in public schools in the United States in 2006.

The NCEF data also give us some sense of where we are going. The projected growth in enrollment between 2004 and 2016 is a 9 percent increase for public school kids in elementary and secondary schools; private schools are expected to increase during that time period by 6 percent, and college enrollment between 2005 and 2016 is expected to increase by 17 percent. If we look at averages and not medians, for 2005–2006 the average number of students in primary schools was 377; in middle schools it was 630; in high schools it was 1249 students. On average, then, students, at least in high school, seem to have a large school experience. But what is a large school? A small school?

At some point, and now seems to be a good time, we need to talk about what we mean by school size. The NCEF Web site of data and statistics tackles the problem of definitions. The Web site provides answers to "What is the definition of a large school?" "What is the definition of a small school?" "What is the recommended size for a school site?" This document, using a definition from Paul Abramson, an often-quoted school planner, says a large elementary school has more than 850 students; a large middle school more than 1220 students; and a large high school more than 2000 students. Small schools are generally under 300 students. The document also cites the definitions used in the influential document about the cost-effectiveness of small schools called *Dollars and Sense*.[48] *Dollars and Sense* gives us the following parameters for small schools: elementary schools from 150 to 200 with no more than 25 students per grade level; middle schools of no more than 200 students with no more than 50 students per grade level; and high schools of no more than 300 students with no more than 75 students per grade level. It should come as no surprise to readers that practitioners often differ in their operational definitions.

Regarding the physical site itself, the recommendations on the NCEF site come from the Council of Educational Facility Planners International (CEFPI). Elementary schools are to be 10 acres plus 1 acre for every 100 students; junior high/middle schools are to be 20 acres plus 1 acre for every 100 students; senior high schools are to be 30 acres plus 1 acre for every 100 students. More recently, CEFPI has produced documents sensitive to the issue of renovation and historic preservation. These recommendations provide exceptions to the recommendations for such issues as small schools, green

---

[48] Lawrence et al. (2002).

schools, urban schools, and historic preservation.[49] The general guidelines I have provided paint a picture that is not what I would call neighborhood-friendly. Especially with regard to siting, we are building schools for a lot of students, and the siting guidelines make it difficult to fit these schools within existing neighborhoods. Until recently the regulations have in general favored new schools as opposed to school renovation.

What Are We Spending?

So what are we spending and to what extent are the decisions we make constrained by regulations at either the state or federal level? According to a 2007 report titled *Smaller, safer, saner successful schools*, updated from a 2001 version[50] and offering case studies of 22 public schools from 11 states, more than $20 billion annually is our current level of expenditure on public school construction in this country. From 2007 to 2009, about $51 billion was expected to be spent.[51] Although construction has slowed somewhat due to the economic downturn, with the fourth quarter of 2007 at its lowest level in this decade in terms of construction spending for schools and colleges, there was still an increase in the amount school districts spent on new construction, from $13.7 billion in 2006 to $14.7 billion in 2007.[52] Between 1998 and 2007, new construction in billions for school districts went from 12,097 to 21,942. If additions and modifications are tallied, the amount in billions "fell" from 12,328 to 10,997.[53] You can see that the bias, reflected in dollars spent, is toward new construction as opposed to additions and modifications. For a period of 23 years, from 1979 to 2001, more than half of the money spent on school construction problems was for enlarging and modifying existing structures. Since 2002, that pattern has changed; we now spend more on

[49] Council of Educational Facilities Planners International (2004). *A primer for the renovation/rehabilitation of older and historic schools.* Scottsdale, AZ: Council of Educational Facilities Planners International. See also, Council of Educational Facilities Planners International (2004). *Schools for successful communities: An element of smart growth.* Scottsdale, AZ: Council of Educational Facilities Planners International, U.S. Environmental Protection Agency.

[50] Nathan, J., & Febey, K. (2001). *Smaller, safer, saner, successful schools.* Washington, D.C.: National Clearinghouse for Educational Facilities, and Minneapolis, MN: Center for School Change, Humphrey Institute of the University of Minnesota. http://www.edfacilities.org/pubs/saneschools.pdf.

[51] Nathan, J., & Thao, S. (2007). *Smaller, safer, saner, successful schools.* Washington, D.C.: National Clearinghouse for Educational Facilities, and Minneapolis, MN: Center for School Change, Hubert H. Humphrey Institute of Public Affairs, University of Minnesota.

[52] Agron, J. (2008, May). *34th Annual Official Education Construction Report.* http://asumag.com/Construction/34th Education Construction Report.pdf, p. 27.

[53] Ibid., p. 28.

new construction.[54] Another interesting aspect of the dollars spent on education for K–12 is that only 2 percent is spent on the site purchase, whereas 67 percent is invested in the construction process itself.

How much do new schools cost per student? Using median figures, the cost per student for elementary, middle, and high schools is $21,176, $28,889, and $23,873, respectively; the number of square feet per student is 134, 158, and 110, respectively; the number of pupils is 600, 800, and 950, respectively; the school building size is 62,000 sq. ft., 135,000 sq. ft., and 110,000 sq. ft., respectively.[55] Other reports, although citing slightly different statistics, reiterate that we are spending more money on construction but realizing less "building" for the same dollars.[56] Fewer buildings were completed in 2007 relative to 2006 because the cost of construction increased at a faster rate than monies allocated to construction. School districts face real problems with the rising costs of construction. In 1995, the square foot cost for high schools was reported as $104.17. In 2008, it was reported as $171.43. The author points to inflation as the likely culprit, although sensitivity to green concerns (which cost more initially), which can raise costs, may also be involved.[57]

Sources disagree on how much money is spent on K–12 school construction. You read different figures when you consult McGraw-Hill Construction, the *American Planning and Management Magazine*, and the *School Planning and Management Magazine*. There is less consistency in reports about what school buildings cost than about what we actually include in new school buildings. In terms of minimums, what we include is consistent: classrooms, offices, physical education facilities, libraries (sometimes called media centers).[58]

If you focus solely on costs, data presented in *The 2008 Annual School Construction Report*[59] seem to favor smaller schools for high schools (880 or fewer vs. 1830–4000), but larger schools for the elementary level (450 or fewer versus 800 or larger). If the data are presented for medians for elementary schools, where 25 percent were designed for 450 students, the cost per square foot is $162.50 and per student is $23,477. If you look at the elementary schools designed for 800 or more students (1 in every 4), the cost per

[54] Abramson, P. (2008, February). More dollars spent, less construction completed. *The 2008 Annual School Construction Report. A Supplement to School Planning and Management. School Planning and Management*, CR1-CR16. http://www.peterli.com/spm/pdffs/constr_report_2008.pdf, p. CR2.

[55] Agron (2008, May), p. 34.   [56] Abramson, P. (2008, February).

[57] Ibid., p. CR15.   [58] Ibid., p. CR8.

[59] Ibid.

square foot was $146.83 and cost per student is $16,489, but the smaller schools provided more space per student (137.7) than did the larger schools (111.8).

Here we see some of the difficulties in reaching conclusions about school size and cost; the variables are hardly ever identical (in this example more space per student was provided in the smaller schools). But if we look at high schools the data for small and large schools are more similar. The median cost for high schools of 600 students is $15.1 million, or $25,166.67 per student, whereas the median cost of the larger school of 2,295 students is $55 million, or $23,965.14 per student.[60] With regard to the cost of schools per pupil, it depends whom you ask. Might it be better to focus on what you are trying to achieve with your construction dollars and what kinds of school sizes and arrangements address your educational mission?

PRINCIPLES TO SHAPE SCHOOLS AND SCHOOL DESIGN

A quotation from Gump may set the stage: "Education is an environmental enterprise. Some have thought that it could be advanced by reliance on learning theory or principles from child development, but these thoughts arose out of social science's inability to deal with environments."[61] Of course Gump's conception of the environment included far more than just the physical environment, but the behavior setting includes identification of the space in which the behavior occurs.

We know how many kids we have, we know how many schools we have, and we know the condition of those schools and their sizes. What is it that these school buildings are trying to support? What do our educators say they want to accomplish? We know what Conant said in 1959 about the need to consolidate our schools to provide greater depth of offerings in math and science. We also saw that there were alternative voices, such as Propst, stressing the role of community, although I think the alternative voices had little impact at the time. What is the thinking now?

There is no lack of principles that specify what it is our schools should be, because there is no lack of problems to address. At the Franklin Conference for School Design in 2005, sponsored by the editorial board of *The Philadelphia Inquirer* and the Institute for Urban Research at the University of Pennsylvania, what are known as the Franklin Principles were established.

---

[60] Ibid.

[61] Gump, P. V. (1974). Operating environments in schools of open and traditional design. *The School Review, 82*(4), 575–593, p. 593.

One can hardly argue with the list of principles. Schools are to be welcoming; they need to be safe and secure ("it's a school, not a prison") and to do so through smart design that encourages interaction. Schools need to be flexible to change for the future; they need daylight, they need good air flow, they need to provide healthy food and exercise programs; they need to be sensitive to environmental concerns; and they need to think of school design as a process that includes the community.[62]

A major effort to improve schools has come from a collaboration of The American Architectural Foundation (AAF) and the KnowledgeWorks Foundation and presenting sponsor Target. These foundations and corporations have laid out a program for creating better schools called "Great Schools by Design,"[63] which is discussed in the findings of the report *Design for Learning Forum: School Design and Student Learning in the 21st Century*. In fact, this collaboration led to the National Summit on School Design in 2005. Another force shaping school design mentioned in this AAF report is the work of the Educational Facilities Laboratory (EFL).[64]

The Great Schools by Design program seeks to address the problems of our schools, their age and lack of maintenance, and their slowness to respond to changes in our world, particularly to technology. The report presents a case that 59 million learners, teachers, and administrators in 120,000 school buildings across the United States are not being supported by buildings that are old, crowded, and have a backlog of deferred maintenance. The demographic data predict a rise in student enrollment through 2013, with school spending at $30 billion annually. The report attacks the "bigger is better" movement propelled by Conant's book.

The report addresses a number of important issues. The design of workspaces within schools will need to reflect the role of technology, but technology in and of itself cannot be the pedagogical driver. A second issue are the needs of an increasing number of poor students, who are often members of minorities or immigrants, for a range of social services. Accommodating the delivery of social services, whether for health or other needs, requires attention to space.

Further, if schools are to be part of communities, which is essential for their survival starting with funding, they must offer spaces the community

---

[62] The Franklin Principles for School Design. http://www.upenn.edu/penniur/civic/ franklin/doc/principles-final.doc.

[63] American Architectural Foundation (2007). *Design for learning forum: School design and student learning in the 21st century: A report of findings.* Washington, D.C.: American Architectural Foundation.

[64] Ibid., p. 10.

can use, from lifelong learning to recreation and wellness. "In the coming decade, we will reach a point where 75 percent of all Americans have no direct link to schools."[65] If this majority is to support town budgets and vote for school bonds, then in our increasingly pragmatic world, they need to see a benefit to themselves for this investment with their retirement dollars. One room type, one building type will no longer suffice.

This study on *School Design and Student Learning in the 21st Century* points out that decisions about education, like those about health care, are to become increasingly data-driven (what the health care community calls evidence-based outcomes), and those involved in making decisions in education will have to figure out additional outcomes to measure. What is surprising to me is that the educational sphere hasn't made more progress in this domain. Arguably it is much harder to do randomly controlled studies dealing with facility design in health care (see Chapter 2) than it is in schools. There seems to be an acknowledgment that we have accumulated knowledge about what we in environmental psychology call the "ambient" environment in schools and its relationship to educational outcomes. These ambient factors include natural light, temperature, noise, and air quality. These factors have been examined in relationship to test scores and teacher retention, for example. We have done less well in providing convincing evidence that variables like the design of the school itself or classroom size make much of a difference in learning outcomes.

Another well-known set of principles comes from the Coalition of Essential Schools (CES). CES was created by Ted Sizer, whose book *Horace's Compromise*[66] set out the challenge of reforming education in the United States. The Horace of the title is the prototypical teacher at "Franklin High," Horace Smith, who, although talented and motivated, ultimately makes the "compromise" to work within a system that has dehumanized him and his students. Although the design of the school building itself is not a fundamental focus of CES, one of the 10 common principles[67] that form the basis of the identity of CES is that the educational process needs to be personalized as much as possible. To that end, many schools described as successes in the CES movement, such as those in the Boston Pilot Schools project, are small schools.

Another set of principles comes from Kenneth Stevenson, professor at the University of South Carolina Department of Educational Leadership

[65] Ibid., p. 6.

[66] Sizer, T. R. (1984). *Horace's compromise: The dilemma of the American high school.* New York: Houghton Mifflin Company.

[67] The Common Principles. http://www.essentialschools.org/pub/ces_docs/about/phil/10cps;print10cps.html.

and Policies, who in 2002 was asked by the National Clearinghouse for Educational Facilities to outline what he saw as major trends in the design of schools. His predictions are quoted here:

1. School choice and equity will redirect facilities planning.
2. Small schools may trump larger schools in future construction.
3. There is continuing debate over reduced class size, and cost is a factor.
4. Technology may replace teachers as a cost-saving measure.
5. The changing mission of schools may require greater flexibility in the use of space.
6. Classrooms are being reconfigured.
7. Schools go 24/7. They will be kept open longer to extend learning time and for greater community use.
8. Paper-based learning materials will disappear, particularly in higher grades.
9. Grade spans are changing: K–8 schools are staging a comeback.
10. Special education will go mainstream, requiring design modifications.
11. Early childhood programs will expand and become the norm.
12. Schools as we know them may disappear, as more children are home schooled and use virtual media to learn. The traditional school may morph into a production and broadcast center.[68]

What I take away from this list is that the pendulum has swung back toward the idea of smaller schools, or at least toward the idea of what has been called small school culture. Among its ideas is the notion that a school should be a welcoming and stimulating place, not a prison. A critical concern is how to use technology appropriately to advance learning. These ideas also stress the importance of interaction as a primary focus of learning. The role of the community, for support of the school process and as a source of learning itself, is also championed.

One sees the idea of small school culture through the emphasis on personalization, for example, and through the idea that schools need to be welcoming and flexible in meeting individuals' needs now and in the future. There is a sense that smaller schools may be able to more rapidly respond to changing educational approaches. There are fewer people to organize and convince. The schoolhouse as we know it is not the only space in which learning occurs; learning is not necessarily connected to a permanent site, nor is where we work (see Chapter 4). Learning is no longer bounded in space and time, and a multitude of influences, from technology to charter

---

[68] American Architectural Foundation (2007), p. 14; also, Stevenson, K. (2007). Educational trends shaping school planning and design: 2007. http://www.edfacilities.org.

schools and home schooling, have contributed to this freedom.[69] In a sense, we have moved beyond the behavior setting as bounded in space and time. The report from the National Summit on School Design quotes Jeffrey Lackney, a prominent educational facilities architect, who states, "The self-contained classroom can no longer provide the variety of learning setting necessary to successfully facilitate 21st-century learning."[70]

School Design: A Closer Look

In addressing the issue of facilities and pedagogy, I will focus on the principles that speak most directly to the issue of architecture and design. School design is being forced to evolve. With the impact of technology, the emphasis on learning by doing through projects and internships, the competition from charter schools, and the home schooling movement, the school facility has to live; its spaces need to be sufficiently flexible to meet a variety of approaches to learning. The days of rows of school desks facing "front" are fading. With our plummeting graduation rates where almost a third of students fail to receive high school diplomas, we need to think differently about how students spend their time.

The authors of the National Summit on School Design talk about the idea of the academic village, where resources from the public library to the Y and the dance and art studio are combined into a campus that brings together all age groups and interests. For funding to be approved, schools will need to become centers open year round to the entire community. The concept of a village community that involves education is not an abstraction; it is a concrete idea given that one can imagine more fully integrated housing complexes with educational facilities than has been the case in recent years. And although we are not focusing on the issue of children's health in this chapter, we cannot ignore the impact neighborhood schools might have on children's exercise patterns. I am sure we will continue to see a change in the emphasis in the curricula of schools to promote healthy eating patterns and weight awareness and to encourage and even demand more exercise during the school day. But beyond the curriculum itself, providing the opportunity for children to walk to school will encourage greater expenditure of energy and help maintain appropriate weight.

---

[69] American Architectural Foundation and KnowledgeWorks Foundation (2006). *Report from the National Summit on School Design: A resource for educators and designers*, p. 3. http://www.archfoundation.org/aaf/documents/nssd.report.pdf.

[70] Ibid., p. 3.

Each of the eight principles from the National Summit on School Design has implications for bricks and mortar.

1. **Design schools to support a variety of learning styles**. If some kids learn better in teams, others individually, some by hands-on activities, others by reading, then the classroom or learning space has to accommodate a large range of activities.

2. **Enhance learning by integrating technology**. Careful thought must be given not only to how technology works for pedagogical purposes, given its evolution on a daily basis, but also to its use in monitoring HVAC systems, for example.

3. **Foster a small school culture**. This principle was viewed as an issue requiring further study and debate, given the pressures many school districts face with growing enrollments and a perception that larger schools are more cost-effective to build.

4. **Support neighborhood schools**. Among the many advantages of neighborhood schools are walking to school, which is a health benefit. In addition, property values can be boosted by good neighborhood schools, and a sense of commitment through identity can be fostered.

5. **Create schools as centers of community**. Questions involve how to open up schools to serve the broader community while at the same time ensuring student safety.

6. **Engage the public in the planning process**. Greater public involvement in the planning process is recommended, and it needs to start early, perhaps in a visioning activity.

7. **Make healthy, comfortable, and flexible learning spaces**. Participants agreed that the "quality, attractiveness, and health of the learning spaces and communal spaces" in the nation's schools must be improved.[71] Beyond the implications for learning of such issues as natural light, air quality, and appropriate temperature ranges, an attractive facility boasts "our community cares."

8. **Consider nontraditional options for school facilities and classrooms**. Especially with regard to real-world activities so important for students, particularly high school students, there was advocacy for looking at civic and other spaces in the community (e.g., museums, colleges) that might present opportunities for learning. And there is some evidence these principles generalize across educational settings and missions. For example, postoccupancy evaluations of 16 schools of architecture revealed that good designs should emphasize

---

[71] Ibid., p. 9.

personalization, a central gathering space, a layout promoting legibility, attention to acoustical privacy, and appropriate HVAC systems. Further, participatory planning was endorsed.[72]

One final set of design principles I would like to mention is derived from the work of Christopher Alexander and his notion of patterns in the environment. Nair and Fielding give us a volume based on Alexander's ideas and apply these patterns to the educational environment.[73] The back cover of this book asks questions we often ponder: "Why do schools look the way they do? Why is there a chasm between widely acknowledged best practice principles and the actual design of a majority of school facilities? Why has the disconnect between learning research and learning places been so difficult to repair?"

Using Christopher Alexander's pattern language as a vehicle, the authors talk about four dimensions of human experience central to the design of schools: the spatial, the psychological, the physiological, and the behavioral. To explain their concepts, the authors often rely on the notion of semantic differentials, where qualities are juxtaposed at the ends of a continuum. For example, the spatial emphasizes such qualities as open-closedness, and particularly the opportunity for intimacy and connection to nature.[74]

There are then 25 patterns, that is, types of spaces that can create "places." Here are some of the patterns I think are most relevant to our discussion of schools: small learning communities, welcoming entry, interior and exterior vistas, flexible spaces, connection to the community. I think the 25 patterns can be reduced to an emphasis on smallness, transparency, flexibility, and connection.

There are some revealing comments. For instance, in the section on classrooms, learning studios, advisories (small groups of students and faculty who work together consistently to talk about personal and academic issues), and small learning communities they say, "The classroom is the most visible symbol of an educational philosophy."[75] Then they state what they think that philosophy is presently and ultimately how it must change. They say that in the present educators have assumed that the same number of students will be in the same place at the same time learning the same

[72] Nasar, J. L., Preiser, W. F. E., & Fisher, T. (2007). Lessons learned and the future of schools of architecture buildings. In J. L. Nasar, W. F. E. Preiser, & T. Fisher (Eds.), *Designing for designers: Lessons learned from schools of architecture* (pp. 72–91). New York Fairchild Press.

[73] Nair, P., & Fielding, R. (2005). *The language of school design: Design patterns for 21st century schools.* Minneapolis, MN: DesignShare.

[74] Ibid., p. 8.   [75] Ibid., p. 17.

material from the same person for the same number of hours each day. This is hardly a recipe for a passion for lifelong learning.

The old-fashioned model of schools from the early 20th century they call "cells and bells." You know this model. It's the model of a double-loaded corridor off which, for the length of the hallway, are similarly sized classrooms. This model is essentially what Propst talked about when he said that when asked to draw a school every school child would produce a large box around a series of smaller, equal-size boxes, set side by side. They argue that we need a new spatial metaphor for what the learning of the 21st century (and beyond) demands of our kids. Not surprisingly, if the old metaphor for learning stressed sameness, the new learning model emphasizes difference – different teachers, different places, different things to be learned, different ways of learning those things, in different ways, at different times, and with students of different ages.

Cells and bells will fail us, they say, because of the format's lecture-based assumptions about how learning will happen. In its place they want spaces that can be used as zones for learning, like an L-shaped classroom, where small learning communities (SLC) can operate. One model they offer is a finger plan, where spaces off a corridor (e.g., at right angles) are themselves subdivided and subdividable (envision a tree graph).

The authors are admirers of the educator David Thornburg and his four "primordial learning metaphors": the Campfire, the Watering Hole, the Cave, and Life. "Campfires are a way to learn from experts or storytellers; Watering Holes help you learn from peers; Caves are places to learn from yourself; and Life is where you bring it all together by applying what you learn to projects in the real world."[76] Not surprisingly, they say educators fear the Watering Hole because who knows what can happen when kids get together; but this kind of exchange of culture is part of growing up, they argue. And Cave-like spaces are not just the library, but can happen outdoors, under a tree or by a fountain. They also bring in the way in which Howard Gardner's multiple intelligences can be accommodated in the kinds of school spaces they have in mind.

Examples of "New" Schools

We have looked at a lot of principles; let's look at some schools based on these principles. First, what happens when good ideas and money converge? We get some sense of the possibilities by looking at a collaboration between

[76] Ibid., p. 61.

Microsoft and the school district of Philadelphia. In 2003, these two forces created a blueprint for the "school of the future,"[77] a part of the Partners in Learning initiative that Microsoft established. The school opened in fall 2006. Key principles for the learning environment of this school were to be continuous, relevant, and adaptive. The idea of continuous learning is that learning happens everywhere, not just in the classroom. Relevancy has to do with the connections of the curriculum to the outside world, including the community. In a learning environment that stresses adaptation, each student has the chance to engage in a manner that best fits his or her learning style.

Although technology obviously plays a central role in Microsoft's interest in education, the physical facilities are a corollary of that interest. Of five factors critical to success (involved and connected learning community; proficient and inviting curriculum-driven setting; flexible and sustainable learning environment; cross-curriculum integration of research and development; professional leadership), the emphasis on physical environment emerges most clearly in the proficient and inviting curriculum-driven setting.[78]

Not surprisingly, the major emphasis is on information technology, with an entire chapter devoted to principles of IT infrastructure planning. The guiding principle for creating an IT infrastructure that might work 10 years out was flexibility. But the challenge is keeping technology from becoming the driver; it is an enabler of learning, not the focus of learning.

What role does architecture play? "The design and deployment of IT infrastructure needs to occur collaboratively alongside the design and construction of the building itself."[79] Wireless technology has its own requirements, from materials used to construct walls and ceilings, to theoretical signal patterns and fields, to wall and ceiling clearances to accommodate fixtures, AV systems, security systems, and so on.

In describing a prototypical classroom of 800 sq. ft., the emphasis is on flexibility, not desks in rows facing a podium. Spaces can be transformed from a lecture hall to a circular discussion section. Movable walls are also incorporated in some spaces to create the flexibility to move from large group to single learner–size enclosures. Daylight that can be controlled through screens to manage glare is a part of classrooms, and of course the classrooms are wireless. Propst's ideas from 1972 seem relevant to the emphasis on flexibility.

---

[77] Building the school of the future: A guide for the 21st century learning environment. http://www.microsoft.com/educaiton/sof.

[78] Ibid., p. 8.   [79] Ibid., p. 14.

The school has a streetscape on the first floor or main level to create a "social spine" for the facility, running its length. It has two gymnasiums, a performance center (which can be subdivided into smaller usable spaces), food court, science lab, and interactive learning center (ILC; open to the community). The second floor houses an art studio and an IT and Web design lab; the third floor houses classrooms.

Some schools "get" that architecture can be central to student learning. One example is a federally funded magnet school for 500 students in Roanoke, Virginia, the Roanoke Academy for Mathematics and Science (RAMS), which opened in 2005. The school received positive press for using architecture as a teaching tool.[80] The school is for students pre-K through fifth grade as well as for disabled adult students who have mental illness. Situated in a 27-acre residential park, the school complex is 84,000 sq. ft. What is special about the school is that its architecture was conceived as a form of *teaching* students about the subject matter that is the focus of the school. The building elements themselves, the types of brick and mortars, the trusses, beams, and purlins (members of the roof horizontally placed that support the rafters), are used to teach about mathematics as well as design. The building blocks of structure are visible and can teach students about principles of geometry. Floor tiles have patterns that illustrate a number of principles, including the Pythagorean theorem. Along a main street that connects three sections or "neighborhoods" in a kind of village arrangement, there are fluorescent lights at irregular angles (called the "train wreck" by the kids) to stimulate interest. Every classroom has replicas of windows by Frank Lloyd Wright and can be used to illustrate geometric and other principles. And the school has lots of vistas to help people understand what they might encounter if they choose one route rather than another. This transparency is comforting and supportive. And to illustrate that great design does not have to raise costs, the school was built at $100 per square foot, no more than the average cost for elementary schools in the state.

At the same time there is frustration on the part of architects in terms of the role they often play in the conceptual process. In the summer of 2008 I spoke with Eric Ward, an architect with Einhorn Yaffee Prescott (EYP) in Boston, whose firm is involved in higher education projects. His view is that the funding system and the way communities are reimbursed for educational expenses hamper what kinds of buildings are designed and constructed.

---

[80] Boniface, R. (2006, July). A school building designed to teach. *AIA Architect.* http://www.aia.org/aiarchitect/thisweek06/0714/0714pw_roanoke.cfm.

Moreover, the architect generally comes rather late to the table, and the role of the architect in Ward's view is to "give shape to ideas that are already formed by the people in authority, whether in local or state government or in academic institutions, in the case of private secondary education." The sad reality, he says, is that the role of the architect in such projects is much less than architects were taught in their architectural programs. Cost is still the primary driver of projects, and communities will resist what they consider "extras" in the project, even if those extras are supported by educational theory. Ward is a resident of Massachusetts and mentioned the idea that the high price tag of school construction in his state, particularly Newton North High, with a cost of $192.5 million including design work, led to the suggestion on the part of some state officials, in particular the state treasurer, that standardized school design is the answer. The thinking is that such a school prototype program (i.e., standardization) would curb what some officials perceive to be competition among communities regarding what are described as perks, in particular swimming pools and field houses. As you might imagine, architects have not taken kindly to the suggestion of such standardization.[81]

IS SMALLER BETTER?

Many principles we have reviewed and the schools that illustrate those principles involve the word "small." And one of the central controversies in the debate about enhancing learning is school size. For example, in the report from the National Summit on School Design, the principle "Foster a 'Small School' Culture" was essentially "referred back to committee." The participants in the summit indicated that more study was needed about the issues and that political pressures in communities, highlighted by increasing numbers of students, often led some school districts to build larger schools. To quote the report, "School size issues are still a leading area of conflict in the national discussion on education and school design."[82]

Is there a controversy over small schools, or is the controversy over what are perceived to be the higher costs of small schools, say, high schools of 500 and fewer and elementary schools of 200 and fewer, relative to their larger peers? I think there are two basic issues at the core of the small school debate, and measurement is fundamental to each of them. The first

[81] Schneider, G. (2008, August 29). Guest blogger: Should public-college buildings be standardized? *The Chronicle: Buildings & Grounds.* http://chronicle.com/blogs/architecture/2376/guest-blogger-should-public-college-buildings-be-standardized.

[82] American Architectural Foundation and KnowledgeWorks Foundation (2006), p. 8.

question is whether small schools are "better" for our youth; the second is whether they cost more. And the question then becomes if they cost more, are the outcomes from smaller schools sufficiently impressive to justify the additional expenditure of funds? I am struck by the layers of subjectivity in these kinds of judgments.

Earlier in the chapter we reviewed how the terms "small" and "large" are defined. Although there is no universal definition for "small," a number of sources point to the range of around 500 or fewer students for high schools and 200 or fewer for elementary schools, although there are recommendations for even smaller schools.[83] The literature seems to agree that schools of 1000 are large. That categorization of the space between 500 and 1000, however, often seems fuzzy.

Regarding the cost, conclusions are different depending on the outcome employed. If the outcome is cost per pupil, then small schools often are more expensive. However, if the cost is measured in terms of the *cost per graduate*, then it has been argued that small schools are often less expensive.[84] And measuring the cost in terms of students who actually graduate speaks to the issue of what small schools accomplish relative to large schools.

Sometimes embedded in the principles discussed in this chapter, sometimes more directly stated, there is a theme that smaller schools (i.e., elementary schools under 200; high schools under 500) provide the opportunity to create learning environments that are much more difficult to establish in larger schools. These learning environments are about sense of community and getting to know students in a way that is more difficult in larger schools.

What do the data say? The benefits of small schools have been identified as student involvement, and related to that a sense of personal efficacy, relationships built on knowing each other, and a high level of parental involvement.[85] Academic achievement in large schools is never superior to that of small schools, and in small schools it is often better. The other areas in which "positives" occur are social behavior, attitudes toward academic subjects, levels of extracurricular participation, attendance, dropout rate, sense of belonging, self-concept, interpersonal relationships, teacher

---

[83] Ibid.

[84] Stiefel, L., Latarola, P., Fruchter, N., & Berne, R. (1998). *The effects of size of student body on school costs and performance in New York City High Schools.* New York: New York University Institute for Education and Social Policy.

[85] Cotton, K. (1996, May). School size, school climate, and student performance. Northwest Regional Educational Laboratory. School Improvement Research Series. Close-Up #20. http://www.nwrel.org/scpd/sirs/10/c020.html.

attitudes toward work, more positive outcomes for students of low socio-economic status (SES), and students who are racial and ethnic minorities. Of the 18 conclusions listed in an influential, often-cited paper by Cotton, 13 indicate more positive outcomes for small schools, and the other 4 simply indicate aspects of the way in which research has been done or facts about school consolidation.

A number of benefits to smaller schools are discussed in the report *Smaller, Safer, Saner, Successful Schools*[86] published in 2007. The report makes points about outcomes that are similar to those discussed in the paper by Cotton. The report also points out that being small in and of itself is not sufficient (think about my comments related to architectural determinism; perhaps we need to call it size determinism). Small schools *plus* an emphasis on forming interpersonal relationships matters, and I think the first step in forming those relationships is having the chance to get to know someone, which is certainly easier when there are fewer students. I know from my own teaching that when I work with individuals or pairs of students on group projects in my research methods course, time spent together helps me get to know them as people, as distinct individuals. Without such projects, that kind of personal relationship is much less likely to occur.

Smaller schools can share resources, for example, which in turn can build a sense of community that involves constituencies beyond the school itself. For example, many unexpected alliances may result when schools have programs that involve facilities such as museums, day care programs, senior citizen centers, or even colleges. The learning opportunities may not be those of a typical self-contained high school, but they may be far more personally rewarding. If you are near an aquarium, as is the case in my community, think about internships learning to work with marine mammals. An example in *Smaller, Safer, Saner Successful Schools* is learning about marketing strategies at the Mall of America in Minnesota. Given our cultural emphasis on shopping (see Chapter 5), this internship makes perfect sense.

Another benefit in the report cites providing social services beyond those that may be routine in schools. One frequent criticism of schools today is that they are trying to do too much and address all of a child's needs because those needs are perceived to be unmet at home. If social services are available, but not actually provided by the school, some of those needs

[86] Nathan & Thao (2007).

of children and families can be met in a more pragmatic manner. An ideal co-occurrence might involve a health clinic situated next to a school. The proximity makes the use more likely. In the chapter on health care in this book, I discuss the growth in the location of health facilities in such places as malls. Providing services in locations that are familiar to students and their families can lessen the trepidation people often have about visiting a health care professional.

The third benefit discussed in the report is that it stretches a school's dollars. That is, services and facilities in the community are available at a cost the school itself could not carry. When entities such as schools, senior centers, and arts programs band together, facilities can be created that no one entity by itself could afford. The fourth benefit they cite is the expansion of time spent together by families. Such expansion often happens in what is known as "work site" facilities, where a school is located in or next to a work site, such as a mall.

One of the featured schools in the report is Amistad, in New Haven, Connecticut, which is close to me and has a variety of features, including a longer school day.[87] The academic results at Amistad on Connecticut's Mastery Test (CMT) have been impressive, including much higher than the district average for eighth graders and achieving at least at the state average, and in some areas, such as writing and math scores, above it. From this success a nonprofit Achievement First was formed. It has recreated the successful Amistad program in New Haven and Bridgeport, Connecticut, and at several schools in Brooklyn, New York.

A second nearby program included in this report is the MET (Metropolitan Regional Career and Technical Center) in Providence, Rhode Island, which had its first graduating class in 2000. The original MET campus in Providence included four small schools, with shared facilities for performing, fitness, and technology. The successful program has been expanded and is represented in 20 states. Support has come from the Bill and Melinda Gates Foundation. The Learning through Interests program is the foundation of the school, where what interests kids forms the basis of how their learning occurs, with more than 2000 internship sites, from an aquarium to a television news station to the mayor's office. These kids do well, with more than 80 percent of those who graduated in 2007 in college and a 98 percent college acceptance rate.[88]

---

[87] Ibid., p. 28.   [88] Ibid., p. 62.

The Boston Pilot Schools Project[89] has been profiled as a success in creating successful small inner-city schools. Data covering the period 2001–2005 show that the students in these pilot schools have outperformed their peers in the Boston school district who are not part of the pilot high schools or are not part of what are called exam schools. Exam schools are those that admit students based on entrance exam scores and prior evidence of academic achievement. Established in 1994, the pilot schools are not under the same strictures as other schools in the system regarding curriculum, instruction, assessment, budget, staffing, governance, and schedule. The emphasis in establishing these schools was on research and development, giving them more latitude in what they did and how they did it, so that the innovations that "worked" could be transferred to the wider school district. There are 20 such schools, 10 high schools among them. Two of the schools are Horace Mann charter schools that receive funds from the school district. The enrollment is limited to 450 or fewer students. The student populations are essentially the same as in the rest of the district. Other characteristics include accountability (benchmarks that schools must meet every 5 years); small size and personalization, driven by a vision of equity and commitment to each child's potential.[90] Students in these pilot schools compared to nonpilot schools have higher graduation rates (75.7 percent vs. 52.2 percent)[91] and better performance on state mastery tests than was true of nonpilot schools, although it has to be recognized that the pilot schools have some advantages (lower percentage of students with risk factors). But the pilot schools still have an enrollment profile typical of the racial, economic, and mainstream special education subgroups of the school system. Of the pilot students, 68.4 percent were eligible for the subsidized lunch program versus 69.8 percent of those in nonpilot schools.[92] As a result of these positive outcomes from the Boston Pilot Schools Project, one strong recommendation is to create more pilot schools and to get out the message about pilot schools, that is, to share information about what makes these pilot schools work.

Most research on school size focuses on academic outcomes, but school is about more than mastery tests. There is some research looking at the idea of self-concept or self-worth as it relates to school size, which essentially has its roots in the concepts of overstaffed and understaffed schools described by

---

[89] Center for Collaborative Education (2007, November). *Strong results, high demand: A four-year study of Boston's pilot high schools.* Boston: Center for Collaborative Education.
[90] Ibid., p. v.   [91] Ibid., p. iv.
[92] Ibid.

Barker and Gump. What evidence do we have of the relationship of school size to a variety of outcomes of interest? One project looked at the association between self-concept and school size.[93] In this correlational research (limited to male students), 1058 participants from 12 high schools in Iowa reported on participation in five activity areas and completed a self-concept scale. The enrollment of schools classified as larger had to exceed 580. The results essentially showed that students at smaller schools were more likely to be involved in activities and in a greater number of activity areas than students at larger schools, supporting the earlier work of Barker and Gump and their associates that students in smaller schools were more likely to be involved in more activities, to participate in a greater variety of them, and to feel a greater sense of obligation to be involved in those activities. Moreover, activity levels were linked to feelings of self-worth. Upperclassmen (11th and 12th graders) at small schools who participated in fewer activities were likely to have lower feelings of self-worth. It may be one thing not to make a team or be a leader in a large school where fewer individuals can fill those slots; at a small school among upperclassmen, such "failure" might be problematic in terms of self-worth. This research moves ahead our understanding of the effects of small schools by linking life in the small school to feelings of self-worth, and not simply to perceived pressure to participate in activities. But the data indicate a critical point often overlooked and of some concern to educators. There can be a downside to being *uninvolved* at a small school in term of feelings of self-worth, and educators need to be sensitive to that possibility.

Who supports small schools? Among the notables are Bill and Melinda Gates, whose foundation has contributed more than $1 billion for 1500 smaller schools to be built in the United States. New York City has also endorsed the small school approach by adopting a plan in 2006 to create 36 middle and high schools of between 300–600 students.[94] Philadelphia is also embarking on a plan to reduce school size by creating more schools in the small and middle size range,[95] and Chicago announced plans in 2004, called Renaissance 2010, to create more neighborhood schools by converting about 100 schools, 10 percent of its inventory.[96]

---

[93] Grabe, M. (1975, March). *Big school, small school: Impact of the high school environment*. Paper presented at the Annual Meeting of the American Educational Association, Washington, D.C.

[94] American Architectural Foundation and KnowledgeWorks Foundation (2006), p. 27.

[95] Ibid., p. 28.   [96] Ibid., p. 29.

BUT IS IT REALLY THE SIZE THAT MATTERS?

Is it school size that matters, or the sense of community more likely to be fostered through smaller rather than larger size? There is some support that it is not size, per se, but the sense of community that matters.[97] As we have seen, the small school movement is sometimes traced to the seminal work of Barker and Gump in the 1960s. The core value of the small schools movement, it is argued, is sense of community, not size. A similar argument is made in an article tracing the small schools movement in both the United States and Great Britain.[98] Britain is undergoing its own struggles with the downsides of large schools (those more than 2000 enrolled) that were constructed in the 1950s. And they have their own version of Teach for America, called Teach First, where in the familiar model top graduates work in challenging inner-city schools for 2 years.

"Small schools are a big deal these days."[99] But small schools, as the title of a 2008 article "Small schools: Size or community?" suggests, are not just about size. And it is difficult if not impossible to tease apart the effects of size from curriculum and quality of instruction. For example, Kenneth Strike of Syracuse University, the author of the article, comments that "scaling up is hard," and that as a movement gains popularity, as the small school movement has done, it is hard to maintain a focus on the essence of the ideal.[100]

In Strike's view, it is not size, per se, that is important, but what small size has the opportunity to create: sense of community. And although he argues that what makes a school small, or small enough, sounds like a simple question to answer, it is not. Like most of social science, the answer seems to be: It depends. What are the outcomes? If the answer is achievement, then how is achievement, certainly not a unitary concept, measured? Small enough to know people's names? Or to know when people are absent, he asks? One response given is that schools must be personalized, and to do this requires that they both feel small and function as small units. There are competing views of what a small school is: "One view emphasizes size and personalization. But it is no longer clear that size has to do altogether with the number of students in a building. It may have more to do with the pattern of interaction between adults and students. A second view emphasizes instructional transformation focusing on a themed curriculum

---

[97] Strike, K. A. (2008). Small schools: Size or community? *American Journal of Education,* *114,* 169–190.

[98] Tasker, M. (2008). Smaller schools: A conflict of aims and purposes? *Forum, 50*(2), 177–184.

[99] Strike (2008).   [100] Ibid., p. 170.

and programmatic coherence."[101] He points out that although at least some educators link the interest in small schools to the pioneering research of Barker and Gump, their book was primarily about rural schools, which the author points out become small schools by default rather than by design.

Small schools have been one suggestion to address the notion of inadequacy in the schools, caused by a system that is a public monopoly and that can be fixed, in the view of some, by introducing competition. Others think that emphasizing standards as part of a system-wide reform is the answer. Still others think the problem is that schools and education itself alienate learners.[102] In Strike's view, the essence of the small school movement is addressing the alienation and lack of involvement that characterize many of our students.

The solution he identifies? Community. Caring is central to community. Operationally, caring seems to involve a relationship with at least one adult in the school; personalization is seen as the way to establish this base of caring; further, size is the instrument to create this base of caring. But Strike wants this solution to involve a broader community and not just an individualized experience of caring. His vision is caring set within the context of community; he describes it as a communitarian view of the purpose of small schools. The antidote to alienation is being a member of a community. The advantage of community membership is the shared vision of the educational goals the community seeks to achieve. Strike goes on to say, "People, particularly young people, come to share the values and commitments of people who care for them.... Belonging begins and ends in caring. Hence, community and caring become mutually reinforcing."[103]

He also has a word or two to say about standards, which are a hot button topic in education today. With regard to standards, he thinks the emphasis should be on excellence rather than on standards that allow a non-expert to judge performance. He argues, and I agree: The language we use is important.

Strike argues that school size in and of itself is not responsible for positive learning outcomes. Other authors strongly argue that the debate over school size is not really about educational outcomes but rather about control. "To be blunt, it appears that educational control, rather than educational quality is of most importance in the 'appropriate' school size debate."[104] The author questions who really is in power with regard to the schools – the local community, the state, federal monetary policy, or even designers? The

[101] Ibid., p. 173.   [102] Ibid., p. 176.
[103] Ibid., p. 181.
[104] Smith & DeYoung (1988), p. 9.

questions aren't simply about educational philosophy but encompass our views on socioeconomic status, the role of the private sector, and morality on some level. Their argument is that looking at school outcomes will not explain why small and rural schools nationally and globally look as they do; rather, we have to look at decisions that relate to much broader questions about how our society is structured.

WHY ISN'T EVERY COMMUNITY BUILDING SMALL SCHOOLS?

Whether it is smallness per se, or smallness that fosters sense of community, as Strike argues, why don't we see more small schools? What are the challenges? Growing enrollment coupled with political pressure seems to be one reason that communities resist the small school argument, as indicated in the voices of participants at the National Summit on School Design mentioned earlier in this chapter. Eric Ward, the architect from EYP mentioned earlier in the chapter, reiterated the view that cost is the primary driver of many projects, and that most communities resist the notion of "extras."

I am reminded of the transformation that has taken place in health care, where hospitals are now embracing the concept of single-room occupancy because the bottom line shows that single rooms can be more cost-effective in terms of occupancy rates, lowered risk of infection, and a variety of other convincing indicators (see Chapter 2). My sense is that over time, town governments, the bodies that often propose the referenda that fund school projects, will be convinced by data that show small schools are actually less costly in the long run if the outcomes used to measure cost are the cost per pupil to graduate rather than simply the cost per pupil.

Communities often resist small schools because of the financial arguments that large schools are more cost-effective. A finding frequently cited because it helps undercut the economics argument is the research by Stiefel in New York City, cost per pupil to graduate is lower in smaller schools that than in larger schools. Here the emphasis is on getting the student to the finish line, which is a goal that society needs to embrace.[105]

Speaking about large public high schools with as many as 3000 to 4000 students, Thomas Toch, author of *High Schools on a Human Scale*,[106] argues that the economies of scale envisioned by early supporters of Conant's

---

[105] Stiefel, L., Latarola, P., Fruchter, N., & Berne, R. (1998). *The effects of size of student body on school costs and performance in New York City high schools.* New York: New York University Institute for Education and Social Policy.

[106] Toch, T. (2003). *High schools on a human scale: How small schools can transform American education.* Boston: Beacon Press, p. 9.

plea for consolidation to enhance curriculum have not really emerged. He mentions research by New York University faculty that if you compare high schools with fewer than 400 students with high schools of more than 2000, the initial findings that small schools spend, on average, only 5 percent more than the large schools disappear when you calculate the cost per student to graduate, as opposed to the cost of simply attending the school. Using cost per student to graduate, small schools actually spend less than large schools. Toch says, "James Conant was well intentioned when he wrote *The American High School Today*. But he was wrong."[107]

School Size and Siting Regulations

Other factors that must often be addressed in deciding school size are location and siting. What might otherwise be considered a good location may be dropped because insufficient land is available according to local and state regulations. One problem with trying to build small schools has been that regulations often promote "sprawl schools."[108] The Council of Educational Facility Planners (CEFPI) based in Arizona has standards and cost ratios for siting schools that are followed by a number of states. For example, the standards operating over the last 30 years until 2004 stated that 15 acres were required for an elementary school of 500, and 50 acres for a high school sized at 2000. The cost ratio rule was known as the two-thirds rule: "If the cost to rehab a school exceeds 60% of [the] cost of replacement, build a new school."[109] The article mentions a study from South Carolina stating that in every decade since 1950, the site size for schools has increased. As I mentioned earlier in this chapter, in 2004 CEFPI issued a number of publications that recognized the importance of older and historic schools, as well as the importance of following smart growth principles in siting schools. These documents reflect a positive step in understanding that there are alternatives to simply building increasingly larger schools in locations at a distance from the community hub. An alliance has grown between those who support Smart Growth principles and educators who see the advantages of schools centered in the community.[110]

---

[107] Ibid., p. 10.

[108] Goldberg, D. (2005, winter). Of sprawl, schools and small schools. *On Common Ground*, pp. 6–11.

[109] Ibid., p. 9.

[110] CEFPI (2004). *Schools for successful communities: An element of smart growth*. Scottsdale, AZ: CEFPI and U.S. EPA.

Near the beginning of this chapter, I talked about the change in how few children walk or bike to school relative to those statistics from 40 years ago. The siting of schools and suburban sprawl certainly have a relationship to those transportation choices. Fortunately, there are inklings of change, such as the Safe Routes to School program in California, which focuses on improving the crossings, sidewalks, bikeways, and other contributors to safe walking by using federal money.[111] And perhaps with greater impact, the standards from the Council of Education Facilities Planners have been reformulated.[112]

Rather than viewing siting as a hurdle, it can be viewed as an opportunity. Another intersection of housing and education is the realization that schools can support Smart Growth principles discussed in Chapter 1. If a neighborhood school is built, walking can be supported. One such example is the San Diego Model School, where what has been described as an urban village will provide housing for low- and middle-income families, recreational facilities, a health clinic, parks, day care, and underground parking, in addition to the school.[113]

WILL COMMUNITIES PAY FOR SMALL SCHOOLS? MAKING THE CASE

If educators and parents with school age children are to make the case for smaller schools they may need to expand the outcomes measured in relationship to school size. The findings from the *Design for Learning Forum: School Design and Student Learning in the 21st Century* report suggest that we must expand the research agenda to include student mobility, delinquency, graduation rates, and the role special education accommodations play in affecting the education of all school students.[114]

I would argue that the outcome measures can be expanded beyond that list. School, as many educators seem to be arguing, is more than a vessel for education about the three Rs. It is also a vehicle for education about relationships, about sexuality, about health in general, about life. Schools provide everything from lunches to films about sexually transmitted diseases. If we are going to provide such expanded services, then our outcomes need to include this broad range, whether it is the drop in the number of teenage pregnancies or sexually transmitted diseases or the number of students on medication for attention-deficit disorder.

---

[111] Ibid., p. 27.
[112] http://cefpi.org:80/creatingconnections/index.html.
[113] CEFPI (2004), pp. 24–25.
[114] American Architectural Foundation (2007), p. 40.

Making the case for good design is often viewed as an uphill battle, given the lack of evidence supporting the effects of "good design," and a number of participants in the Design for Learning Forum lamented the problem of school board resistance to what are viewed as "Taj Mahal" schools. One might argue that the architects and designers have not sufficiently made their case if school boards respond to proposals in this manner. However, if architects come late to the table where most of the pedagogical decisions have already been made, it is not they alone who must make the case about good design.

What is obvious to many is that good design for a school has spillover effects into the community, where it lifts the community's image and makes a case for home purchase. Obviously it helps if good test scores accompany this image, but a community's willingness to invest in its schools also says something about whether the community embraces the life cycle.

But the aging and graying of America is bringing another kind of tension between the increasing number of those without school age children and those who have kids yet to educate. In the chapter on health care, I discussed the impact of the retirement of the baby boomer generation on social programs like Medicare. The aging of America has a dramatic effect on education as well, with 70 million Americans over the age of 65 predicted in 2025, up from 35 million in 2011.[115] Only 25 percent of the general population will have children of school age at that time. Who will vote to pay for schools? When I wrote this the price of gas had only recently dropped from well more than $4/gallon and millions of Americans had lost their homes through foreclosure related primarily to the subprime debacle.

The Design for Learning Forum report argues that the way to address this divide between those with school age children and those without is to reinforce the idea of the school as community center, a place where retirees can go for lifelong learning, as well as for recreational facilities.

ARE SMALL LEARNING COMMUNITIES A SOLUTION?

Can you have your cake and eat it, too? Can you create small schools "within" large schools to build a number of different distinct communities and the sense of "small school culture," in the process maximizing economies of scale? This approach can be operationalized in a number of ways, but at its core is the notion of a small learning community (SLC). In fact, Cotton

[115] Ibid., p. 29.

provides definitions for 18 different kinds of small learning approaches.[116]
One of the better known approaches is the School within a School (SWAS),
in which one or more schools operates within a structure, each with its own
students and teachers, but reporting to one principal. Such programs are
fairly new and are typically limited to urban environments; we do not yet
have enough data to determine the success of such approaches, which are
being tried in my community. One research summary suggests that schools
within a school do not necessarily achieve the same effects as creating small
schools themselves,[117] and that we must consider the findings tentative at
best, as extensive research has not yet been conducted. One fundamental
problem seems to be creating enough separateness and autonomy to create
a distinctive identity for each school.

There are a variety of approaches to creating small learning communities.
Charter schools can be considered in this category, as well as plans that involve segregating ninth graders to ease the transition into high school, often
called a "house" plan. It is hard to evaluate the outcomes of small learning
communities because researchers do not always indicate how self-contained
the program is within the larger setting. But some research shows benefits in
the areas of academic achievement, social behavior, attitudes, satisfaction,
relationships between students and teachers, and attendance.[118]

One success story is the Julia Richman Education Complex in New York
City. This complex contains six unique and distinct schools, and a number of
steps were taken to create that sense of distinct identity. This complex probably would be considered to contain autonomous small schools, according
to the definitions that Cotton provides, because there is independence of
organization, finances, and instruction.[119] An entire chapter is devoted to
this school in Toch's book on how small schools can transform American education.[120] One critical step in creating distinct identities was called
hot-housing, in which schools were started in other facilities so that the
glitches could be worked out before "transplanting" them to the Richman
complex. In addition to creating a sense of community within these schools,
the schools were made physically distinct, which is a decided advantage in

---

[116] Cotton, K. (2001, December). *New small learning communities: Findings from recent literature.* Portland, OR: Norwest Regional Educational Laboratory.

[117] Cotton, K. (1996, May). School size, school climate, and student performance. Northwest
Regional Educational Laboratory. School Improvement Research Series. Close-Up #20.
http://www.nwrel.org/scpd/sirs/10/co20.html.

[118] Ibid.   [119] Cotton (2001), p. 8.

[120] Toch (2003).

my view. "Though as many as three of them share floors of the building, there are no common hallways and the swinging double doors that connect the schools might as well be cinderblock walls; students and teachers simply don't go into other schools' space – a fact that has required a lot of instructional gerrymandering, including the moving of a chemistry lab so that its students don't have to enter Vanguard's area to go to class."[121] Further, the author notes that a common trouble spot, the bathrooms, are physically contained within each school and are "off-limits" to students in other schools in the complex. Moreover, the students and teachers in at least one of the schools use the same bathrooms, which in itself may send a signal about being part of a community. There are shared facilities, to be sure, and they include what one typically considers the expensive spaces (recital hall, athletic facilities, art facilities, auditorium, and theater), but only the library and cafeteria are in use at the same time by students from the six different schools.

An educator in the Urban Academy, one of the six schools, is quoted as saying, "Houses don't work because you need autonomy for teachers for them to feel truly responsible for kids and houses don't create enough autonomy. You can't go halfway. If teachers don't feel responsible they don't invest themselves."[122] It seems evident that the educators at the Richman complex have taken steps to create the autonomy necessary for schools within a school to succeed.

GROTON'S SOLUTION

The impressive and admittedly glamorous schools highlighted in this chapter (MET; Microsoft School of the Future) are smaller rather than larger. But will America build such schools? Americans seem to be asking themselves whether they can afford to do so and whether size really makes a difference.

In May 2002, the Groton Public Schools in Groton, Connecticut, released its Vision Committee Report,[123] which outlines the work of 29 teachers, parents, board of education members, and administrators, across the elementary, middle school, and high school levels, to articulate the needs of the Groton school system through 2025. Page 2 of the document states, "We believe, and the research shows, that architecture affects learning;

---

[121] Ibid., p. 25.   [122] Ibid., p. 26.

[123] Groton Public Schools (2002, May 20). *Vision Committee Report.* Groton, CT: Groton Public Schools.

therefore, the proposed design of our schools enhances and brings to life the educational programs for our students and community." The report talks about the importance of creating smaller communities at the elementary level, of fostering interaction that in turn builds a sense of community at the middle school level, and of implementing a school within a school strategy at the high school level. Further, the report emphasizes the central role that flexible spaces play in meeting needs in a changing educational landscape.

Although the plan outlines steps to be taken at the elementary, middle, and high school levels, I will focus on the high school, where commitment to a smaller learning community is most evident. During the summer of 2008, I spoke with Groton School Board member Elizabeth Gianacoplos, who had been chairperson of the board of education when the Vision Committee Report was drafted. She has served on the board of education for 13 years. Among the options the board considered, including building an entirely new school, the notion of building or having two high schools was never considered, presumably because of cost, she thought. The final plan for the high school included building a new section, renovating parts of the older building, and demolishing some of the original facility to keep the school square footage within parameters allowed for state reimbursement. At the same time, the Vision Committee recognized the advantages of the small learning community model.

The school within a school model that has been implemented involves three different floors in the new section, each floor constituting a separate school with an assistant principal and guidance counselor. The teachers will stay with the students in that school for all 4 years, and there is heterogeneous grouping of ability in each school. The core subjects are taught in each school, but some courses with unique facility demands, such as art, are taught in specialized but shared spaces, and students who are few in number taking advanced courses such as AP Physics would also be taught "out of school" together.

The Groton Vision Committee Report states that "architecture affects learning and the design of this facility enhances educational programs and brings them to life. Our vision is a high school that has common and administrative areas at the center, or hub of the school; wings that serve as four houses (academic clusters); and a fieldhouse, theater, and cafetorium on the outside of the design, making them easily accessible to the community. The school has climate control, state-of-the-art security, and as much natural light as possible. The facility also serves as a community

FIGURE 3.6. Fitch High School

center."[124] In researching this book I have learned that a cafetorium combines the functions of a cafeteria and an auditorium (typically physically realized as a stage at one end of the cafeteria).

The guiding principles, from smaller learning communities to dynamic spaces, sense of welcome, sense of safety, energy efficiency, support of technology, and community access to and use of facilities, come directly from research reviewed in this chapter.

What I have described was the vision. What is the reality (see Figure 3.6)? I spoke to C. Wesley Greenleaf, director of buildings and grounds for the Groton Public Schools in September 2008 to better understand the match between vision and reality. We had a wide-ranging conversation that covered the role of cost as a driving factor, the impact of demographics, the reasons for the failure of a house program at the high school some 10 years ago, and hopes he has for the success of the SWAS program at the new (and renovated) high school. Like architect Eric Ward and school board member Elizabeth Gianacoplos, he reiterated the role of cost in educational decisions. "Locals only care about the bottom line," he said, and it takes a considerable amount of creativity and perseverance to match the vision to the funding. The role of demographics is also inextricably intertwined with cost. In 1973, he noted, there were approximately 10,000 students enrolled in the Groton Public Schools. Today, there is roughly half the number of students. The situation in Groton is even more pronounced than the situation nationally where children comprised 25 percent of the population in 2007. In Groton, public

---

[124] Ibid., p. 34.

school enrollment was 12.5 percent of the town population in 2000.[125] What this demographic change means is that it becomes increasingly difficult to persuade voters about the necessity of supporting school bond issues as the percentage of voters with children in the public school system shrinks. Within that context, it is easier to understand why the concept of the small school had to be accommodated within the physical reality of a larger structure and why having two high schools was never considered as an option.

Greenleaf's assessment of the failure of the house system about 10 years ago was strikingly similar to comments made by teachers at the Julia Richman Education Complex in New York City discussed earlier in this chapter. Autonomy was identified as a critical variable in the success (or failure) of the house approach. Greenleaf indicated that the house system was doomed for failure from the start because the teachers did not buy into the concept, and the school had not been designed to physically support a separate entity. The house program was never sufficiently separate to establish the autonomy needed for success.

But it is a tribute to the vision and perseverance of the Board of Education and the parents in the community that they returned to the concept of the small school in this recent high school construction involving both new and renovated components. With regard to the SWAS concept, Greenleaf said he was absolutely convinced that it was the right thing to do, even though he knew that the town was a number of years away, through one 4-year generation as a minimum, of being able to assess the impact of the SWAS approach. The identity of each individual school emerges through its academics, and that is where the bulk of construction funding was focused. Deciding to replicate science labs (biology, chemistry, physics) in each of these schools (where each school is on a separate floor) was an expensive choice, he said, but it helps to maintain the integrity of the SWAS concept. This expenditure of funds to maintain the academic integrity of each school may be critical to its success; only time will tell.

We also discussed what kinds of measures would be used to assess whether the approach was succeeding. Attendance? Graduation rates? Level of vandalism? Educational achievement? In all likelihood one of the primary outcomes will be the state's assessment of achievement, the Connecticut Academic Performance Test (CAPT), in conjunction with graduation (and dropout) rates. Fitch High School in Groton, Connecticut, is an example of

[125] Groton Public Schools (2007, December 10). *Strategic profiles: 2006–2007.* Groton, CT: Administration Offices.

the small school movement applied to a nonurban area. In this respect, it is an example of the strength of the small school movement and the realization that architecture and educational outcomes go hand in hand.

Not everyone is impressed by the new look and feel of the school, of course. Society has changed, education has changed, and schools themselves have changed over the last 50 years. A letter to the editor from our local paper speaks to the perception of that change from a graduate of Fitch High School 50 years ago:

> We journeyed to Groton to attend the 50th anniversary of our graduation from Fitch Senior High. It was fun to reminisce with our "old" classmates. Unfortunately, we made the mistake of touring the much-modified high school. The Fitch we remember was a school of about 500 students, one principal, one assistant and one guidance counselor. There were five buildings, all with large classrooms with views of the Sound and surrounding hills. The school was devoted to teaching fundamentals and the ability to independently reason. Entry to the new school is through a metal detector into a bleak cavernous masonry hall, evoking the feeling of entering a prison. Classrooms are small, cluttered and inward oriented – no sweeping vistas. Each of the three floors contained an administrative office, with vice principal, guidance counselor and staff. Frivolity abounds, such as a credit union (for thugs to practice robbing, one person quipped). "Art work" and propaganda posters made it clear that instruction is oriented more to indoctrination than academics and reasoning. The school has expensive bells and whistles, but lacks any feeling of community. It is a sad commentary. I wouldn't have sent my children and I'm glad to have moved elsewhere.[126]

When I asked Wes Greenleaf about this letter to the editor, he laughed. "There is no metal detector; there is no propaganda." And the reality is that the high school now must accommodate 1400 students, not 500 as it may have had in 1958. The challenge that communities like Groton face is to figure out a way to incorporate the small school concept within the constraints of a reticent voter base and a changing demographic profile. The SWAS that Groton has embraced has potential. Stay tuned.

A FINAL WORD ABOUT SCHOOLS AND OUTCOMES

As I have indicated, I am not a physical determinist; that is, I do not believe that a place, designed in one way rather than another, can *determine* a

---

[126] Robison, J. (September 5, 2008). Groton school lacking a sense of community. *The New London Day*, A6.

particular academic (or any other kind of) outcome. But I do believe that spaces and places can make certain kinds of outcomes more probable than others. It has been far easier for educators to show that certain kinds of variables are more likely to have a causal relationship to academic outcomes than is true of other kinds of variables. The kinds of variables that have been linked to academic outcomes are indoor air quality (including ventilation and thermal comfort), lighting, acoustics, building age and quality, as well as the ubiquitous two, school size and class size.[127] With regard to the ambient environment, the factors of air quality, temperature and humidity, and light, the research comes closer to providing causal evidence than is the case when we look at the school building or even classroom size. The impact of ambient factors has been more clearly demonstrated. Those kinds of variables (light, heat, air quality, noise) lend themselves much more easily to experimental manipulation than school size or classroom size, for example. This chapter has not reviewed the research on ambient factors because their impact is not generally debated.

When we come to the issues of school and classroom size, the research pendulum has a challenge producing what we would call "hard evidence" because there are many commingled variables when you talk about the issue of size. Schools are set in neighborhoods, they have a demographic profile, they are located in a particular space in the community and that community within a region, and they may have a special curriculum. Further, no one can argue about the unique qualities of teachers, and the school building has a configuration and an age, and so on and so on.

You will notice that I have not included a discussion of the role of class-room size in this chapter. Given limited pages, I chose instead to focus on the parameters of the school building itself. I do want to mention something about the issue of classroom size in the context of the challenge of doing good research. At the opening session of the 2008 American Psychological Association Convention in Boston, Malcolm Gladwell, author of such best sellers as *The Tipping Point*[128] and *Blink*,[129] delivered the address. I was in the audience. In his address, Gladwell spoke about the premise of his new book *Outliers*.[130] Essentially he said that we need to do a better job of

[127] Schneider, M. (2002, November). *Do school facilities affect academic outcomes?* Washington, D.C.: National Clearinghouse for Educational Facilities.

[128] Gladwell, M. (2002). *The tipping point: How little things can make a big difference.* Boston: Back Bay Books.

[129] Gladwell, M. (2007). *Blink: The power of thinking without thinking.* Boston: Back Bay Books.

[130] Gladwell, M. (2008). *Outliers: The story of success.* Boston: Little, Brown and Company.

understanding people who succeed against formidable odds and to reexamine the role of motivation and hardship. He was unhappy with what he perceived to be the dominant view of economics in explaining behavior: that our resources largely determine what happens to us.

In his address he mentioned data on classroom size and educational outcomes that suggest that classroom size doesn't make as big an impact on educational outcomes as one might think unless the classes become quite small (fewer than 18 students), highly unlikely to happen in this country, even *in* small schools. Further, the positive effects of small classrooms are not universal and seem more pronounced for low-income and minority students.[131] One thought he had about the failure of classroom size to predict educational achievement was that perhaps kids in larger classes benefited from learning coping skills necessary to achieving in larger rather than smaller classes.

I mention Gladwell's point of view because I think it demonstrates just how many variables undoubtedly influence educational outcomes. And it is fair to say that a good deal of the controversy surrounding the debate about the relationship between class size and achievement has to do with measurement and methodology.[132] But unlike Gladwell, I place much more faith in the idea of the personalized relationship in the classroom than his remarks suggest that he does, and I think such relationships are more likely to occur in small than large schools. In an article about the challenges of reestablishing a school system in New Orleans after Hurricane Katrina, one student named Ronnie comments about a Teach for America member who expected more from him and his friends in the classroom than he had ever experienced. He is quoted as saying, "I finally got a teacher that really cares about me."[133] The development of relationships takes time, and schools

---

[131] Class size and achievement. The Center for Public Education. http://www.center forpubliceducation.org/site/c.kjJXJ5MPIwE/b.1533647/k.3B7C/Class_size_and_student_achievement.htm; see also research from Tennessee's STAR program, Nye, B., Hedges, L. V., & Konstantopoulos, S. (1999). The long-term effects of class size: A five year follow-up of the Tennessee class size experiment. *Educational Evaluation and Policy Analysis, 21*(2), 127–142; Nye, B., Hedges, L. V., & Konstantopoulos. S. (2004). Do minorities experience larger lasting benefits from small classes? *Journal of Educational Research, 98,* 94–100; Krueger, A. B., & Whitmore, D. M. (2000). The effect of attending a small class in the early grades on college-test taking and middle school test results: Evidence from project STAR. Working paper number w7656. Cambridge, MA: National Bureau of Economic Research.

[132] Schneider (2002).

[133] Tough, P. (2008, August 17). A teachable moment. *The New York Times Magazine,* pp. 30–37, 46, 50–51, p. 46.

that promote a sense of community are more likely to be the product of interactions among a smaller rather than larger number of students. Small schools foster a sense of involvement, and involvement is the hallmark of relationships. In a way we have come full circle to the lessons of Barker and Gump's seminal work *Big School, Small School.*

4

The Landscape of Work: Visible or Virtual?

PERSONAL REFLECTIONS

For 4 months in 2009, I lived and worked in Rome (*ho abitato* and *lavorato*, as I learned to say). I lived in the renovated convent of the Sant' Agnese in Agone church (see Figure 4.1), and the circular window in the study of my apartment overlooked Bernini's famous Fountain of the Four Rivers (Fontana dei Quattro Fiumi) in the Piazza Navona. Those moviegoers who have seen the 2009 film *Angels and Demons* will remember that the fountain is the scene of the rescue of the last Vatican hostage. What made this experience even more special was that I worked in this building; the classroom where I taught was one floor below my apartment. If I forgot a notebook or the adaptor for my computer, it was only a flight of stairs away. If I needed a coffee break, it was down the stairs and around the corner to Café Tor Millina, in my neighborhood. Between my morning and afternoon classes, I could simply walk upstairs and fix lunch in my own apartment. My situation reminded me very much of the benefits of living in a city that Jane Jacobs described in her book *The Death and Life of Great American Cities*. But we are not in Kansas anymore, which is my way of saying that very few Americans live and work in one place, as I did in Rome. When I returned to the United States, one of the greatest shocks for me was how much I had to rely on my automobile to get anything done. I fought back, including walking to and from my car dealer to have my VW repaired, until I discovered a deer tick on my arm, the price I paid for walking along a rural road without sidewalks. That was the end of my attempt to make the America I know a pedestrian environment.

The work we do and where we do it has changed dramatically over the last 100 years. This chapter will primarily explore where work is done, which is arguably a result of the kind of work we now do. That work is strikingly

FIGURE 4.1. Facade of Sant' Agnese in Agone, Piazza Navona, Rome

different than at the start of the 20th century. In 1900, 43.5 percent of us were employed in farming, whereas in 2000, 2.4 percent of us were. The second most dramatic change in how and perhaps where we work is in the services sector. In 1900, 25.4 percent of us were employed in services; in 2000 that percentage was 62.5 percent.[1]

This chapter seeks to address a question posed by architect and researcher Kent Spreckelmeyer concerning the way building types affect the traditions and patterns of work in America.[2] As he argues, not only does the functional nature of work matter, so does the emotional or spiritual nature. Spreckelmeyer thinks that the "containers" for workers (office buildings) are the chief contribution of designers to building types in the United States,[3] and he argues that commercial interests have substantially affected the design and function of cities in North America. Further, he discusses what we saw in the chapter on residential environments when we looked at the concept of edge cities; that Americans have spread out, or decentralized, to some extent to create opportunities to control their environments, that is, for personal control. Edge cities, those bounded commercial suburbs, "extend the single-family sprawl into low-density corporate headquarters, shopping malls, and recreation centers."[4] What happened during the 1980s, Spreckelmeyer said, was the extension of the workplace into suburbia, its "suburbanization," and a concomitant segregation or isolation of these office buildings in commercial parks. But this movement, he argues, has not resulted in self-control for the worker; rather "this continued fragmentation and isolation of the workplace" has led to "the gradual breakdown in the collective sense of purpose associated with a commonly defined work ethic" for individual workers.[5] At least some of the dissatisfaction with the modern American workplace, in his view, is the loss of a sense of community with regard to work, or the loss of the sense that we are in this together. In his view, our national work ethic is bound up with this idea of a collective sense of work. Commenting on the areas that are related to low levels of satisfaction in the workplace and are a focus of this chapter (privacy issues related to hearing and seeing; size and degree of control over one's workspace), he suggests the way American designers have gone about the creation of the workplace does not fit well with a mature and established economy.[6]

---

[1] Employment Trends: Data Presentation (2000). http://socialjrank.org/pages/849/Employment-Trends-Data-Presentation.html, p. 1.

[2] Spreckelmeyer, K. F. (1995). Places for a work ethic: An appraisal of American workplace design and research. *Journal of Architectural and Planning Research, 12*(2), 104–120.

[3] Ibid., p. 105. [4] Ibid., p. 106.

[5] Ibid., p. 107. [6] Ibid., p. 109.

This chapter deals with America's work environments, and not simply the traditional physical manifestation of work, the office. Of necessity the chapter also addresses how technology is shaping not only how, but also where and when we work. Certain companies and research teams, in particular Herman Miller, Inc. and the late Michael Brill and the Buffalo Organization for Social and Technological Innovation (i.e., BOSTI) receive considerable attention; Herman Miller for its innovation and design aesthetic and BOSTI because that group arguably did groundbreaking research on space and productivity in office design. In addressing the issues of technology and work, the role of working in isolation versus collaboratively is highlighted in this chapter given the pressure of what has come to be known as the virtual office, which tends to physically isolate workers, and the pressure of collaboration and working in teams, which binds them together.

To a certain point, perhaps the last 10 years, the great concern in the research literature was whether office space, particularly the open plan and the cubicle, supported the way in which people work. Now, the omnipresence of technology has added a dimension that makes space an elastic concept. The concept of working "from anywhere" perhaps says it best, and technology has been its driver. I typed my dissertation on a secondhand IBM Selectric typewriter in 1976. My first computer, purchased in the early 1980s, was a Commodore 64, the best selling personal computer of all time, and when I think back to it, I can't believe how incredibly primitive it was compared to the equipment available today. I remember learning my first word processing program on a Mac Classic. I also remember, much to my students' horror, using a mimeograph machine when I first arrived to teach in 1973, and having to do some statistical calculations by hand, next using a large Unix system, and finally moving to a PC-based program, SPSS, now on something like version 17.0. I typed this chapter while teaching in Rome, Skyping, and chatting on Gmail to stay connected. We do indeed work from anywhere.

This chapter starts with issues related to offices themselves, in particular looking at the impact of what might be called the open plan and the cubicle revolution. The cubicle has fundamentally transformed the interior configuration of offices. Then the issues move outward to address the impact of technology on the less traditional workspaces (places) emerging. Essentially all writers on workspace design and its impact start by saying that about 90 percent of the cost of doing business is related to personnel. To lower costs, you need to make people more effective in their work. From the standpoint of facilities, the question then becomes what role the physical environment plays in increasing effectiveness. Not only can the physical aspects of the office directly affect your work, but offices can also be used as rewards,[7] for example, awarding high performers with private office space. And inefficient offices cost money; estimates in Britain are that the British economy has lost about 135 billion pounds annually due to inefficient offices.[8] The nature of our physical facilities regarding where, how, and how well we work is not a trivial concern.

NOMENCLATURE: SPACES AND THEIR NAMES

Before plunging much further into where Americans work and why, it may be useful to provide definitions of concepts that appear in this chapter. I have already used the terms traditional office and cubicle. Let me define these and other related terms.

Action Office. The Action Office was introduced by Herman Miller, the furniture company, specifically through the work of Robert Propst, who designed the Action Office. Propst wanted to create an office system consisting of modular components that could be rearranged at much less expense and with greater ease than renovation of a conventional office. Herman Miller introduced the Action Office in 1968, hence the cubicle's 40th anniversary in 2008. Although Propst created the Action Office, the idea of systems furniture and modularity predates him, as indicated by the Union Carbide headquarters designed in 1959 by Skidmore Owings and Merrill (SOM).[9]

Bullpen. A bullpen is most often described as a room of desks, typically in fixed rows, with no partitions or other dividers.

Modified conventional plan. In this iteration, the conventional plan is modified by the use of private offices necessitated by function, with everyone else placed in open areas. This configuration provides more flexibility than the conventional plan, but may not fit in all spaces (especially narrow or small spaces).[10]

Office landscape (Bürolandschaft). The term office landscape is sometimes used interchangeably with the term open plan. But office landscape, a concept introduced in 1959 by Quickborner, a firm in Germany that

[7] Wineman, J. (Ed.) (1986). *Behavioral issues in office design.* New York: Van Nostrand Reinhold Company, p. xv.

[8] Wheeler, G., & Clements-Groome, D. (2006). Office design and productivity. In M. K. Chapin (Ed.), *Edra 37: Beyond conflict. Proceedings of the 37th Annual Conference of the Environmental Design Research Association* (p. 312). Edmond, OK: EDRA.

[9] Shoshkes, L. (1976). *Space planning: Designing the office environment.* New York: Architectural Record Books.

[10] Saphier (1978).

specialized in planning consulting,[11] refers to the idea of "landscaping," or laying out the office in a way that promotes better communication. As conceived by the Quickborner team, files being actively used were stored in mobile carts that were on the floor and could be moved.[12] The concept spread to the United States in the late 1960s. Although over time it seems that people have equated office landscaping with decorations, typically plants and posters, the original purpose had more to do with internal communication and interdependencies.[13] There is agreement that the original European implementation of office landscaping or *Bürolandschaft* only vaguely resembles its original implementation, because the vistas, movement of air, and other qualities that were part of the original concept may be obscured or limited by the installation of partitions.[14]

Open plan. An open plan office is one in which there are work stations (desks or other work platforms) enclosed by partitions to some degree; typically each station has three panels that may vary from waist to shoulder height. Systems furniture, or furniture consisting of components made to work together, is typically an element of the open plan, but need not be. Systems furniture can also be found in traditional offices.[15]

Traditional office. A traditional or conventional office or closed plan,[16] as it is sometimes called (or, when very small, a cell office), refers to a space enclosed by floor-to-ceiling walls (often permanent), with a door that closes and typically locks. One or more people may occupy traditional offices. The perimeter office and the corner office are related concepts. Perimeter offices are on outside walls of the building with a single wall of windows. A corner office has two window walls. Typically one person occupies a perimeter office; corner offices almost universally have one occupant, as they reflect a high level of status. In fact, the window, which is a hallmark of the corner office, has historically been an important reflection of one's status.[17]

[11] Palmer & Lewis (1977), p. 5.

[12] Klein, J. G. (1982). *The office book: Ideas and designs for contemporary work spaces.* New York: Facts on File, Inc., p. 36.

[13] Palmer & Lewis (1977), p. xii.

[14] Vischer, J. C. (1989). *Environmental quality in offices.* New York: Van Nostrand Reinhold.

[15] Brill, M., Weidemann, S., & BOSTI Associates (2001). *Disproving widespread myths about workplace design.* Jasper, IN: Kimball International and BOSTI Associates, p. 17.

[16] Saphier, M. (1978). *Planning the new office.* New York: McGraw-Hill.

[17] Palmer, A. E., & Lewis, M. S. (1977). *Planning the office landscape.* New York: McGraw-Hill.

HERMAN MILLER: TRUTH IN ADVERTISING

Herman Miller figures prominently in this chapter for a number of reasons. First, I admire the commitment to research and design aesthetic, which are hallmarks of the Herman Miller Corporation. Of the manufacturers of contemporary furniture, both Herman Miller and Knoll stand out as having made significant contributions to the design aesthetic of offices, and of many homes for that matter. The showrooms of both Herman Miller and Knoll were said to have had a role in shaping clients' tastes and educating them about design.[18] Second, my sister used to work at Herman Miller doing internal communication. Third, Robert Propst's children and I went to the same high school, and I thus became familiar with his work early on. I had the pleasure of interviewing Propst many years ago when he worked in Ann Arbor. For those reasons, you will hear more about Herman Miller than about some of its competitors (e.g., Steelcase and Haworth).

THE OFFICE: ITS HISTORY

One writer summarizes some 300 years of workplace evolution as follows:

- When we were primarily an agricultural economy, we had no choice but to bring all the workers to the workplace – that's where the dirt was.
- When we became primarily an industrial economy, we had no choice but to bring all the workers to the workplace – that's where the assembly lines and machines were.
- When we became primarily an information economy, we initially had no choice but to bring all the workers to the workplace – that's where the desks, typewriters, file cabinets, and all the other work resources were. But towards the end of the 20th century, we realized that for the first time in the history of the workplace, we now *did* have a choice – and we could use technology to bring some of the work to some of the workers.[19]

The number of offices increased substantially during the Industrial Revolution, but it was not until the 20th century that the number of people

[18] Ibid., p. 2.
[19] Gordon, G. E. (2000). Employer scheduling, staffing, and work location issues. In *Telework: The new workplace of the 21st century* (pp. 105–115). Washington, D.C.: U.S. Department of Labor, p. 105.

working in offices outpaced those in manufacturing.[20] Although the first half of the 20th century is arguably important as the nation moved to a more services-oriented economy, this chapter focuses on the period over the last 4 decades that has been dominated by the open plan and by technology.

ROBERT PROPST AND THE ACTION OFFICE

Before discussing the research on open plans and cubicles, I want to talk about the person credited with creating the cubicle: Robert Propst. Propst is often linked to the cubicle, perhaps because he created the Action Office, essentially a furniture system that has work surfaces of various heights and panels for varying degrees of enclosure. Although Propst introduced the Action Office, George Nelson (George Nelson & Associates), who worked with the Herman Miller Company, is tagged with the design of the first workstation, or at least its precursor, with an L-shaped desk, in 1947.[21]

For Propst the office has a number of critical qualities. It is a thinking place, where "the management of symbolic representation of reality is the function of offices."[22] In other words, the reality of what we do is symbolically represented in our communication, whether it is in person or via some stream of information transmitted via audio or visual means. Propst's design emphasized the vertical display of information through shelving, rather than filing information out of sight in filing cabinets.

What Propst wanted, which he outlined in his book *The Office – A Facility Based on Change*,[23] was to enhance the connection between the action of the worker and productivity. He created a workspace where "acting," in the sense of doing work, was enhanced because of the features of the workspace. These included the ability to work at stations of different heights; the display of materials used frequently (as opposed to the invisibility of those materials in filing cabinets); and of course the nonpermanent walls and opportunity for varying degrees of enclosure. Herman Miller thinks Propst's ideas are viable today;[24] over the 35-year period from 1968, when the Action Office was introduced, to 2003, the number of people working in offices grew from 34 million to 56 million.[25]

---

[20] Klein (1982). [21] Ibid.
[22] Propst, R. (1968). *The office – A facility based on change.* Zeeland, MI: Herman Miller, Inc., p. 19.
[23] Ibid.
[24] Herman Miller (2006). *Forward thinking: Why the ideas from the man who invented the cubicle still make sense.* (Web pdf)
[25] Ibid., p. 1.

Propst's rules were (1) the Forgiving Principle; (2) Grace with Change; (3) On-line Planning and Expression; (4) Choice and Variety; (5) Enriching Work Experience.[26] These principles focus on flexibility (the forgiving principle means you can easily change the arrangement if it doesn't work). Similarly, the idea of grace with change emphasizes the ease with which the modular components can be rearranged.

Propst did recognize that there are always tensions in the office, and he wrote that one of the primary tensions was between access and enclosure. With regard to these dimensions, the extremes (either four-sided enclosure or open space) were to be avoided. About the worker who is completely enclosed by four sides he said, "He is isolated, insulated, and remote. His ability to be part of an organizational family is diminished."[27] Propst recommended enclosures of three panels set at about 120 degrees at each corner.

What Propst may not have fully taken into account was the difficulty with privacy related to hearing and seeing. But he was of the opinion that if you were in the office working, what you were doing should be "available" for someone to check on at any time. There are no secrets in the office, from his point of view. During the time period when my sister worked for Herman Miller, I remember visiting their showroom in Boston in the Sears Crescent building in 1978. In addition to a handsome display of all kinds of seating and fabric options, the salespeople had workspaces (cubicles, if you will) comprised of Herman Miller components (of course). A number of these workstations included a white globe on a pedestal (see Figure 4.2), which, as I learned, was a white noise emitter. Human speech causes the most distraction in the office; it is hard to tune out the human voice. To that end, these emitters produced background noise that helped filter the sound of the human voice so that beyond the range of about 12 feet, people could not hear the conversation. Thus, even in Herman Miller's own facilities the acoustical privacy issues had to be addressed. As you might imagine, these acoustical issues are managed in a more sophisticated manner today. For example, in Resolve, one of Herman Miller's systems furniture lines, small acoustical inserts are installed overhead between screens used to configure the workspace.[28]

Propst also may have underestimated the pressure of costs in the workplace, leading to smaller spaces for work. Such a financial influence in the 1960s was a change in depreciation laws that favored furniture, with a

---

[26] Ibid., pp. 1–6.   [27] Propst (1968), p. 43.

[28] Herman Miller (2003). *Sound masking in the office: Reducing noise distractions to increase worker productivity.* Herman Miller Solution Essay. (Web pdf)

FIGURE 4.2. Cubicle installation, Herman Miller Sales Office, Boston

depreciation in 7 years, over buildings (typically with conventional offices), which had a longer depreciation. What this means was that laws essentially pushed companies to invest in cubicles because they could recover their costs much more quickly.[29]

SOME REFLECTIONS ON HERMAN MILLER: THEN AND NOW

Arguably the creative environment fostered by Propst's employers, the Herman Miller Corporation, set the stage to realize his considerable talents. Founded in 1923, Herman Miller is a highly regarded furniture manufacturing company that has historically emphasized excellence in modern design, and its products are represented in the collection of the Museum of Modern Art in New York. Charles and Ray Eames[30] were designers for Herman Miller of such iconic pieces as the Eames Lounge chair and ottoman, from the mid-1950s. More recently, readers may recognize the name of the Aeron Chair introduced in 1994, a Herman Miller design for an ergonomic and

[29] Schlosser, J. (2006, March 15). The great escape (from *Fortune Magazine*). CNNMoney .com, para. 10. http://money.cnn.com/magazines/fortune/fortunearchive/2006/03/20/ 8371767.

[30] Albrecht, D. (Ed.) (1997). *The work of Charles and Ray Eames: A legacy of invention.* New York: Harry N. Abrams.

relatively expensive office chair. In fact, Herman Miller settled a claim in 2008 against an accusation that its anticompetitive conduct was designed to increase the prices of these chairs.[31] The design aesthetic of Herman Miller even carried into the factory, where sculptures of workers, crafted from papier-mâché, dotted the walls and ceilings.[32]

Not only is the Herman Miller Company a leader in office systems research and a champion of design aesthetics, it also communicates effectively with its constituency, in my opinion. It also sees the future, and with the slowing of sales in the office furniture industry, its research has helped to develop projects for the health care industry: for example, a chair with an adjustable seat (the Nala) designed for patients recovering from surgery.[33]

In addition to its design prowess, the Herman Miller Corporation emphasized the importance of research and established a separate research facility in Ann Arbor, Michigan (the headquarters are in Zeeland, Michigan, across the state) where inventor Robert Propst could think and create, as long as there were no projects related to the military or to furniture (although this second stipulation was bypassed, and with it the advent of a component office system). Propst was a versatile designer with more than 120 patents when he died in 2000, credited with such innovations as the Action Office, introduced in 1968 and a focus in this chapter. Propst also designed a modular system for hospital containers and carts, called Co/Struc. In addition, he is credited with designing a vertical tree harvester, an electronic tagging system for livestock,[34] and a heart valve.

The Herman Miller Web site has a large number of articles available to users (and potential users) covering a range of issues from evolutionary psychology and the workplace to support for the baby boomer generation and work. These articles are one reflection of the company's emphasis on research. Here is a sampling of titles:

Third places: The social side of work (2004)
Making room for collaboration (2008)
Measures of success: The facility's role in effectiveness (2007)

---

[31] Herman Miller settles claims (March 26, 2008). *Wall Street Journal Abstracts*, Section B, Column 4.

[32] Franz, D. (2008). The moral life of cubicles: The utopian originals of Dilbert's workspace. *The New Atlantis: A Journal of Technology and Society*, winter, 132–139, p. 136.

[33] Jana, R. (2008, June 16). Herman Miller's clinical trials. Inside Innovation. *Business Week*, vol. 4088, p. 60.

[34] http://www.hermanmiller.deour-business/research-and-design/design-biographies/robert-propst/.

Evolutionary psychology and workplace design: Doing what comes nat-
urally (2004)
Set them free: How alternative work styles can be a good fit (2007)
It's a matter of balance: Acoustics in the open plan (2007)

What is not surprising, perhaps, is the reiteration of the ways in which furniture systems can support open plans. Herman Miller is also sophisticated
in its presentation of materials. The presentation does not come across as
a "sales pitch." Rather, the company uses research from the literature to
support the points related to the systems it sells. For example, one of its
Web articles entitled "Third places: The social side of work"[35] cites an article
by Lesser and Storck[36] that shows how generating communities can benefit
an organization by making it easier for new employees to learn the ropes,
and to help people avoid starting from scratch (i.e., reinventing the wheel)
because they are part of a group that shares information. Further, new ideas
are generated from the interaction of group members. The article makes a
point that communities are built through providing places where people can
walk and talk. In other words, communication can be enhanced through an
open plan.

The article further includes a quotation from Martha O'Mara's book
*Strategy and Place: Managing Corporate Real Estate and Facilities for Com-
petitive Advantage.*[37] The quotation reads: "Some corporate offices now
resemble Italian piazzas. Aisles widen into streets with places to stop and
talk. Rather than being relegated to a hidden corner or closet, the water
cooler and coffee machine now are celebrated in centrally located cafes
where people are encouraged to meet each other."[38] This example reminds
me of the Pfizer Central Research building in Groton, Connecticut, and the
W.C. Decker Engineering Center, part of Corning, Incorporated, in Corning, New York (also mentioned in Chapter 3). On a tour, one of the aspects
of the design that impressed me in the Pfizer Central Research Building was
a large central space that looked like a hotel lobby, replete with a coffee bar
and other amenities. Scientists' labs overlooked this interior courtyard and
in a sense created the transparency we are talking about. This central space
was a crossroads for the facility. Similarly, the W.C. Decker Engineering
Center includes spaces along the corridors equipped with whiteboards and
other props to encourage the exchange of ideas.

[35] Herman Miller (2004). *Third places: The social side of work.* (Web pdf)

[36] Lesser, E., & Storck, J. (2001, April). Communities of practice and organizational performance. *IBM Systems Journal, 40*(4), 839–842.

[37] O'Mara, M. (1999). *Strategy and place: Managing corporate real estate and facilities for
competitive advantage.* New York: Simon and Schuster.

[38] Herman (2004). *Third places,* p. 4. (Web pdf)

Collaboration comes up in a number of these Web pages because it is a central component of the kinds of systems Herman Miller and other office furniture manufacturers provide. Although some of these systems may work in traditional offices, the components are more clearly geared for variation of an open office plan. In a survey of more than 1500 executives from 100 countries, employee incentives have been used to encourage collaboration, and collaboration is referred to as a "survival skill" and the equivalent of "knowledge sharing."[39] "In fact, evidence suggests that 'co-location' may be the single most effective way to promote and support communities of practice, simply because nonverbal behavior plays such a central role in the transfer of tacit knowledge.... Co-location also affords the opportunity for spontaneous encounters that promote social relationships and collaboration."[40] Tacit knowledge, mentioned on the Herman Miller Web page "Making room for collaboration," is practical knowledge that you learn that is difficult to document. You learn it by being exposed to it, by living it. Having people close together (through proximity) enables people to share tacit knowledge.

Surprising to me is how in tune the Herman Miller Company seems to be to some of the research in my field, environmental psychology. Consider, for example, the article entitled "Evolutionary psychology and workplace design: Doing what comes naturally."[41] This article refers to the seminal work of Roger Ulrich (see Chapter 2) and also talks about the Center for Health Design and the role of evidence-based results in health care (we have to demonstrate that the physical environment matters through objective measurements, such as length of hospital stay). The emphasis in this article is really the importance of views from windows and the role that nature can have in well-being and performance in the work environment. Research is cited showing higher performance on assessments of cognitive functioning when workers had the best possible view, described as a combination of size and visible vegetation, contrasted with no view. Researchers Steve and Rachel Kaplan and their work on environmental preference, geographer and landscape theorist Jay Appleton (the importance of vista, or prospect, and shelter, or refuge), the biophilia hypothesis, and the savanna hypothesis make an appearance. In other words, a case is made that where we evolved (on the savanna) has some relationship to the kinds of environments we prefer.

---

[39] Herman Miller (2008). *Making room for collaboration*, p. 2. (Web pdf)

[40] Ibid., p. 3.

[41] Herman Miller (2004). *Evolutionary psychology and workplace design: Doing what comes naturally*. (Web pdf)

The Web site then translates how these properties linked to our evolutionary heritage can be recreated in the workplace. For example, prospect (a vista) and refuge (a place to retreat) can be thought about as reaching out for communication as well as having a place to call one's own. The open plan and the cubicle can be argued to bear a relationship to prospect and refuge. So, fabric canopies are mentioned (think treetops), and open areas around pathways provide vistas for surveillance and escape.[42]

As another example of how in tune the company is with current research in psychology, consider the article "Making room for collaboration."[43] Collaboration is not going away, and the article suggests that solving problems collaboratively is a survival skill and a way to expand brain function. The article quotes what is known as the "30-Meter Rule," associated with work at MIT, that "the frequency of one person's interaction with another person sitting more than 30 meters (about 99 feet) away is about the same as if the two people were located in different buildings (or cities)."[44] The floor plan of the W.C. Decker Engineering Building, previously discussed, is an example of a design that tries to support the possibility of collaboration in nearby spaces.

But even Herman Miller has to deal with the problems inherent in open plans and in cubicles: distractions from visual and auditory channels. What do they currently have to say about those bugaboos, disruptions of acoustical and visual privacy? I think aspects of what they say are somewhat misleading, given the evidence. For example, they quote an article supporting the idea that knowledge workers were expected to spend upward of 70 percent of their time in collaborative work by the year 2005.[45] It is one thing to have work that involves collaboration, and quite another to be spending 70 percent of your time collaborating. Research from the Buffalo Organization for Social and Technological Innovation (BOSTI) suggests that people spend 75 percent of their time in their own workspace.[46] Further, the BOSTI research suggests that even in team-oriented software companies (characteristic of what has been called The New Economy), people work alone from one-half to two-thirds of the time.[47] To be sure, Herman Miller cites useful information, but it is obviously building a case for its products.

Despite its leadership position in the furniture systems industry, Herman Miller seems to have faced some of the very problems having to do with such issues as personal space and territoriality that other (nonoffice furnishings) companies routinely experience. In a traditional Herman Miller

[42] Ibid., p. 4. [43] Herman Miller (2008).
[44] Ibid., p. 4.
[45] Herman Miller (2004). *Third places.* (Web pdf)
[46] Brill et al. (2001), p. 24. [47] Ibid., p. 51.

office, 80 percent was individual space and none was collaborative; in its MarketPlace facility (a showroom and working office), 55 percent was individual space and 21 percent was collaborative. The people who spent less than 25 percent of their time in the MarketPlace office were labeled "voyagers" and were not assigned to a workstation. They had a place (dock) to park their belongings but worked at one of the "campsites" located throughout the building. But "office squatting" became a problem, which occurs when personal belongings are put in the same campsite daily so coworkers can "find you." The company addressed office squatting by giving workers cell phones (to forward calls to their work location that day), providing whiteboards at docks for notes to tell others the workers' location that day, and instituting a game called "campsite bingo" to reward workers with prizes once their card was full (working at different campsites was the equivalent of a location on a bingo card).[48]

In recent years, furniture manufacturers such as Steelcase and Knoll, as well as Herman Miller, have attempted to address some of the distraction issues with smaller, capsule-like "cockpit" spaces (a term used by BOSTI as well).[49] Unlike the point made by some journalists criticizing the cubicle on the occasion of its 40th anniversary, the real problem with cubicles does not seem to be size, per se, given these small cockpit-like spaces, but the ability of those spaces to provide the acoustical and visual privacy people need to do their work. Systems furniture manufacturers such as Steelcase and Knoll have created products such as the Personal Harbor and A3, respectively, to address the need for these small cockpit workspaces. How much space does the "average" worker have? A table of the square footage of commercial buildings for 2003 indicates that if the principal activity in the building is offices, the mean square footage per worker is 434. For comparison, if the principal purpose is religious worship, that number is 2200; if the principal purpose is warehouse and storage, that number is 2306.[50]

Office systems are big business. For example, Herman Miller's revenue for 2008 was more than $2 billion,[51] and office manufacturers have created upward of 100 variations of systems furniture in the last 3 decades, according to an article in *Fortune* magazine.[52] The system Herman Miller introduced in 1999, called Resolve, has been described by Herman Miller as

---

[48] Herman Miller (2003). *Taking on workplace change.* (Web pdf)

[49] Brill et al. (2001), pp. 46–47.

[50] Commercial Buildings Energy Consumption Buildings (CBECS) Detailed Tables. U.S. Energy Administration, Table 968. Commercial Buildings – Summary: 2003. http://www .eia.doe.gov/emeu/cbecs/cbecs2003/detailed_tables_2003/detailed_tables_2003.html.

[51] http://www.hoovers.com/herman-miller/-id_13676-/free-co-factsheet.xhtml.

[52] Schlosser (2006), para. 1.

"the biggest breakthrough in office systems since 1968."[53] What the Resolve system is supposed to combine are aspects of both nature and geometry to create relatively open workspaces that invite interaction and collaboration while being space efficient. In a book on space planning for commercial and residential interiors, Resolve is described as working for companies that have flatter hierarchies (i.e., where there is less distance between the top and bottom personnel in the company structure). Sam Kubba, the book's author, goes on to say, "The Resolve system is an innovative new product that is designed to meet the needs of companies that are technologically advanced, fast moving, and collaborative in nature. It is also designed to help companies respond quickly and inexpensively to high churn rates, reduce real estate costs, accommodate new and emerging technologies, and develop a sense of community among employees. However, the Resolve system is not suitable for all work situations."[54] Systems furniture has to match the office culture for which it is purchased. One size does not fit all.

Although I have focused on Herman Miller, I would be remiss if I did not mention the contributions of other systems furniture manufacturers. Steelcase, described as the world's largest manufacturer and provider of office furniture, offers a variety of components that can work together, including furniture, technology, and worktools (see http://www.steelcase. com/en/fidex.jsp). Following Steelcase is Haworth (http://www.haworth. com/index_fhome.asp), another major contributor to the field of systems furniture.[55] Whatever their creative and design contributions, all of the companies have something in common: "the problem."

THE "PROBLEM"

The problem that all systems furniture manufacturers face is managing the distractions that accompany open office plans. Even in Kubba's book, which is less research oriented and focuses on issues in space planning, he mentions the "story," that is, the need to resolve the tension between privacy and communication. A claim has been made that there are generational differences in this tension between privacy and communication, which can be seen in employees' responses to cubicles. The claim is that people under the age of 35, the Millennials or Generation Y-ers, born after 1980, enjoy the open environments because they like the "communal buzz;" members

---

[53] Kubba, S. (2003). *Space planning for commercial and residential interiors.* New York: McGraw-Hill, pp. 256, 259.

[54] Ibid., pp. 259–260.   [55] Ibid., p. 265, 268.

of my generation, the baby boomers, born between 1946 and 1964, need "quiet places for reflection" because we grew up in what seems to be an environment marked by sensory deprivation![56] I doubt this; I haven't seen any solid research that suggests these differences, and there is no reason to believe that people under the age of 35 have any less need for privacy and territoriality and a place to do distraction-free work than do those in the boomer generation. It is possible that Generation Y-ers are more comfortable with group work and places for group meetings, but as research has shown, even in dot.com companies, the majority of time is spent working alone.[57]

Herman Miller reports on an interview with members of Gensler, an architecture and design firm in Chicago, in which a number of comments were made about the new generation of workers and the way they like to work. A principal in the firm commented that young people have a fear of isolation "because they will fail unless they can collaborate. In some companies it is a challenge – younger people are put in private offices and they don't like it. They actually want to be in open plan –and they're used to concentrating in very distracting environments. I think we are going to be designing spaces that are extremely diverse. I think a good workspace will be like a town with an interesting character – it will not be like Levittown – it will be Boston or London."[58] Although I am not convinced that Generation Y-ers fear isolation, I agree with the idea that successful workplaces offer choice in the kinds of spaces where work can be done.

WHY OPEN PLAN? WHY CUBICLE? THE IMPACT OF THE OPEN PLAN

In late summer 2008, a reporter called me for an interview about the cubicle, which was celebrating its 40th anniversary. The first question she asked me was, "Do you have an office with a door?" I answered, "Yes." I work in an old-fashioned environment, a traditional office with permanent walls, a door that locks, and even windows to nature. I am in the minority. Many of us remember the film *Working Girl*, starring Melanie Griffith and Sigourney Weaver.[59] Melanie played Tess, who aspired to and ultimately earned a perimeter office with a spectacular view and a door that locked. She was

---

[56] Whittaker, S. (2008, February 2). Confined in a cube? *The Gazette (Montreal) Business Working*, p. G1, paras. 20–22.

[57] Brill et al. (2001), p. 24.

[58] Herman Miller (2007). *21st-century work habits: A conversation with Gensler*, p. 3. (Web pdf)

[59] *Working Girl* (1988). Written by Kevin Wade; directed by Mike Nichols. Twentieth Century Fox Film Corporation. http://www.imdb.com/titlett0096463.

no longer a member of the bullpen and the cubicle pool. Although I have never shared an office or worked in a bullpen, my office is hardly impressive (roughly 100 sq. ft.). But it has that view to nature (a wall of windows facing south with a large maple tree right outside the window) and that lockable door. As one team of researchers commented, "Privacy protection may well arguably be one of the defining issues of our time."[60]

Why has American business embraced the idea of the open plan, and its typical installation, a floor full of cubicles? Is it the reduced cost? The speed of change in business such arrangements can accommodate? What role did the predicted concomitant, an increase in the frequency and quality of communication, play as a justification of the open plan?

The flexibility that allowed offices (and particularly the desks or workstations where work was done) to change as changes in work demanded (e.g., different work groups, different assignments) was undoubtedly a driving force. With the absence of permanent barriers, communication was predicted to increase.[61] Some research indicated that costs related to alterations in open landscape installations were on average about 3 percent of the costs of alterations in conventional offices.[62]

There seemed to be such a push for the open plan in the 1970s. But soon thereafter questions arose about some of the drawbacks that accompanied the open plan. "There are those who will argue that this country's most oppressed minority group consists of those who operate in an open plan office,"[63] and its success has been less than convincing.[64]

Why was the open plan thought to be desirable? Saphier lists a number of reasons, which include the following[65]:

1. eliminating department barriers to enable better functional flow
2. simplified communication across work units
3. ease and inexpensive cost of reconfiguration of the open plan
4. comparability of status with equal office type (i.e., no private offices)
5. reduced cost of air conditioning

[60] Kupritz, V. W., & Bellingar, T. A. (2007). Quantitative assessment of individual and group privacy needs. In J. M. Bissell (Ed.), *Building sustainable communities. Proceedings of the 38th Annual Environmental Design Research Association Conference* (pp. 208–209). Edmond, OK: EDRA, p. 208.

[61] Brennan, A., Chugh, J. S., & Kline, T. (2002). Traditional versus open office design: A longitudinal field study. *Environment and Behavior, 34*, 279–299.

[62] Palmer & Lewis (1977).

[63] Planas, R. E. (1978). Perfect open plan priority: The human element. *Buildings*, March, 74–75, p. 74.

[64] Stone & Luchetti (1985), p. 104.   [65] Saphier (1978), p. 95.

He also lists the disadvantages, which include the need for relatively large open floors (50–60 feet wide), which ideally do not include columns. He also mentions the need for new furniture and equipment when creating a new open plan office. Finally he mentions that familiar challenge: acoustical control.

Although "the merger of flexible planning principles and office technology brought about the biggest changes in office design in 100 years," at the same time the open office was described as the "most controversial feature of office planning" in the 2 decades leading up to the mid-1980s.[66]

REFLECTIONS ON THE 40TH ANNIVERSARY OF THE CUBICLE: A HUMOROUS INTERLUDE

With the 40th anniversary of the cubicle in 2008, journalists and others reflected on the impact of the cubicle, still with us after 40 years. The "monolithic insanity"[67] Propst is said to have called the cubicle before he died is not what he had in mind. Another comment about the cubicle is that "it is the Fidel Castro of office furniture,"[68] in the sense that it has lasted a very long time. Still another tongue-in-cheek description is "the cubicle celebrates its 40th anniversary this month. A party is unlikely."[69] And of course the comic strip *Dilbert* by Scott Adams draws humor from its setting, the office cubicle.[70]

In a 2008 article, writer David Franz argues that cubicles were intended to create a more egalitarian work environment because uniformity made everyone an equal; supervisors and supervisees had physical environments that were the same. "Empowering and humane, cubicles seemed to create a workplace with a soul."[71] Franz argues that the revolution in office design that fostered the cubicle was fundamentally a revolution about ideology. But the lines between what was intended and what was achieved diverged. Franz comments, "For many, this soullessness of office life is now most aptly represented by the cubicle – that open, wall-less, subdivision of office space" and goes on to point out that the average amount of space devoted to each

---

[66] Klein (1982), p. 36.   [67] Schlosser (2006).

[68] Ibid., para. 3.

[69] Eveld, E. M. (2008, July 21). Office cubicles mark their 40th anniversary. *The Kansas City Star.* http://www.mcclatchydc.com/256/story/45027.html.

[70] http://www.dilbert.com.

[71] Franz, D. (2008). The moral life of cubicles: The utopian originals of Dilbert's workspace. *The New Atlantis: A Journal of Technology and Society*, winter, 132–139, p. 133.

worker is dropping, down from 250 sq. ft. in 2000 to 190 sq. ft. in 2005, with an expected drop of 20 percent the end of the decade.[72]

There are a plethora of derisive terms used to describe cubicles, among them "cube farms."[73] "Cube farms. Ridiculed and maligned everywhere from comic strips to movies, the seas of office cubicles that have defined the work landscape for three decades have few, if any, admirers."[74] Or the writer who titled his article "Arrgh! Not the smelly socks again" to illustrate some of the problems of being...close.[75] The article describes what happened when the dream of more open communication and interaction "soured as workers were cooped up in smaller and cheaper cubes like battery hens."[76]

WHAT THE RESEARCH TELLS US ABOUT OPEN PLANS AND CUBICLES

Many empirical studies on the issue of open office design began to appear in the 1970s and grew in strength in the 1980s, when two issues of the journal *Environment and Behavior* were devoted to the topic "Office design and evaluation."[77] These issues were edited by Jean Wineman, whose book *Behavioral Issues in Office Design* was published in 1986.[78] With the introduction of the cubicle, it took little time for social scientists to investigate the impact of the cubicle on work life, primarily issues of satisfaction, with a secondary emphasis on productivity (perhaps because productivity is harder to measure in white collar workers than satisfaction). The Action Office that Propst introduced, and the furniture systems that followed, prompted research because they introduced office components and possibilities for new configurations. Further, I think research was undertaken because indications of dissatisfaction began to emerge.

What is it about the open plan and cubicles themselves that might cause dissatisfaction? Some dissatisfaction is related to change itself. Other aspects

---

[72] Ibid., pp. 132–133.   [73] Whittaker (2008), p. G1.

[74] Kelley, D. (2008, February 13). Cubicle conundrum: Personal space or livestock pen. *National Post Canada*, p. WK4, para. 1.

[75] Munro, P. (2008, August 31). Arrgh! Not the smelly socks again. *Sunday Age*, Melbourne, Australia, p. 13.

[76] Ibid., para. 6.

[77] Wineman, J. (1982). Office design and Evaluation, Part 1. Special Issue. *Environment and Behavior*, 14(3) and Office design and Evaluation, Part II. *Environment and Behavior*, 14(5).

[78] Wineman (1986).

are related to the physical structure of the open plan and of the cubicle. Humans are adaptable, and they habituate. But they are also territorial. Given that territoriality, it should come as no surprise that people required to move from a traditional office to an open office plan experience a number of changes and losses, including the extent to which they control their privacy. A series of studies points to losses experienced as dissatisfaction, primarily concerning visual and acoustical privacy.

When we have visual privacy, we can control who sees us, and in turn whom we see. Similarly, when we have acoustical privacy, we control who hears us, and in turn whom we hear. Even a study published as early as 1980 contained citations of nine earlier articles that show people who worked in open plans generally reported less privacy, spent more time talking, heard more noise, and also experienced more distractions than those not in open plans.[79]

It is also the case that the nature of one's job interacts with the structure of the physical space one inhabits. If your job is simple and repetitive, the presence of others in a nonprivate space may result in social facilitation. Social facilitation refers to the idea that the presence of others facilitates and enhances the activities in which one is engaged. However, in this research, even among people with relatively routine tasks, greater job satisfaction was associated with being in areas viewed as somewhat private. In this research, people preferred to be "invisible" (physically) to their supervisors and to be in a location removed from major corridors where foot traffic occurred. Importantly from the view of one theme in this book, the authors state that " . . . these results go squarely against the idea of architectural determinism" in that the architecture does not seem to determine the kind of interactions that occur over time.[80]

It is beyond the scope of this book to review every study dealing with the effect of open plans, but a sample will indicate patterns that emerged. Several studies trace what happens when employees leave conventional offices and move to open plans. In an early study (1979), employees who made that kind of move were assessed three times; before the move and twice following it. The new office space for these employees of a newspaper organization in the Midwest was experienced as a "'fishbowl,' 'cage,' or 'warehouse.'"[81] Other

---

[79] Sundstrom, E., Burt, R. E., & Kamp, D. (1980). Privacy at work: Architectural correlates of job satisfaction and job performance. *Academy of Management Journal, 23*(1), 101–117.

[80] Ibid., p. 114.

[81] Oldham, G. R., & Brass, D. J. (1979). Employee reactions to an open-plan office: A naturally occurring quasi-experiment. *Administrative Science Quarterly, 24*, 267–284, p. 280.

comments compared the space to noisy Grand Central Station where concentration was difficult. What makes this study somewhat more convincing than many others published during the same period is the fact that the study at least used a control group (employees in the pressroom), although they were obviously not randomly assigned to their condition (i.e., their job) and are considered what is known as a nonequivalent control group. People (employees in the pressroom) who began in a conventional office and moved to another one were contrasted with those who moved from conventional to open plan space. Whereas motivation and satisfaction decreased in those who moved to the open plan, there were no such significant decrements in the reactions of the pressroom employees who moved to another conventional arrangement. This research is a reasonable indication that the physical environment has at least some impact on employees.

Repeatedly we see complaints about distractions related to acoustical and visual privacy; at the same time we may see reports that the open plan improves communication. At least one influential researcher and practitioner has claimed that privacy is the critical variable related to workplace satisfaction; at the same time, it arguably is the most difficult to control.[82] The features usually linked to satisfaction relate to providing privacy *as well as* communication. It seems that we cannot simply adopt the open plan lock, stock, and barrel, nor can we return to an approach that provides conventional offices for everyone. Over and over we see the question, "How might we make work spaces 'work?'"

Although open office plans were touted to increase communication because the environment was more open, studies that evaluate such open plans do not routinely show those increases in communication. There may be increases, but also decreases or no change. Or one kind of communication may increase while another decreases.[83] Basically, open offices are not a panacea, but then why should we have expected them to be?

What the promoters of open plans may have underestimated is just how important privacy is to getting complex work done. In a thorough and helpful review of the literature, Rashid and Zimring differentiate between

[82] Spreckelmeyer, K., Rashid, M., & Angrisano, N. (2008). Workplace change and perceptions of privacy. In B. Rodriguez & M. Chapin (Eds.), *Linking differences/defining actions. Proceedings of the 39th Annual Conference of the Environmental Design Research Association* (p. 334). Edmond, OK: EDRA.

[83] Rashid, M., & Zimring, C. (2005). On psychosocial constructs in office settings: A review of the empirical literature. In H. Chaudhury (Ed.), *Design for diversity: Proceedings of the thirty-sixth annual Conference of the Environmental Design Research Association* (pp. 107–122). Edmond, OK: EDRA.

psychological privacy (dealing with social contacts and the control of information) and architectural privacy (how the physical environment is structured; interruptions related to sound and speech). They list a number of conclusions about privacy, some of which are indicated here:

1. The number of enclosed sides and the height of those panels may be related to perceived privacy, but this perception is not uniform across job categories (read a lack of architectural determinism).
2. A door to your own workspace is the best characterization of architectural privacy.
3. If your work is complex, you are more likely to be satisfied in a private rather than nonprivate setting.
4. Privacy appears to be elevated in importance above such variables as lighting, temperature, and ventilation; the view; and even the general aesthetics of workspaces.
5. As the privacy level increases, so does the level of satisfaction; at the same time, differences in social and cultural factors as well as in personality may be associated with privacy preferences.
6. The downside of privacy is the potential to limit social facilitation by screening people from each other.
7. The lack of acoustical privacy is the top complaint.
8. Over time, the relationship between job satisfaction and privacy is maintained; that is, we do not seem to habituate to the effects of privacy.[84]

THE ROLE OF TERRITORIALITY

Implicit in this list of variables related to privacy is the concept of territoriality. The creation and defense of territories is arguably a fundamental human behavior, and it exists where we are, and that means in the places where we work. We use the term territoriality to label the space over which we exert control, and it is a concept closely related to privacy. It is not difficult to see why. The best way to create privacy is to have a space over which you reign supreme; it is your eminent domain. Rashid and Zimring also summarize research findings about territoriality. Among them are that personalizing the office and demarcating it in some way are approaches to establishing your territory. Moreover, as has been indicated by any number of researchers, when territoriality has been established, conflicts

---

[84] Ibid., pp. 110–111.

may be reduced because there are no questions about who governs the space.

On some level, a question that has to be asked is whether the office as configured when the open plan was introduced really meets human needs, one of those needs involving territoriality. As territorial animals, an interesting question is the losses people feel when they no longer can call a space their own. Or, as other observers put it, "Do we need a home base?" Their response is, "A modest-sized private home base should be an employee's entitlement."[85] With regard to territoriality, the structure of space within buildings, and this includes cubicles, can communicate not only a sense of ownership but also a sense of organizational culture. For example, the steward of the Prada fashion house, Miuccia Prada, is reported to tolerate no clutter in cubicles, no visible coats, and definitely no pets.[86]

Miuccia Prada clearly exerts wide-ranging stylistic control; territoriality provides an opportunity for that control, as Rashid and Zimring (and many others) point out. Freedom and status are associated with this control; essentially we can do what we want more or less when we want to if we exert that control. When we don't have this control, the results may be strain, both psychological and physiological.[87]

To me, a fascinating part of Rashid and Zimring's literature review has to do with the percentage of studies on particular constructs published in each decade beginning with the 1950s. They were looking at a particular set of psychosocial constructs (communication and interaction; privacy; territoriality; control and supervision), and they report a publication record that shows 3 percent in the 1950s; 6 percent in the 1960s; 36 percent in each of the 1970s and 1980s; declining to 16 percent in the 1990s; and 3 percent in the 2000s (their study was published in 2005). In other words, the research on these psychosocial constructs reached its apex in the 1970s and 1980s, declining dramatically thereafter. Moreover, the bulk of the articles seem to be related to privacy and communication (not surprisingly), with control and territoriality receiving less emphasis. The concepts of privacy and communication are essentially the standard bearers of research on open plans and cubicles.

But why did the number of articles published on these topics drop off so precipitously? Many times I think researchers come to a point where

[85] Stone & Luchetti (1985), p. 111.
[86] Camilli, D. (2008, April 1). Window shades of insanity; Prada honchos have design on cubicle etiquette. *Arts & Life, The Gazette* (Montreal), p. D7.
[87] Rashid & Zimring (2005), p. 113.

they have exhausted what they have to say about a topic, and the research on privacy and communication as those topics relate to offices may have been "heavily mined" by the end of the 1980s, particularly because the same results emerged repeatedly. As a research community we pointed to consistent problems with open plans in terms of distractions and threats to visual and acoustical privacy not easily resolved. Most of the research shows a decrement in satisfaction when employees move to an open plan from a traditional office, which is usually defined as floor-to-ceiling walls and a door that closes. Almost as soon as researchers began to study employees' reactions to changes in office design, this decline in satisfaction began to appear. What is beginning to replace this work and research focus on open offices is the work on telecommuting, or working from anywhere (more on that later).

Although research on communication in work environments has declined since the 1980s, as Rashid and Zimring's summary shows, research on the topic still appears, and by and large the same message typically emerges. What is different, I think, is that the current research often uses new analytical tools, such as spatial analysis. Space syntax is one such tool; it shows how spaces are related to one another in terms of connectivity and integration. For example, research in 2007 on four federal offices examined the degree to which the qualities of the environment would support interaction of a private nature, and the degree to which the environment fostered a sense of community. Taking a spatial analysis perspective, the authors show that the kinds of connectivity, or connections of spaces to each other in the environment, and the sense of accessibility to others and sense of community are linked to job satisfaction. But the research also showed the familiar tension between privacy and communication. As the authors state, designers face a dilemma in "how to provide the connectivity to enhance interaction, yet the privacy for concentrated work."[88]

IS PRODUCTIVITY ENHANCED IN OPEN PLANS?

In balancing what kind of difference the open plan makes in the lives of workers *and* of the company, the issue of productivity has been targeted almost since research started on the topic of open plans. In a large study of almost 650 respondents, there was little suggestion that productivity

---

[88] Wineman, J., & Adhya, A. (2007). Enhancing workspace performance: Predicting the influence of spatial and psychosocial factors on job satisfaction. In J. M. Bissell (Ed.), *Building sustainable communities. Proceedings of the 38th Annual Environmental Design Research Association Conference* (pp. 205–206). Edmond, OK: EDRA, p. 206.

increased in an open plan, and what was called a "'privacy and distractions' factor" was presumed to be the explanation for the difference between what workers wanted to accomplish and their actual work output.[89] Other research points to a relationship between ratings of performance (granted, this is not the most objective indicator we might have) and greater degree of enclosure as well as fewer neighbors.[90] These data suggest that the open plan office may have to offer a good deal of enclosure to facilitate work. These authors state, "If the findings generalize, employees in a variety of jobs may prefer more privacy than was afforded by many of the workspaces found in this study. This could explain why so many of the companies that have introduced open plan offices have had complaints from employees."[91] At the same time, there is research with both public and private employees from five different organizations showing that perceived distraction has little impact on perceived performance, that is, as indicated by self-ratings.[92] Although there is little doubt about the positive relationship between job satisfaction and greater personal control in the environment, I don't think we fully understand the factors that may mediate the relationships between distraction and performance, as reflected in the variability in these research findings. More work looking directly at the effects of distraction on productivity and performance is needed.

STATUS, CULTURE, AND OFFICE DESIGN

Privacy means a lot; one of its primary messages is status, and one of the important status markers is control over the access people have to you.[93] Other status markers are reported to be the degree to which you can personalize, the amount of space, and the types of furnishings you have, which reflect something about you and perhaps about the culture of the company where you work.

[89] Hedge, A. (1982). The open-plan office: A systematic investigation of employee reactions to their work environment. *Environment and Behavior, 14, Special issue: Office design and evaluation, Part II*, 519–542, p. 537.

[90] Sundstrom, E., Burt, R. E., & Kamp, D. (1980). Privacy at work: Architectural correlates of job satisfaction and job performance. *The Academy of Management Journal*, 23(1), 101–117.

[91] Ibid., p. 115.

[92] Lee, S. Y., & Brand, J. L. (2005). Effects of control over office workspace on perceptions of the work environment and work outcomes. *Journal of Environmental Psychology*, 25, 323–333.

[93] Konar, E., Sundstrom, E., Brady, C., Mandel, D., & Rice, R. W. (1982). Status demarcation in the office. *Environment and Behavior, 14, Special issue: Office design and evaluation, Part II*, 561–580.

Recently, with mergers forced by casualties in the financial industry, reports have emerged about the conflict of organizational culture between such groups as Bank of America and Merrill Lynch.[94] Some of these reports point to differences in dress code, for example, and one can imagine there might be different approaches to the use of the physical environment in these firms. Possible clashes of corporate culture were described when a merger was proposed for Dupont and Monsanto; where Dupont's culture was reflected in business suits and paneled offices replete with dark wood, the culture for Monsanto ran more to khakis and cubicles.[95]

Employees who are higher up relative to their peers (i.e., supervisors vs. nonsupervisors) are more attuned to the ways in which their workspace communicates their status. In other words, we realize that in addition to location, for example, office square footage "says" something about us. Bigger is presumed to be better (more impressive). Status markers go with the territory, pun intended.

Ironically, even a cubicle can confer status when considered in the context of losing it.[96] Taking the perspective of environmental deprivation, the author argues that if the cubicle is considered owned and occupied, then losing it can result in a variety of emotional responses. I would imagine the responses discussed, involving sorrow and anger, create a kind of cognitive dissonance or issue of inequity. To lose even a cubicle through a move to a less desirable location, for example, could produce stress. The article provides an anecdote from an employee who essentially said he had worked a decade to rise to a certain level of status and exclaimed, "Sir, please do not take away my cubicle."[97] The physical environment has meaning for us, and there is every reason that strong feelings about the physical environment should emerge at work. Yes, there is a culture and symbolic attachment to the physical environment of the workplace. This point has often been overlooked, in the estimation of some.[98] In other words, we cannot separate the social processes of the workplace from the forms in which they occur.

[94] Smith, R., & Fitzpatrick, D. (2008, November 14). Cultures clash as Merrill herd meets "Wal-Mart of Banking." *The Wall Street Journal*, p. C1. http://online.wsj.com/article/SB122662188273026611.html#.

[95] Barboza, D. (1999, March 3). Monsanto visionary in a cubicle; could his company's special culture survive a merger? *The New York Times*, p. C1. http://www.nytimes.com/1999/03/03/business/monsanto-visionary-cubicle-could-his-company-s-special-culture-survive-merger.html?pagewanted=3.

[96] Mazumdar, S. (1992). "Sir, please do not take away my cubicle": The phenomenon of environmental deprivation. *Environment and Behavior, 24,* 691–722.

[97] Ibid., p. 705.   [98] Spreckelmeyer (1995), p. 116.

We like to let people know who we are, on some level. I remember doing some consultation for a new housing project for the elderly in downtown Providence. One of the design features of this high rise was what was euphemistically called the window on the world. In each apartment there was a small window over the kitchen sink that fronted the hallway. Although blinds were provided and used, many residents displayed collections of objects between the blinds and the window, so that residents who passed by could admire the collection. When we display personal objects in the office, we, like the elderly in this high rise, are telling the world who we are, or what matters to us. And there is some evidence that these personal displays in the office play a role in our work satisfaction.[99]

Executives may face their own challenges with regard to the erosion of status, as more executives are moving away from private offices to more open accommodations. Such moves are argued to bring them closer to where ideas are being generated, and this reminds me of the idea of management by walking around (MBWA) touted in *A Passion for Excellence*,[100] the follow-up book to Peters and Waterman's influential *In Search of Excellence*. The biggest obstacle to such change, at least according to the experience at Herman Miller, and there is no reason to think it is unique, is the "I deserve private space" mentality of executives because "I have earned it."[101] This article provides a list of words and phrases associated with the title-and-status versus function-oriented workspace. Some sample contrasts include "architectural solution vs. furniture solution; walls vs. glass; hierarchy vs. teamwork; privacy vs. accessibility; upgraded space and finishes vs. egalitarian; isolated location vs. crossroads location."[102] No longer is the chief executive in a singular role; there is typically an entire senior team that needs to work together.

Personalization

Yes, the office is functional, but it often takes on a ceremonial role as well. One view is that those designations overlap.[103] Estimates are that up to

---

[99] Wells, M. (2000). Office clutter or meaningful personal displays: The role of office personalization in employee and organizational well-being. *Journal of Environmental Psychology*, 20, 239–255.

[100] Peters, T., & Austin, N. (1985). *A passion for excellence*. New York: Random House.

[101] Herman Miller (2003). *New executive officescapes: Moving from private offices to open environments*. (Web pdf)

[102] Ibid., p. 3.   [103] Klein (1982), p. 20.

70 percent of American employees[104] engage in some kind of personalization of their workspace, with those of higher status more likely to do so, and there is some evidence that personalization is more a reflection of the organizational culture of the company than of the individual.[105] Research involving more than 170 office employees from almost 20 businesses reflects this pattern. If you have higher status, and a private, enclosed place to work, you are more likely to personalize. Using the competing values framework, which categorizes cultures into four types (clan $\sim$ like an extended family; adhocracy $\sim$ visionary leaders and innovation; hierarchy $\sim$ leaders who are monitors; and market $\sim$ leaders who are hard-driving), research indicated that companies that were clan-like had more personalization than companies characterized by hierarchies. It was fascinating that 90 percent of the companies had no explicit policy about personalization, but 98 percent of the employees in the study still personalized in some fashion. But the company has a lot to do with the degree of personalization; if the company allows personalization, it is more likely to occur. Further, there are gender differences; women do it more than men. Women display trinkets, and their possessions tend to reflect more sentimentality; men display sports memorabilia, and their displays are often utilitarian.[106]

Personalization extends to cubicles, and even in companies with a large number of employees, people figure out ways to make their cubicle space distinctive. Ways to make one's cubicle unique include having a lawn (something like indoor/outdoor carpeting) or a display of McDonald's Happy Meal figurines.[107] The journalist writing about such identifiers in the office mentions a book entitled *Cube Chic: Take Your Office Space from Drab to Fab!*, which lists amenities you can purchase for your office, such as a cartoon that presents you in front of your computer in your cubicle.[108]

Some employees have thoroughly embraced the idea of personalization. Writing about his cubicle on a Web site, Jared Nielsen talks about the hardwood floors, large wooden desk, and leather chair . . . in *his cube*. To combat what he sees as the socialism represented in the cube farm, he has chosen

---

[104] Wells, M., & Thelen, L. (2002). What does your workspace say about you? The influence of personality, status, and workspace on personalization. *Environment & Behavior, 34,* 300–321.

[105] Wells, M. M., Thelen, L., & Ruark, J. (2007). Workspace personalization and organizational culture: Does your workspace reflect you or your company? *Environment and Behavior, 39,* 616–634.

[106] Wells (2000); Wells & Thelen (2002).

[107] Wheatt, D. (2007, April 22). My workspace. Section: Working. *St. Petersburg Times,* p. 1F.

[108] Moore, K. L. (2006). *Cube chic: Take your office space from drab to fab!* Philadelphia, PA: Quirk Books.

the trappings of capitalism, specifically a big wooden desk and a leather chair.[109]

In an odd way, one could also argue that bringing a pet to work is a kind of personalization. Although some firms permit this, research suggests both an upside and a downside to pets in the workplace. A study using more than 190 employees from 31 companies looked at the role of pets in the workplace. It should be noted at the outset that there was considerable self-selection bias in the companies that chose to participate. What the study showed was that having a pet in the workplace was more likely to occur in small companies (those with fewer than 10 employees) and that the job status of the individual who brought a pet to work was likely to be high, that is, an owner or manager.[110] Not surprisingly, owners and managers were more enthusiastic about having pets at work than were employees. Although the percentage bringing pets to work was 14 percent, a relatively small number, issues related to cleanliness and health exist whatever the percentage and deserve consideration for their impact on group cohesiveness, if not for legal reasons.

Status Symbols

Americans typically work longer hours than workers in any other country, and our vacations are painfully short relative to those in other nations (especially in Europe).[111] One might say that we are our work. Given this investment in work, it is not surprising that our status in the workplace matters to most of us. "A title on the door rates a Bigelow on the floor" is a familiar applicable refrain.[112] The choices an organization makes about where it is located and the attributes of its physical facility communicate a great deal about "who" that organization is.[113]

What are the status symbols we recognize? The location of the office itself; whether you have windows and, if so, what they overlook; the square footage of space you control; the kind of accoutrements you have (e.g., kind of carpet, executive chair, artwork), screening from others (whether you

---

[109] Silverman, C. (2008, July 7). Yeah, that's hardwood in my cube. Global Life; The Office: A weekly look at work culture. *The Globe and Mail (Canada)*, p. L3.

[110] Wells, M., & Perrine, R. (2001). Critters in the cube farm: Perceived psychological and organizational effects of pets in the workspace. *Journal of Occupational Health Psychology, 6*, 81–87.

[111] Brett, J. M., & Stroh, L. K. (2003). Working 60 plus hours a week: Why do managers do it? *Journal of Applied Psychology, 88*, 67–78.

[112] Steele, F. I. (1973). *Physical settings and organization development.* Reading, MA: Addison-Wesley Publishing Company, p. 19.

[113] Ibid., p. 45.

have a private office); your "desk"; and your support staff (number and location) are a few symbols.[114] The number of people reporting to you is a reflection of status, as is the number of gatekeepers you have, that is, the number of people who control access to you.

"Issues related to status symbols and appropriate cues generate emotions far in excess of their actual importance to the work of the system."[115] There are books devoted to this topic, for example, *Symbols and Artifacts: Views of the Corporate Landscape.*[116] And sometimes when efforts are made to provide standardized offices, people are insulted because you have damaged their status.[117]

A cousin of personalization and status is etiquette, in this case the behavior(s) required or expected in cubicles. Peter Post, the great-grandson of Emily Post, recommends that when people are talking and their conversation interferes with your work, simply ask them nicely to find another location for the conversation.[118] A less well-known authority on office etiquette has suggested "don't prairie-dog (or meerkat) over the tops of cubes or peek in as you walk past each one" and "eat quietly. Avoid gum-popping, humming, slurping and pen tapping."[119]

WORK, BUILDINGS, AND CUBICLES: BAD FOR OUR HEALTH?

We work long hours, and there is no doubt that Americans feel job stress, as 80 percent of workers surveyed in a Gallup Poll in 2000 admit to feeling stressed on the job.[120] Moreover, if we add in visits to primary care physicians for stress-related reasons, reported to be on the order of 75–90 percent for first time visits, rising health care costs in the United States, and the cost (estimated in excess of $1 billion annually) to America's employers for substance use (e.g., alcohol and tobacco),[121] we might ask how the environment can alleviate rather than exacerbate stress.

---

[114] Ibid., p. 48.   [115] Ibid., p. 53.

[116] Gagliardi, P. (Ed.) (1990). *Symbols and artifacts: Views of the corporate landscape.* New York: Walter de Gruyter.

[117] Berg, P. O., & Kreiner, K. (1990). Corporate architecture: Turning physical settings into symbolic resources. In P. Gagliardi (Ed.), *Symbols and artifacts: Views of the corporate landscape* (pp. 41–67).

[118] Post, P. (2008, April 27). Even top executives need a gentle hint sometimes. *The Boston Globe, Sunday 3rd edition, Business,* p. G8.

[119] Munro (2008), paras. 30, 38.

[120] Russ, R. R. (2007). The impact of design elements on wellness in the built environment. In J. M. Bissell (Ed.), *Building sustainable communities. Proceedings of the 38th Annual Environmental Design Research Association Conference* (p. 206). Edmond, OK: EDRA.

[121] Ibid., p. 206.

In looking at the relationship between office settings research and health care environments, a point is made that although physiological outcomes may need to be targeted in hospital settings, the primary factors in the office environment may well be psychosocial.[122] In a linkage of influences, the physical environment is tied to personal motives, attitudes, and background characteristics; relevance in a context; and ultimately to outcomes. These outcomes, things like more noise, higher temperatures, headaches, helplessness, lowered task performance, loss of privacy, and lack of group involvement, in turn lead to stress.[123]

Although an in-depth review of the literature on office settings and health is beyond the scope of this chapter, it might be useful to highlight major findings. With regard to the effect of noise, the overview from Rashid and Zimring indicates that uncontrollable noise is more harmful than continuous noise; that intelligible speech is more harmful than sounds without information content; telephones and talking are a problem; and novel sounds are troublesome in terms of efficiency. The issue of control seems to emerge from the literature.

Lighting has been extensively studied. "In fact, direct physiological and psychological benefits of daylight in workplaces are so great that many countries in Europe require that workers be within [a] certain distance from a window."[124] Lighting can affect our mood, our sleep, our productivity, and our accident rate.

On a dire note, those of you who spend a considerable amount of time text messaging and using personal digital assistants (PDAs) may develop text messaging injury (TMI), which is linked to thumb soreness occurring with the repetition of motion, force, and awkward position involved with texting.[125] Further, what about this digital generation, the next generation of office workers? An astounding statistic is that in the United States in 2002, although 500,000 people had to take time off from work to address work-related musculoskeletal disorders (WRMDs), the Social Security Administration provided disability payments to more than 50,000 teenagers and young people not yet 30 for MDs![126]

---

[122] Rashid, M., & Zimring, C. (2008). A review of the empirical literature on the relationships between indoor environment and stress in health care and office settings: Problems and prospects of sharing evidence. *Environment & Behavior, 40*, 151–190.

[123] Ibid., p. 153.   [124] Ibid., p. 161.

[125] Herman Miller (2005). *All thumbs: The ergonomic implications of text messaging.* (Web pdf)

[126] Herman Miller (2004). *Primed for injury: What happens when the digital generation becomes the next generation of office workers?* (Web pdf)

With regard to temperature, the results are intuitive. Extremes of hot and cold are unwelcome. When people are in environments with higher temperatures, their sense of being crowded increases, and they feel less attraction to the people around them.

Air quality, in the form of the air supply, the odors in the air, and pollutants, have an effect on workers. Poor air quality has caused stress. Sick building syndrome is mentioned; the quality of the air, in terms of volatile organic compounds, has been linked to sick building syndrome. One's history of allergies, one's personality, and other factors also may play a role.[127]

In evaluating how work affects our health, one new concept appears to be a discipline called macroergonomics, with a focus on WRMDs. As a way to avoid these disorders, you can train people to modify their own workspaces, for example, the height of their chair, and to understand the kind of movement that will ease back and joint pain. In research with groups trained in how to create a flexible workspace and adjust their furniture as needed, those with the intervention reported gains in a variety of areas: decrease in WRMDs and increases in environmental satisfaction, communication, and collaboration, as well as sense of community and the time and cost of doing business (called business process efficiency).[128]

Although MDs have received a fair amount of attention in the workplace, another concern is computer vision syndrome (CVS), which involves eye strain, which in turn is often associated with headaches. These kinds of symptoms have been reported to occur in upward of 90 percent of computer workers.[129] Furthermore, as an article on the Herman Miller Web pages points out,[130] the labor force is getting older, and coupled with the crisis in the current economy, we are likely to have older workers working longer because they cannot afford to retire (amen to that). The projections in this article were a labor force of 55 and older of 20 percent by the year 2020, up from 13 percent in 2000; my guess is that it will be even larger given the state of the economy. One recommendation to combat this eye strain is to use products that let you adjust your monitor to combat glare, and to manage lighting, especially overlighting, peripheral lighting that is bright, and reflected light (glare).[131] The fact is that older workers (and I

---

[127] Rashid & Zimring (2008), p. 173.

[128] Robertson, M. M., Huang, Y-H., O'Neill, M. J., & Schleifer, L. M. (2008). Flexible workspace design and ergonomics training: Impacts on the psychosocial work environment, musculoskeletal health, and work effectiveness among knowledge workers. *Applied Ergonomics, 39*, 482–494.

[129] Herman Miller (2004). *Vision and the computerized office.* (Web pdf)

[130] Ibid., p. 2.   [131] Ibid., p. 7.

am one) are with us for the foreseeable future. Although we are experienced, reliable, and so on, our physiological functions are declining[132] (ask my students how many times I respond "What?" to a question I did not anticipate).

One enhancement to health in the workplace is to find ways to let people have more control over their environment. As mentioned previously, chair adjustability is one possibility. Another advance that may improve health at work, at least for some people, is the idea of the "work-walker," a workstation that allows you to walk on a treadmill while working. This idea of Dr. James Levine, an endocrinologist at the Mayo Clinic, emphasizes the idea of figuring out a way to integrate movement while doing routine tasks. The "Walkstation" costs approximately $4000 and comes in 36 laminate finishes. There are even work-walking blogs.[133] The potential exists for this piece of equipment to improve concentration as well, at least for some. Built-in treadmills may join other innovations to improve workstations of the future.[134]

Other companies have integrated personal trainers into the cubicle work routine, a popular approach in Australia and New Zealand, where a trainer comes to the office and provides motivation as well as designing a plan for the employees' health and fitness.[135] At least some employers, such as Google, see relaxation as a support for creativity, and for that reason they have ping-pong tables in their offices.[136]

People have vested interests in the buildings they construct (i.e., those they authorize to have constructed), and sometimes interests conflict and the health of the user may suffer. There are land development costs, depreciation considerations, leasing, selling and operating costs, considerations of gross-to-net ratios, technology, zoning, and of course profit.[137] But who are the users? Arguably, people who work in the building are the users. Even when we think we are doing our best job to create a satisfying work environment by

---

[132] Herman Miller (2006). *Embracing boomers: How workplace design for maturing knowledge workers benefits everyone.* (Web pdf)

[133] Katz, M. (2008, September 18). I put in 5 miles at the office. *The New York Times*, E8.

[134] Tutton, M. (2008, October 16). Work is a pleasure in tomorrow's office. http://www.cnn .com/technology. http://www.cnn.com/2008/TECH/science/10/16/future.office/index .html.

[135] Young, E. (2007, October 10). Office workout: With cubicle fitness sessions, there is no need to leave the office to exercise, and no more excuse not to. *The Straits Times* (Singapore), Mind Your Body-Living Well.

[136] Lehrer, J. (2008, July 28). Annals of science: The eureka hunt. *The New Yorker*, 40–45.

[137] Vischer, J. C. (1989). *Environmental quality in offices.* New York: Van Nostrand Reinhold.

incorporating attractive atriums and such amenities as waterfalls, artwork, and pedestrian bridges to other buildings, users may suffer. How? Researcher Jacqueline Vischer mentions the recycled pollutants, the dry itchy throat and watery eyes from dust particles, headaches from high-wattage lights, and a variety of other physical ailments. We also may experience psychological irritation from high density in elevators, lack of personal space in our work environment, and even a dearth of parking.[138] Stuffy air quality, the extent and quality of light, and bothersome noise have been related to high depression and anxiety scores.[139] Vischer summarizes the situation:

> Most of the knowledge and technology to improve environmental design in office buildings exists in the building industry, but for reasons having to do with the structure of the industry, the nature of the building commissioning process, and the ignorance of building users, much of it is not applied.[140]

THE STRESS OF GETTING TO AND FROM WORK

Many Americans who work long hours and are subjected to a variety of stresses when we actually *arrive* at work also commute some distance to get there. One of the points made in the chapter on residential life (Chapter 1) is that the American landscape is in some measure a product of government subsidies, for example, the Interstate Highway Act of 1956 that created our 41,000+ miles of federal highways. Given America's love affair with highways and the automobile, the idea that employers, either private or public, would subsidize commuting seems unlikely. After all, Americans love to drive. In fact, subsidies for commuting were available to only 5 percent of those who worked in private industry in 2007. But public transportation is part of a pattern of getting to and from work for those for whom such transportation is available. Of the 9.8 billion trips on public transportation in 2005, those used for travel to and from work constituted about 50 percent.[141] More than 100 million Americans commute to work each day of the workweek, and

---

[138] Ibid., p. 18.

[139] Carlson, K., & McDowell, K. (1984). The effect of attributes of office environments on employee mood. In D. Durek & D. Campbell (Eds.), *Edra 15: The challenge of diversity: Proceedings of the 15th Annual Environmental Design Research Association Conference* (p. 310). Edmond, OK: EDRA.

[140] Vischer (1989), p. 27.

[141] Long, G. I. (2007). Employer-provided "quality-of-life" benefits for workers in private industry, 2007. Bureau of Labor Statistics. http://www.bls.gov/opub/cwc/cm20071022aro1p1.htm, para.7.

FIGURE 4.3. Parking, Via S. Maria dell'Anima, Rome

the length of that commute increased substantially between 1980 and 2000, with nearly 20 percent of those spending more than an hour commuting.[142]

What do we know about the benefits and drawbacks of the different forms of transportation and the choices Americans make about getting to and from work? These questions are of more than a passing interest to me personally with my recent 4-month stay in Rome overlooking the Piazza Navona, which is often thought to be the heart of Rome. Within a 15-minute walk you can reach the Colosseum, the Roman Forum, the Spanish Steps, and the Vatican, arguably the main historical and tourist attractions. You can also reach literally thousands of shops by foot. It's hard to think of a city in the United States that would compare in any way. Perhaps Boston has the walkability of Rome, but it does not have the density of retail environments. Further, because of the price of real estate in Rome, many buildings that were formerly residences have been converted into office buildings, which brings workers closer to the city center. These workers then can meet virtually any need on foot once they arrive at work. Many Romans also drive scooters; some ride bicycles (although scooters dominate). Then there are *very* small cars, Smart cars, and others, and parking occurs . . . everywhere (see Figure 4.3).

[142] Evans, G. W., & Wener, R. W. (2006). Rail commuting duration and passenger stress. *Health Psychology, 25,* 408–412.

Let me return to the idea of walking and public transportation. Almost everything I needed in Rome was within walking distance – the food market, the butcher, the bakery, the cobbler; all are small markets, and some shops, like the cobbler, no more than 10 feet wide. No, I do not expect the United States to be Italy (thankfully, some might say, given the stereotype of Italian efficiency and punctuality), but I think the proximity to work has many rewards, as I indicated in my opening comments in this chapter. The topic of proximity relates to Chapter 1 of this book, especially in terms of the discussion of new urbanism and the idea of walkable or pedestrian communities. How many remaining communities in the United States can meet residents' needs by *foot*?

What stresses are associated with commuting in the United States, and in particular taking the train to work? The trade-offs? A colleague's husband works in New York City and lives in Milford, Connecticut. Five days a week he rises early to drive to a nearby train stop and take Metro North into Grand Central. He leaves his house before 7 a.m. and returns home just before 9 p.m.; he does this 5 days a week.

Do we feel crowded on the train? Do we claim our territory to avoid an invasion of personal space? It appears that people avoid sitting in the middle seat of a train seating section (with three seats across) "like the plague" and will even stand to avoid that seat. How do you find out about the stresses people feel in a way that moves beyond the idea of self-report (e.g., surveys, interviews)? To address that question, a series of inventive studies has been conducted by Gary Evans and Rich Wener. In one such study involving 139 adult commuters who lived in New Jersey and commuted into Manhattan, participants were given an incentive, a free monthly rail pass.[143] These people were highly educated (83 percent with a college degree) with substantial income (the median was above $95,000). What makes this study more convincing than a typical survey is the inclusion of a salivary cortisol measure. Salivary cortisol is a commonly used measure of stress. Taken from saliva, it reliably indicates stress from 30 minutes to 75 minutes, and the peak levels lag behind a discrete event by about a half-hour.[144] It can be obtained by brushing the inside of the cheek with a cotton swab, and in this research salivary cortisol was obtained by researchers on the participants' morning trip (meeting participants at the end of the commute) and the following weekend at the same time during the day (in participants'

[143] Evans, G. W., & Wener, R. E. (2007). Crowding and personal space invasion on the train: Please don't make me sit in the middle. *Journal of Environmental Psychology, 27,* 90–94.
[144] Evans, G. W., Wener, R. E., & Phillips, D. (2002). The morning rush hour: Predictability and commuter stress. *Environment and Behavior, 34,* 521–530.

homes). To measure motivation, researchers also administered a proofreading task to assess persistence, and to assess mood they used two 5-point semantic differentials, one of which was anchored carefree-burdened; the other, contented-frustrated. As objective measures for the train cars, the researchers counted the number of people in the car and the number of seats; seat density was the number of people sitting in the same row divided by the number of seats in the row. The results indicated that seat density, not car density, is related to all the measures of stress. Think about it: If a train car has high density but by some miracle there is no one sitting in *your* row, you have a much different experience than people who have others sitting next to them.[145]

Men and women differ in many ways, but it appears that the stress, as measured by salivary cortisol, affected them similarly in a related study on commuting.[146] In research with more than 200 men and women who took the train to work in Manhattan, there was a relationship between the length of the commute and stress level as measured by salivary cortisol. The longer the commute, the higher the salivary cortisol levels. The authors see these data as adding to the evidence that Smart Growth (see Chapter 1) makes sense. Although these studies have the drawback of limited generalizability given the demographic characteristics related to education and income, the authors suggest that the results are probably indicative of those who make the commute into Manhattan from New Jersey.

There may be stresses associated with some aspects of commuting by rail, but there are benefits when contrasted with automobile commutes. In addition to the decrease in automobile traffic and in turn carbon emissions related to taking the train and the use of public transportation in general, these actions have personal health benefits. People who take the train walk more than car commuters over the course of the workweek. In fact, in research on those who commute from New Jersey to Manhattan, the participants in a study of physical activity related to mass transit use took "an average of almost 30% more steps per day than did car commuters."[147] In this research the 177 participants wore pedometers for the workweek, which indicated that the train users took about 9400 steps, whereas car users took about 7400 steps. Moreover, the authors indicate that train users were much more likely, even four times more likely, to meet physical activity recommendations of 10,000 steps per day than those who drove their cars to work.

---

[145] Evans & Wener (2007).   [146] Evans & Wener (2006).

[147] Wener, R. E., & Evans, G. W. (2007). A morning stroll: Levels of physical activity in car and mass transit commuting. *Environment and Behavior, 39,* 62–74, p. 66.

Where do train users accumulate this advantage? They have to walk to the train station or from the train station parking lot to the boarding platform, from the train station to the office, and then repeat those movements on the way home. But as the authors point out: "Although mass transit is significant and growing, most Americans still commute by car and have limited mass transit options. . . . "[148] As we move to a new way of working, which involves working from anywhere, including our cars and other modes of transportation, as well as satellite facilities and third places such as airports and cafes, evaluating the stresses related to these new modes of working should be on our research agenda.

BOSTI AND ITS CONTRIBUTIONS

I have saved commenting on BOSTI in depth until this point in the chapter because I think the work of BOSTI provides a good transition from the evaluation of the old way of working (in more or less permanent places) to the idea of working from anywhere. One of the leaders in the behavioral analysis of offices was Michael Brill, who ran BOSTI until his untimely death in 2002. This company was a leader in providing sophisticated analyses of the role of office design and configuration. One small volume challenged the myths BOSTI said were associated with design of the workplace.[149] Again and again we come across the statistic that it is people that cost money in the workplace; that businesses spend more than 80 percent of their cash outflow on people, and BOSTI says only 5 percent on the workplace.[150]

I had the good fortune of meeting Michael Brill at a number of the EDRA (Environmental Design Research Association) conferences. Michael Brill was BOSTI, in my view, and since his death, many former BOSTI employees whom he influenced and mentored continue to do important research on workplaces and spaces. The list of clients served by BOSTI is impressive, including Ernst & Young, Fidelity Investments, Sun Microsystems, Xerox, and a number of U.S. government agencies, among them the Army Construction Engineering Research Laboratory (CERL), the Department of Housing and Urban Development, the Government Accountability Office, and Public Works and Government Services Canada.[151]

BOSTI tackled some of the difficult problems of the office, from the distractions caused by losses of visual and acoustical privacy, to the movement

[148] Ibid., p. 69.
[150] Ibid., p. 15.

[149] Brill et al. (2001).
[151] Ibid., p. 2.

toward working from places other than your assigned office space. BOSTI argues that the importance of teams and the role of technology have led to new ways of working on the part of companies. These new ways of working are often called alternative officing or new officing. "New Officing's goal is to use workplaces, technologies, and work processes as an integrated system of enablers... to work smarter... and wherever work happens."[152] The idea of working smarter is a concept used by the late Peter Drucker, often considered the father of modern management. The idea of working smarter is to be more productive without having to work longer or harder. Working smarter involves defining the work task, concentrating effort on that task, and then measuring performance.[153] The strategies used in new officing, according to BOSTI, are radical redesign, work-from-anywhere, and hotelling. These strategies can be used singly or can be mixed.

What are these strategies? In radical redesign, so much has changed about the way work is done (both its content and the physical nature of the work) that a new approach must be taken. This approach typically involves making changes in the way work is actually done (the process and practice of work); making teams more effective in the way they work, and recognizing that productivity (performance) and satisfaction are related and seeking to increase them. What happens is that the physical environment needs to change from the traditional approach to meet these goals.[154]

The idea of work-from-anywhere equates to the notion that the principal office is no longer necessarily the main site for work. Employees work from home, they work from satellite facilities (as is increasingly the case in the federal government), they work at the client's base, and they work at Starbucks and a host of other places like hotels and airports. Ray Oldenburg wrote about the idea of third places (see Chapter 1) and felt that in the process of creating suburbia and extending commuting times, America had lost what he called her third places[155] – not the home, not the workplace, but the bar, cafe, deli, any place that is inclusive, accessible, has regulars, is homey and home-like. Ironically, these third places may be making a reappearance in the form of the work-from-anywhere movement. One clear advantage of this movement is the need to lease or construct less space for your

[152] Ibid., p. 7.
[153] Drucker, P. (1991, November–December). The new productivity challenge. *Harvard Business Review*, pp. 69–79.
[154] Brill et al. (2001), p. 7.
[155] Oldenburg, R. (1989). *The great good place: Cafes, coffee shops, community centers, beauty parlors, general stores, bars, hangouts, and how they get you through the day.* New York: Paragon House.

employees, given that the main facility never houses everyone at the same time.

Hotelling is a related concept "where the office is still the base for work, but much of it happens elsewhere." The label "hotelling" comes from the idea that the office is like a hotel, in that employees who are away from the office a good deal of the time share spaces in the home office as needed. These are spaces that can be reserved, but that no one "owns." What happens in a hotel is the rental of rooms. What happens in hotelling is the reservation of workspace. In hotelling, people are out of the office as much as 60 percent of the time.[156]

Just as Drucker talked about defining the task, BOSTI describes its approach to helping clients as looking at the business first, not simply at facility issues, and showing how the factors that lead to business success involve key behaviors, which in turn are related to the way the workplace is configured. Then BOSTI works backward to show how the way in which the workplace is configured affects the objectives that a company has identified for itself.

BOSTI says it distinguished itself in the marketplace by moving beyond interviews and surveys. "The results are the product of direct research on 13,000 workplace users, using rigorous objective measurements. They are the findings from structured questionnaires, responded to by these office workers in multiple industries and 40 business units."[157] Although one could criticize the kinds of measures, essentially self-report, that BOSTI employed, the sheer number of participants in its research across a wide array of industries adds reasonable generalizability to its findings. BOSTI's focus on the user echoes the theme addressed by Peters and Waterman, in their well-known book *In Search of Excellence: Lessons from America's Best Run Companies*. This important theme is productivity through people.[158] Yes, people are the critical component, but people work in spaces and places. Workplace design can and does make a difference in the productivity of employees, as BOSTI has shown. In terms of the nomenclature, BOSTI differentiates between workplace, which is the entire working environment (the parking lot, the building, etc.), and the workspace, which is the place where the employee spends most of his or her time.[159]

BOSTI's research shows a varying impact of the workplace on subjective and objective dimensions. On job satisfaction, a subjective variable, that

[156] Brill et al. (2001), p. 9.   [157] Ibid., p. 11.

[158] Peters, T. J., & Waterman, R. H., Jr. (1982). *In search of excellence: Lessons from America's best run companies*. New York: Harper and Row.

[159] Brill et al. (2001), p. 17.

impact is reported to be 24 percent; on individual performance, an objective (or at least a more objective) variable, it is 5 percent; on team performance (also a more objective variable), 11 percent.[160] But it is worth remembering that issues like job satisfaction do matter. Although it is a subjective variable, job satisfaction is correlated to turnover ($-.40$) and absenteeism ($-.25$), both of which are objective measures, perhaps the most easily quantifiable measures in the workplace.[161] And they cost the organization significant amounts of money.

To me one of the ironies in the broader research on work is the relatively low correlation typically found between job satisfaction and productivity. Estimates for that relationship are between .17 in a meta-analysis[162] (a study of studies) in 1985 and .30 in a more recent study.[163] Why? People have to be productive at work to keep their jobs, and they may need their jobs for a variety of reasons: family support, health and retirement benefits, a poor economy and no other job choices, and so on. Whether they are satisfied may have little to do with their work performance. Thus, one might argue that the absence of job satisfaction means little because it has a relatively low correlation with productivity. On the other hand, job satisfaction correlates with absenteeism and turnover, both of which cost the organization money. For that reason, and surely for a host of others, it makes sense to determine how to create office environments related both to job satisfaction and productivity. Other research teams have estimated that the impact of the physical environment on productivity in the office is small but meaningful, from 5 to 15 percent.[164] More than any other researcher or research team, BOSTI has been able to provide clarity about the relationship between the physical space of the office and what it does to workers – their satisfaction, their morale, and their productivity.[165]

There is a wealth of material to digest in BOSTI's two research volumes (*Using Office Design to Increase Research Productivity*), but one of the major messages about open plans is the importance of privacy and how to manage

[160] Ibid., p. 18.

[161] Muchinsky, P. M. (2006). *Psychology applied to work: An introduction to industrial and organizational psychology*. Belmont, CA: Thomson Wadsworth.

[162] Iffaldano, M. T., & Muchinsky, P. M. (1985). Job satisfaction and performance: A meta-analysis. *Psychological Bulletin, 97*, 251–273.

[163] Judge, T. A., Thoresen, C. J., Bono, J. E., & Patton, G. K. (2001). The job satisfaction–job performance relationship: A qualitative and quantitative review. *Psychological Bulletin, 127*, 376–407.

[164] Vischer (1989), p. 24.

[165] Brill, M., Margulis, S. T., & Konar, E. (1984). *Using office design to increase productivity* (Vols. I & II). Buffalo, NY: Workplace Design and Productivity.

it, because privacy is related to environmental satisfaction, job performance, and job satisfaction.

In the 2001 volume *Disproving Widespread Myths about Workplace Design*, Brill and his colleagues describe the kind of workspace that supports people, and in the process "bust the myths" people have about open plans. Here is their list of the characteristics of workspaces that support people[166]:

- ability to do distraction-free solo work
- support for impromptu interactions (in one's workspace and else-where)
- support for meetings and undistracted groupwork
- workspace comfort, ergonomics, and enough space for work tools
- workspace supports side-by-side work and "dropping in to chat"
- located near or can easily find coworkers
- workplace has good places for breaks
- access to needed technology
- quality lighting and access to daylight
- temperature control and air quality

The kind of work that people do, BOSTI says, has remained relatively similar over the time period 1994–2000. Their research shows what you might expect. People do quiet things, such as work on their computer; they do louder things, such as talk on the telephone (or cell phone); they have formal meetings; they have informal interactions in their own workspace; they have meetings outside their own workspace; they have other informal interactions outside of their own space; they have lunch (in their workspace or elsewhere); and they take breaks. In BOSTI's research involving managers, professionals, engineers, and administrators, most of people's time is spent in their own workspace, approximately 75 percent of it, and BOSTI says that the individual's own workspace is the *"primary spatial tool for work, even in highly interactive, team-based organizations."*[167] It should be noted that these percentages are based on self-report and may be an overestimate according to observational data.[168]

So, what does that mean? It means that we haven't really moved away from the notion of the importance of personal space, privacy, and territoriality. Nor should we expect that to have happened, given our evolutionary heritage. What it also means, as BOSTI and everyone else points out, is

---

[166] Brill et al. (2001), p. 19.   [167] Ibid., p. 24.

[168] Ellen Bruce Keable, Principal, Workplace Strategies, Advance Planning Group, Jacobs Global Buildings, personal communication, May 30, 2009.

that being able to work free of distractions is paramount. Two-thirds of the people in BOSTI's research reported being "often distracted," which is not surprising, really, when you consider that most noise in an office comes from the sounds generated in people's own workspaces, basically from communication devices, like their own voice.[169] But the conundrum is that people also say they gain most from informal learning, which typically occurs through informal, not formal, interactions. More than 85 percent say that informal learning is more beneficial than formal learning.[170] It is intriguing that these statistics hold across office types, including conventional offices, so that the advantage in communication thought to accrue in open plan offices doesn't emerge here.

If individual workspaces that offer floor-to-ceiling walls and a door for each employee are the best match for at least a good portion of the work that people do, BOSTI then asks, why is America filled with open plans? It then provides a list of six myths, which it demonstrates are just that – myths – about open plans[171]:

Myth 1: "We can't have *both* distraction-free work and easy interactions. They're opposites."

Myth 2: "We can provide a distraction-free *open* office."

Myth 3: "We are moving towards being a more *open organization*, one with better communications."

Myth 4: "We *learn* more in the open from overhearing others' conversations."

Myth 5: "We can't have all enclosed workspaces . . . our *space utilization rate* will skyrocket."

Myth 6: "We *can't afford the cost* associated with providing enclosed workspaces."

BOSTI argues that assumptions about the benefits of the open plan have not been really tested, and that its research suggests that the assumptions linked to open plan offices are "backwards." BOSTI sees the reverse of what was hypothesized; it sees that greater physical enclosure can lead to easier communication and communication of higher quality; a low degree of physical enclosure produces the opposite.[172] In fact, BOSTI's two-volume work based on 10,000 participants demonstrated that the highest degree of enclosure (full walls, fours sides, a door) had the greatest support for communication (98 percent), whereas the lowest degree of enclosure

---

[169] Brill et al. (2001), p. 27.   [170] Ibid., p. 29.
[171] Ibid., p. 33.   [172] Ibid., p. 38.

(1–2 sides, low-full walls, or bullpen) had the lowest support for communication (58 percent).[173] And the individual office isn't disappearing. Some estimates indicate that the ratio of individual to collaborative spaces will be about 60/40 in the years 2006–2010.[174]

SOLUTIONS?

Given these myths about the open plan, the solutions BOSTI offers involve a greater emphasis on enclosure. They suggest a kind of main street/side street layout in which the main street carries the major traffic, and the enclosed offices open off "side streets," which branch off this main thoroughfare. The focus is on making sure individual workspaces are separated from the circulation spaces. When distractions (noise) are produced by work groups adjacent to each other, they recommend enclosing each work group within an enclosed workspace of its own, but within that group's workspace providing open workspaces if the work demands it. Within one's own work group, within an open plan, you can still enclose each individual's workspace if noise is likely to be generated from the kind of work people do.[175]

Similar to the BOSTI configuration of main street and side streets, one recommendation from Herman Miller is to locate space for collaboration out of the main traffic areas, that is, to the side or in a corner. Its rationale is that central space may be perceived as open to everyone, that is, more public, and hence people will have difficulty "reading" that space as a place where they do not belong.[176]

In summary, the qualities of the workplace that have the strongest effect on work satisfaction and productivity are the ability to do distraction-free work and support for informal interactions. The qualities at the "bottom" of the list (meaning the least strong effects) are quality lighting and daylight access and temperature control and air quality, at least according to BOSTI's work.[177]

"The office is more than just a cost center,"[178] BOSTI says, pointing to the importance of looking beyond the cost per square foot of housing

---

[173] Ibid., p. 39.

[174] Madsen, J. J. (2006, August). The cause and effect of shrinking workspaces. *Buildings*, *100*(8), 50–52.

[175] Brill et al. (2001), pp. 52–54.

[176] Herman Miller (2002). *Making teamwork work: Designing spaces that support collaborative efforts*, p. 4. (Web pdf)

[177] Brill et al. (2001), p. 56.   [178] Ibid., p. 56.

your employees. Employers need a paradigm change, in a sense. They need a different way of thinking about the role of the physical environment for their employees; they need to believe that "**carefully designing your workplace to support what your people and teams actually do is an investment that pays off in both business terms and in positive changes in corporate culture.**"[179]

One connection I see between what is desirable in the office setting and the other topics in this book (schools, housing, health care, and retail) is a kind of smaller-is-better configuration. Even when we have to build "big," as is the case for some communities that cannot persuade voters or town councilors to build multiple small schools, you can create smallness within that bigness. In the case of office environments, the smallness has to do with the importance of privacy and personal space. People need to be able to exert some control over their "territories." The work environment, although not as important as the home territory, is significant because we spend so many of our waking hours there. "The trend underlies the preference for smaller, more controllable working environments in which identity is not lost or smothered by the corporation. Privacy will always remain an issue, especially in open-plan offices."[180] This description reminds me of the small school idea, in which smaller units can be created within larger units by designing various self-contained sections (see Chapter 3).

TELECOMMUTING, TELEWORK, AND THE MOVE TO MOBILITY

Propst makes the point that the physical manifestation of the office has not kept pace with the evolution of work,[181] and certainly if he were writing today he would add that the office as a physical entity is no match for technology. Writing in 1968, Propst was already talking about the deluge of information we were experiencing, and at the time he wrote he was essentially limited to commenting on journal articles and other print publications. The Internet and World Wide Web were not yet tools of office workers.

Technology is arguably one of the biggest influences on the kinds of work environments we create in the United States. Simply put, technology has provided choices. Just as some educators are questioning whether the school building will continue to exist, the office as we have known it will never dominate the landscape of the 21st century as it did in the 20th century. More than 20 years ago, researchers questioned whether the office as it had

[179] Ibid.   [180] Klein (1982), p. 44.
[181] Propst (1968).

been known for a large measure of the 20th century would essentially go the way of the dinosaur. In particular, the question was asked, "Is the office as we know it obsolete? Are its artifacts obsolete?" and the author answered his own question, "Chances are that both are obsolete."[182] The explanatory variable: technology. Whereas gasoline may restrict travel or curtail changes in location, says the author, telecommunication does not.

The ideas of telecommuting and telework were introduced in the mid-1970s by Jack Nilles, who, when he confronted the traffic congestion of Los Angeles, thought about alternatives that would accomplish a number of things: reductions in office space costs, reductions in commuting costs, and greater flexibility for the people who you want to keep in your company.[183] Nilles is credited with the first demonstration project for telework, funded in part by the National Science Foundation (NSF).[184] It seemed like a great idea, and although it did not catch on as fast as many people thought,[185] it is gaining steam.

There are many terms used to describe workers who are no longer tethered to a company office (more on that shortly), but two such terms need to be defined now. In *Telework Trendlines 2009*, a report from the WorldatWork, teleworking is defined as doing all of one's work either from home or another remote location (either for an employer or through self-employment), whereas telecommuting is more restricted, either "periodically or regularly" doing work for an employer from one's home or from a remote location.[186] I might also add that these definitions are not universally adopted, and the literature contains many examples where the terms seem to be used interchangeably or where other definitions are applied.

Some authors argue that although telecommuting has been "known" for almost 40 years now, it had a jump start during two natural disasters, the

---

[182] Kleeman, W. B., Jr. (1982). The future of the office. *Environment and Behavior, 14, Special issue: Office design and evaluation, Part II,* 593–610, p. 593.

[183] Kurland, N. B., & Bailey, D. E. (1999). Telework: The advantages and challenges of working here, there, anywhere, and anytime. *Organizational Dynamics, 28*(2), 53–68.

[184] Van Horn, C. E., & Storen, D. (2000). Telework: Coming of age? Evaluating the potential benefits of telework. In *Telework: The new workplace of the 21st century* (pp. 3–28). Washington, D.C.: U.S. Department of Labor, p. 10.

[185] van der Wielen, J. M. M., Taillieu, T. C. B., Poolman, J. A., & van Zuilichem, J. (1995). Telework: Dispersed organizational activity and new forms of spatial-temporal co-ordination and control. In J. M. Peiro, J. L. M. Prieto, & O. Luque (Eds.), *Work and organizational psychology: European contributions in the nineties* (pp. 263–280). Hove, East Sussex, U.K.: Erlbaum.

[186] WorldatWork (2009, February). *Telework trendlines 2009.* http://www.workingfrom anywhere.org/news/Trendlines_2009.pdf, p. 4.

earthquake in Los Angeles in 1995 and the snowstorm on the East Coast in 1996, when email continued despite the snow.[187] I remember that storm. Connecticut governor Ella Grasso closed the highways for 3 days, with the exception of emergency travel.

I asked a friend, Ellen Bruce Keable, formerly a vice president of BOSTI and now a principal for Workplace Strategies with the Advance Planning Group of Jacobs Global Buildings in the United States, about telework. She responded that there is a "huge upswing in the 'move to mobility,' which goes beyond telework to address working from anywhere – in the community, at home, with clients, and at different locations in buildings and corporate campuses. It is catching on very quickly now given desires for a low cost way to attract and retain people and of course to reduce facilities costs."[188]

When I asked her about whether consulting firms were using BOSTI's approach to provide more enclosure and privacy in offices, she responded that "I don't think that's widespread, *but* the idea of providing alternatives that include places for peace and quiet (and often it's just allowing you to work at home when you need it!) has been wrapped into the mobility concept. The catch is that you may give up having your own desk – you pick what you need when you need it – whether it be a meeting room, a 'touchdown' desk in the open, a very small enclosed office/'phonebooth,' or other settings. This really draws on the history of the landscaped office (a colleague of mine says landscape has variety – and what we've done with open offices is to create office prairies!)."[189]

DEFINITIONS (AND MORE DEFINITIONS)

In research for this chapter, I came across at least five different frameworks to describe work outside the traditional office. Operational definitions (i.e., how we define what we measure) vary. In one scheme seven different types of teleworkers were identified.[190] One sense you get from reading the literature is that the experts don't really know how to count telecommuters (and/or teleworkers), in that the estimates of how many people are in these

---

[187] Riley, P., Mandavilli, A., & Heino, R. (2000). Observing the impact of communication and information technology on "net-work." In *Telework: The new workplace of the 21st century* (pp. 140–154). Washington, D.C.: U.S. Department of Labor.

[188] Ellen Bruce Keable (personal communication, December 11, 2008).

[189] Ibid.

[190] Helling, A. (2000). A framework for understanding telework. In *Telework: The new workplace of the 21st century* (pp. 54–68).

categories vary substantially. Part of the problem related to documenting the number of telecommuters and teleworkers relates to this variability in definition.

In different sources there are variations in the number of days a month you have to work from home to qualify as a telecommuter. Generally that criterion is at least "a few days" (always a tricky translation) a month. With the elasticity in the definition, it is not surprising that estimates ranged from 3 million to 9 million, or 3 percent to 8 percent of the U.S. workforce, in an article published in 1999. In that same article, estimates for the year 2000 were predicted to range from 15 million to 44 million or almost 60 percent of the workforce.[191] To say that those numbers represent a big range is an understatement. The *Telework Trendlines 2009* report indicates that if your measure is employed telecommuters who work at least 1 day a month from a remote location (including home), the figure for 2008 is 33.7 million, an increase of 43 percent over that measure since 2003.[192]

Here is how the government defines telework (or at least what some of the government's publications say): "Telework is defined as work performed away from the principal office under circumstances that reduce or eliminate the employee's commute. Teleworkers typically work at home or at a telework center one or more days a week."[193] You can see a difference between the government's definition and the one provided by *Telework Trendlines 2009* earlier in this chapter. Such differences make it difficult to compare reports, which produces some of the confusion surrounding just how many Americans have adopted some form of the move to mobility.

There seem to be two extremes related to physical space and employment: (1) working completely at home, or (2) working completely at one office (the old way of working). But there are many, many in-betweens. The in-betweens have to do with working at someplace in between home and "the office," and/or working at more than one of these places. For example, one can work at what is called a satellite office, where everyone there is employed by a single employer; or one can work at a telework center, where employees who work for different companies may have office space leased by those different companies, sometimes called neighborhood telework centers. Another category related to being on the move is mobile workers, who essentially have no home base. In one scheme offered by Pratt, satellite offices can be equated to the traditional branch office, and that link, however weak, provides some kind of connection to the culture

---

[191] Kurland & Bailey (1999).   [192] *Telework trendlines 2009* (2009), p. 5.

[193] http://www.gsa.gov/graphics/ogp/BlueFactsheet.pdf, para. 1.

of the parent organization.[194] Yet another term that sometimes appears is the "tethered worker," who has some mobility but reports to the office on a regular basis.

Virtual workplace is a term with broad reach to suggest that people are working almost anywhere (from airports to the client's site).[195] A similar term is "network offices," places such as train stations and airports where you can rent space to work (and Internet connections) on an hourly basis.[196] The term "virtual corporation" has also been used, in which the company exists where the employees are, and not in particular headquarters.[197] Another label used is "nomadic work." "Nomadic work is a radical new mode of work that emphasizes worker mobility both at and away from the company facility; a paperless operation; and integrated technological platforms that enable knowledge work and flexible, project-based organizing."[198] A recent term that has appeared is "white space," which refers to the space where the work is actually accomplished. This space can be in the office, but also, if not more likely, in coffee shops, libraries, and airport lounges. These white spaces are places where people actually "think."[199] In this article in *The New York Times*, the author says that the ultimate benefit of white space is that people can choose where they work best, whether it is onsite or not.[200] I often find that I do a good deal of work waiting for airplanes, because although there may be people around me, they are not related to me or to my work, and I can tune out those distractions.

Thus, whatever *office* means, where work gets done is changing. Almost every writer on the topic talks about how work now can be separated from a specific location, which is the ultimate implication of working from anywhere. Quoting the writer Woody Leonhard, from his *The Underground*

[194] Pratt, J. H. (2000). Telework and society – implications for corporate and societal cultures. In *Telework: The new workplace of the 21st century* (pp. 225–243).
[195] O'Connell, S. E. (1996). The virtual workplace moves at warp speed. *HRMagazine*, March, pp. 50–57, p. 57.
[196] van Meel, J. (2007). On the road: Flexible office space at highways and airports. In J. M. Bissell (Ed.), *Building sustainable communities. Proceedings of the 38th annual environmental design research association conference* (p. 169). Edmond, OK: EDRA.
[197] Froggatt, C. C. (1998). New work directions: Creative environments for the future. http://www.gilgordon.com/downloads/directions.txt, para. 6.
[198] Bean, C. J., & Eisenberg, E. M. (2006). Employee sensemaking in the transition to nomadic work. *Journal of Organizational Change Management*, 19(2), 210–222, p. 210.
[199] Belkin, L. (2007, December 13). You won't find me in my office, I'm working. *The New York Times*, paras. 6, 10.
[200] Ibid., para. 25.

Guide to Telecommuting, one author reminds us: "Work is something you do, not someplace you go."[201]

These terms just described relate to the larger issue of the building or virtual building where the work gets done. A second category of terms relates to movement within a particular facility (e.g., hotelling). In some sense, both categories can be described by the term "distributed work." Work can be distributed offsite; work can also be distributed onsite, that is, within the site.[202] Focusing now on work distributed within a given site, there are a variety of possibilities. As previously mentioned in this chapter, hotelling is the equivalent of renting a room in that the space in the office is not permanently assigned and you have to reserve where you are going to work on a particular day. Another term emerging is hot desking, which refers to switching desks in the office almost daily. Another concept is the phone booth, a small workspace in offices with wireless access and sliding doors where people can go for work that requires real privacy. Although this presentation is not exhaustive, it gives the reader some idea of the options for distributed work within a site and terms used to describe these possibilities.

WHAT THE GOVERNMENT DATA TELL US

In 2000, U.S. Secretary of Labor Alexis Herman convened a national symposium on telework in some measure to pool knowledge about the country's involvement in telework.[203] The presenters at the symposium saw a bright future for telework in terms of contributing to the U.S. economy, to the work–family balance, to productivity, and to global competition. At the same time, an undercurrent in the symposium was that the potential for telework was largely untapped. At the time of the symposium, the teleworker was described as likely to be a man who was White and college educated, who was in his mid-30s to mid-50s, who earned in excess of $40,000 annually, and who owned a computer. That same profile has held up over time. The *Telework Trendlines 2009* report states that most telecommuters in 2008 were likely to be men under the age of 55 (predominantly around 40) who had a college degree and household income of more than $75,000 per year.[204]

---

[201] Gordon, G. E. (2000). Employer scheduling, staffing and work location issues. In *Telework: The new workplace of the 21st century* (pp. 105–115).

[202] Ellen Bruce Keable (personal communication, May 30, 2009).

[203] U.S. Department of Labor (2000).   [204] *Telework trendlines 2009* (2009), p. 8.

Among the most important factors contributing to an increase in tele-work in the United States and outlined at the 2000 symposium are

- declining technology and telecommunications costs
- growing investments in digital technology and digital infrastructure
- increasing demand for information technology sector jobs
- increasing use of computers in the workplace
- increasing leverage of workers in tight labor markets who demand telecommuting opportunities
- encouraging initial research on the financial and environmental benefits of telework.[205]

Interestingly, in the report on the status of telework in the federal government for 2007, a statement was made that telework had moved beyond being a program to improve the quality of worklife for employees to one that could enhance a given agency's recruitment and retention, emergency preparedness, "green" savings (e.g., reduced emissions), and real estate costs.[206]

When I wrote this chapter in spring 2009 I had to laugh at the irony of the remarks prepared by the chief economist of the Department of Labor, William Rodgers, in the introduction to the report on the national symposium in 2000 assessing telework. Rodgers said, "As the century began, America was enjoying the longest, strongest economic boom in its history. Over 22 million jobs had been created since 1993 and unemployment was at a 30-year-low. Record deficits had been transformed into record surpluses, productivity was rising at spectacular rates and inflation remained low."[207] How the landscape has changed. More recently, reports focus on the recession as a factor promoting the growth of telework.[208]

The report explains that the government supported telework by establishing the telecenters program in 1993, which created centers from which government employees could work rather than commute to the central office. At the time of the symposium, there were 17 centers, primarily in the Washington, D.C., Beltway area. In a federal telecenter, office space leased

---

[205] Van Horn & Storen (2000), p. 18.

[206] U.S. Office of Personnel Management (2008, December). *Status of telework in the federal government: Report to the Congress.* Washington, D.C.: U.S. Office of Personnel Management, p. 2.

[207] Rodgers, W. M. (2000). Introduction: Telework in the 21st century. In *Telework: The new workplace of the 21st century* (pp. v–xi), p. v.

[208] Shepard, L. C. (2009, March 1). Economic downturn will spur upswing in telework. *Employee Benefit News.* http://ebn.benefitnews.com/news/economic-downturn-spur-upswing-telework-2670431-1.html.

by a federal agency is made available to its employees. An example closer to me (in the Boston area) was the office space that the General Services Administration (GSA) leased to make it easier for workers to avoid what was called the Big Dig. The Big Dig, which took much longer than anyone ever imagined (and cost a great deal more, as well), was the highway and tunnel construction project in the downtown area of Boston that made commuting a nightmare.

But the sense in the report from the symposium is that although the federal government was making progress, it could do much more to encourage and support teleworking. Although there was a substantial increase in the number of teleworkers during the Clinton administration to about 25,000, that number was only about 2 percent of the federal workforce and compares poorly to the percentage of teleworkers ($\approx$10 percent) in the private sector.[209] Stanley Kaczmarczyk, deputy associate administrator of the Office of Governmentwide Policy of the GSA, testified before the U.S. Senate Subcommittee on Oversight of Government Management and the Federal Workforce, in a session entitled "Improving federal telework participation and current telework activity," on June 12, 2007. In his prepared remarks he stated, "After more than 15 years of continuing efforts to build a robust and vital Federal telework program, levels of participation are still not as high as we believe they can and should be."[210] After explaining how much gasoline and work-years of time could be saved if even 50 percent of the federal workforce teleworked even 2 days a week, he revealed how few federal workers of the 92 percent eligible for telework actually do so.[211,212] In other words, telework's potential has yet to be realized.

THE JUSTIFICATION AND IMPLEMENTATION OF TELEWORK

Although the federal government has not implemented teleworking at the pace expected, it has arguably produced a substantial body of research

---

[209] U.S. Department of Labor (2000). Executive summary. *Telework: The new workplace of the 21st century* (pp. 1–6), p. 2.

[210] Kaczmarczyk, S. (2007, June 12). Improving federal telework participation and current telework activity. Statement of Stanley Kaczmarczak, Deputy Associate Administrator, Office of Governmentwide Policy, U.S. General Services Administration, before the Subcommittee on Oversight of Government Management, the Federal Workforce, and the District of Columbia, Committee on Homeland Security and Governmental Affairs, United States Senate, para. 2. http://www.gsa.gov/Portal/gsa/ep/contentView.do?contentId=23133&contentType=GSA_BASIC&noc=T.

[211] Ibid., para. 11.   [212] Ibid., para. 19.

and discussion on teleworking. Further, the government has policies that govern the "work" of telework. A list of laws that apply to teleworking can be found online (http://www.telework.gov/Guidance_and_Legislation/Telework_Legislation/index.aspx). There is also a GSA Telework Library (http://www.gsa.gov/telework). A new bill, S. 707, the Telework Enhancement Act of 2009, has been proposed that would go beyond creating policies for telework participation in the government to establishing and implementing policies to *enable* such participation and further create two pilot programs to reimburse some teleworking employees.[213]

The fact sheet from the federal government provides many positive outcomes of telework, including a survey of more than 1500 federal workers, of whom more than 50 percent were involved in the care of dependents. Of those 50+ percent, more than 90 percent stated that telework helped them meet those care responsibilities.[214] The government also claims a return on investment (ROI) in technology expenditures in the first year of between 200 percent and 1500 percent![215] There are other facts related to saving money on gas, saving time in travel delays, reducing pollution and congestion, and so on. In other words, there is a good deal of information available to inform us about the state of telework in the United States and the benefits that accrue from telework. Beyond the federal government, organizations focusing on telework have sprouted, including The World at Work (http://www.workingfromanywhere.org) and the Telework Exchange (http://www.teleworkexchange.com).

At its extreme, the office could exist virtually, that is, without a physical presence. That is rarely the case, but some companies have employees on the road more than not and working virtually. Recognized leaders in virtual offices, a kind of telecommuting, are IBM, Hewlett-Packard, and Lotus Development Corporation.[216] Needs addressed are the expected ones: reduce space costs, improve customer service, increase productivity, create better family and work balance and so on. IBM started a Workforce Mobility Transformation Program in the early 1990s. With 20,000 mobile employees, IBM reduced its real estate costs per site by 40 percent to 60 percent, which yielded savings of $35 million per annum. Moreover, these cost reductions were associated with increases in productivity of as much as 15 percent and

[213] S.707 Telework Enhancement Act of 2009 (June 1). http://www.cbo.gov/ftpdocs/102xx/doc10253/s707.pdf.

[214] http://www.gsa.gov/graphics/ogp/BlueFactsheet.pdf, para. 9.

[215] GSA Telework Technology Cost Study, 2006. http://www.gsa.gov/telework.

[216] O'Connell, S. E. (1996, March). The virtual workplace moves at warp speed. *HRMagazine*, 50–57.

more.[217] IBM software also supports the mobility movement. A new software package called Mobility@Work enables users to take a mobile device (e.g., a BlackBerry or iPhone) and run existing desktop applications on it.[218]

As I have indicated, a repeated theme is the underutilization of telework, relative to the number of eligible workers. According to the Telework Technology Cost Study (its executive summary) of 2006, the government has not made the investment in infrastructure that must exist to scale up telework (i.e., to really expand it). Often, workers use their own equipment at home, which may not comply with federal standards in terms of ergonomics or security.[219] "The study findings show that no Federal departments have developed plans specifically to expand their telework infrastructure. IT modernization efforts, in general, have benefited telework, but these have been incidental rather than planned telework infrastructure improvements."[220]

How many potential teleworkers are we talking about? The March 2008 National Compensation Survey, using the standard occupational classification system in 2000 to classify workers, shows that the total number of civilian workers in the United States is: 126,734,200, of whom 107,406,000 are in private industry and 19,328,100 are in state and local government employ. Of these, 35,147,900 are management, professional, and related civilian workers. If we look at sales and office workers, there are 33,676,800 civilian workers.[221] Although we have made some progress in teleworking, the potential is still relatively untapped.

TECHNOLOGY AND TELEWORK

Despite its relative underutilization, one main reason telework has become more feasible is the growth of support in technology, particularly broadband and the Internet. A 10-fold increase in the percentage of broadband users was projected from 1999 (2.5 percent) to 2003 (25.09 percent).[222] To support more growth in telework, it is argued, the income gap as it relates to the technology you have at home needs to be addressed. Americans earning

---

[217] Ibid., p. 52.

[218] Morphy, E. (2008, August 10). IBM kicks mobility into high gear. CRM*Buyer*™. http://www.crmbuyer.com/story/64109.html?wlc=1244757194.

[219] Telework Technology Cost Study (2006, May 2). Executive summary. Washington, D.C.: GSA: U.S. General Services Administration, p. 4. http://www.gsa.gov/telework.

[220] Ibid., p. 9.

[221] Appendix Table 2. (March, 2008). Number of workers represented, National Compensation Survey. http://www.bls.gov/ncs/ebs/benefits/2008/appendixtable2008_02.pdf.

[222] Van Horn & Storen (2000).

more than $75,000 annually are nine times more likely to have a computer at home than those who earn below that level.[223] Cost savings play a role in companies' interest in telework, or at least in reducing office space because employees are there less often. In an article labeling the cubicle the "great mistake," the author cites a survey showing the use of broadband in 2005 by 26 million Americans who could work from home.[224]

In addition to the change in work locations (e.g., the virtual world), there is new technology to support this world. In addition to the mobility software introduced by IBM, there are relatively affordable video conferencing systems and programs from Google (Docs and Glance) that enable the employee to see the work of a colleague at a remote site in real time.[225]

RESISTANCE TO TELEWORK

Somewhat ironically, resistance to telework has come largely from management in terms of concerns about how to manage "remotely." The label "remote manager" refers to the idea of managing employees from a distance. The growth of the virtual office is a fundamental change in the way work is done. More and more work will be under the control of the worker in an unprecedented way.[226]

Resistance seems to have come from established work culture and fears among remote managers that "when the cat is away, the mice will play." In a 2008 report on the status of telework in the federal government, among the top four barriers to the implementation of telework was the resistance of management.[227] Another relevant perspective is the idea that "measure it, or you can't manage it,"[228] and that measuring white-collar performance or productivity is a challenge. If you have trouble measuring performance under normal circumstances, what happens when the employee is invisible in the sense that he or she is not onsite? If, as has

---

[223] Ibid., p. 7.   [224] Schlosser (2006), para. 26.

[225] Koerner, B. (September 22, 2008). Home sweet office: Telecommute good for business, employees, and planet. http://www.wired.com/culture/culturereviews/magazine/6-10/st_essay.

[226] Tutton, M. (2008, October 16). Work is a pleasure in tomorrow's office. http://www.cnn.com/2008/TECH/science/10/16/future.office/index.html.

[227] U.S. Office of Personnel Management (2008), p. 11.

[228] Herman Miller (2007). *Measures of success: The facility's role in effectiveness*, p. 1. (Web pdf)

been argued, temporal–spatial organization is "at the very heart of social theory,"[229] what happens when that spatial relationship is turned on its head? And from the workers' perspective, what happens when you are not visible in terms of issues like promotions? Is it "out of sight, out of mind?"

The resistance of management to the expansion of telework is often listed as one of the reasons telework has been slower to flourish than initially predicted. Froggatt outlines what she calls six layers of management resistance: (1) a misunderstanding of telework, and in particular that not everyone will be doing it every day; (2) misconceptions about current work patterns and not realizing that current work patterns outside of telework do not involve 100 percent presence every single day; (3) acknowledgment by higher management that implementing telework means more "management" work for managers because those they manage are not physically present – this extra work perhaps needs to be compensated; (4) lack of trust about teleworker worker performance (e.g., how teleworkers are actually spending their time) can be addressed if managers understand how to operationalize performance and not just attendance; (5) the personal issues that may need to be addressed, even those of managers, to make telework successful; and (6) corporate culture, which is said to underlie all kinds of resistance. "How work is viewed and rewarded needs to change to reflect emphasis on these new ways of working."[230]

Repeatedly we see evidence of management resistance in the form of a more industrial as opposed to humanistic approach to worker motivation as a reason why the adoption of telework has not skyrocketed. There is some sense that it is easier to manage teleworkers at lower than higher levels of the knowledge worker hierarchy because it is easier to measure what they do, in the form of such outcomes as keystrokes.[231] In the view of one writer, managers seem to perceive telework as an "unnatural act."[232]

Not all companies and not all managers take that view. Best Buy has been written about as one of the leaders in ROWE, or results only work environment,[233] in which it is the output, and not the employee's physical presence, that counts. The approach has been implemented in the corporate offices of the electronics retailer, and by the end of 2007 it was expected that

---

[229] van der Wielen et al. (1995), p. 268.   [230] Froggatt (1998), paras. 18–25, para. 24.

[231] Van Horn & Storen (2000), p. 18.

[232] Vega, G. (2000). Building the case for telework. In *Telework: The new workplace of the 21st century* (pp. 168–174).

[233] Smashing the clock (2006, December 11). *Business Week*. http://www.businessweek.com/magazine/content/06_50/b4013001.htm.

all of the employees in the corporate office would be on the ROWE plan
and that the approach would figure prominently in recruiting efforts for the
company. The company reports dramatic decreases in voluntary turnover
as well as increases in productivity, as much as 35 percent, in departments
that have implemented ROWE.[234]

Still related to the issue of trust and control but with a slightly different
focus is the use of spaces that may be occupied by different companies.
For example, in the view of one telework symposium contributor, telework
centers have not lived up to their forecast because employers are resistant to
lease space that may be shared by competitors. Although they are not paying
for the competitor's leases, having that space available for competitors to
lease is an advantage management does not want to give, and there is the
potential that proprietary information may be compromised. Even on the
federal level, Pratt states that the telework center movement has not been
successful if you evaluate it in terms of the number of potential workers and
the number who actually use such centers.[235] In Pratt's view, we cannot deny
the human predilection for establishing and guarding our personal space
and territory; for that reason, telework faces an uphill battle, particularly
when it involves such leased space.

Other factors that will be critical in the growth curve of telework are such
things as tax incentives, how OSHA policies apply to the home environment
(there is government oversight of teleworking in terms of the regulations
that apply to it), continuing advances in technology, and the costs of such
technology and telecommunications.[236]

We are in the early stages of evaluating how workers react to alternative officing. One theme that has emerged is how important management
understanding and support of telecommuting needs to be if the venture
is to succeed. More than 50 percent of companies responding in one survey pointed to insufficient organizational support as the chief obstacle to
telecommuting.[237] Just as the transformation of the office to the open plan
led to a growth industry in research about those issues in the 1970s and
1980s, I expect to see research on teleworking and alternative officing rapidly
expand over the coming decade.

[234] Ibid, para. 11.

[235] Pratt, J. H. (2000). Employer scheduling, staffing, and work location issues. In *Telework:
The new workplace of the 21st century* (pp. 225–243).

[236] Van Horn & Storen (2000), p. 19.

[237] Piskurich, G. M. (1996, February). Making telecommuting work. *Training and Development*, 20–27.

TELEWORK AND THE ELASTICITY OF TIME

Most of the literature points to the benefits of telework to the employee, the employer, and the environment. But there are some drawbacks to teleworking for the employee. A case has been made that what increases during telework are the stretches of work, canceling the benefit of time flexibility. What often happens is that people just work more and longer hours, rather than using the flexibility that may exist to structure when they do the work.[238] In a small study of 44 workers, of whom 43 percent were employed and 48 percent were self-employed teleworkers, the concept of time was an issue, and in particular the fact that there were no clear boundaries between work and nonwork. Ironically, although flexibility of time was ranked at the top as a justification for doing telework, people didn't live that life; in other words, their work behavior did not reflect that flexibility. What got in the way of that flexibility were society's conventions related to work and the perceived influence of managers to constrain behavior. What happened was the encroachment of work on personal time. In this study "these teleworkers appeared to be strongly influenced by the old conventions of the office, social norms of time, explicit and implicit managerial demands and individual work ethics."[239]

Not every employee may be a good match for telework and the virtual office. The characteristics of employees who successfully adapt to this work style are those who (1) understand and are comfortable with their work, (2) are internally motivated and possess a well-developed work ethic, (3) can manage themselves, (4) can communicate effectively, (5) are open and willing to compromise, (6) understand the company's procedures, (7) are comfortable with technology to the point of being self-sufficient, and (8) are oriented toward results.[240]

Not only is it a matter of figuring out which employees are suited to telework. Certainly that is being done, as at least some companies recognize that individuals who are introverted and unlikely to ask for help may be a poor match working alone a good portion of their time.[241] Beyond the issue of matching individuals to telework, tasks remain to educate those "left behind." At least some attendees at the national symposium on telework in 2000 saw a backlash and for that reason less growth in the numbers of teleworkers, because those employees left behind are jealous and corporate

[238] Steward, B. (2000). Changing times: The meaning, measurement and use of time in teleworking. *Time & Society,* 9(1), 57–74.
[239] Ibid., p. 72.   [240] O'Connell (1996), p. 55.
[241] Ellen Bruce Keable (personal communication, May 30, 2009).

loyalty may be weakened.[242] In comments offered by one of the contributors to the national symposium, the point is made that the central issue behind telework is decentralizing the office, a view proposed in Nilles's 1998 book *Managing Telework: Strategies for Maximizing the Virtual Workforce*,[243] in which he talks about the "edifice complex" and the idea of eliminating it through decentralization. But if we are to decentralize the office, we must address the needs of those who are left without the option or who are a poor match for decentralization. If we do not, it is argued that the resentment felt by those still bound to the office may undermine some of the telework initiatives.[244]

THE FUTURE

One question that has been asked but not answered in my view, and the views of others, is "What is the role of design in a work world unbounded by physical space and linear time?"[245]

In 1986, Jean Wineman wrote about the future of the office, a precursor to a widely read article written on that topic by Turnage in 1990.[246] Wineman's thoughts about challenges in office design were the themes that repeatedly emerged in her book: how to accommodate individual choice and control; how to create a diversity of environments; how to involve workers in the process of workplace design; and how to increase communication across practitioners from different disciplines engaged in workplace design issues.[247] These issues continue to be important in telework, whether the workspace is a remote telework center or a home.

The move to mobility, as it is sometimes called, can transform the way we work; some would argue that it has done so already. But the move to mobility is still relatively new and small if one looks at the total number of

[242] Bowles, O. D. (2000). Comments. In *Telework: The new workplace of the 21st century* (pp. 43–53).

[243] Nilles, J. (1998). *Managing telework: Strategies for maximizing the virtual workforce.* New York: John Wiley and Sons, Inc.

[244] Bowles (2000).

[245] Smith, P. (1996). Big waves in jungle gyms: Alternative officing – alternative disciplines? In J. L. Nasar & B. B. Brown (Eds.), *Public and private places: Proceedings of the 27th Annual Conference of the Environmental Design Research Association* (pp. 190–191). Edmond, OK: EDRA.

[246] Turnage, J. J. (1990). The challenge of new workplace technology for psychology. *American Psychologist, 45,* 171–178.

[247] Wineman, J. (1986). Current issues and future directions. In J. Wineman (Ed.), *Behavioral issues in office design* (pp. 293–313). New York: Van Nostrand Reinhold Company.

workers who might use the flexibility it provides. There is great interest in following the telework movement and the move to mobility more generally. A number of groups monitor changes in work, such as the group Workplace Trends.[248] At its conference in 2008 one presentation was entitled "The impact on flexible working/virtual working – increase or decrease?" and a 2008 report on the status of telework in the federal government actually reported a decrease from 2007, primarily attributable to changes in a number of agencies where data security was an issue.[249]

With the move to mobility, one underlying, tongue-in-cheek response is, "Where is everybody?"[250] A 2007 document from the Atlanta summit on the move to mobility gives the following statistics: outside the United States, 60 percent of employees do not sit in the same facility as the person who manages them, but in the United States that percentage is 40 percent; having at least one team member in another country or another time zone is true of at least 75 percent of managers. Other informative statistics from this document are that there are 100 million cell phones in North America and that almost 50,000 people daily sign up for cell phone service; 10 billion email messages go out each day, and that number is projected to increase to 35 billion in the next 3 to 5 years; surfing the Web now challenges the time we spend watching television. The article reminds us about the typical, familiar "old" ways of working, where employees have been in one place, where we have face time, with supervision, and team members are in the same place. Now, things are turned upside down.

The questions for the future posed in this document are "How will technology be imbedded in the new workplace?" "How will new interfaces and devices be designed to be more simple and intuitive?" "Where are Web services technologies headed in the evolution of integrated workplace management systems?" With regard to the physical environment, the questions are "How will we remain connected to our company's culture while mobile? How will new social network apps like Facebook, Second Life and online Avatars [a]ffect work?"[251]

There is no turning back. We need to figure out how to embrace these choices and make them work for us. There have never been more choices in terms of working from anywhere. The exciting prospect is that we have

---

[248] http://www.workplacetrends.co.uk.

[249] U.S. Office of Personnel Management (2008).

[250] *Move-to-mobility: Workplace Knowledge Community* (2007, October). Workplace Community Presentation, Atlanta Summit.

[251] Ibid.

the chance to change the American landscape with this move to mobility. Office buildings need not dominate the urban landscape, and cubicles need not dominate their interiors. Spaces that better support the fundamental needs of privacy and territoriality are emerging, whether in our homes, our cars, or our cockpits.

5

The Landscape of Retail: Big Box and Main Street

PERSONAL REFLECTIONS

After reading a news article about the Jil Sander clothing store and its elegant design, I visited the store on the edge of Soho in New York City the summer of 2008, shortly after the store had opened. It was a work of art, with the bottom floor devoted to a series of manikins, perhaps five in total, on pedestals. That was it, except for the security guard. There was a small selection of clothing on the second floor, which was reached either by the marble stairs or by elevator.

At the other extreme, I can recount my first trip to IKEA, in Canton, Michigan, 2 years ago to help my sister purchase a desk for her daughter who was starting a job in Chicago. To say that I felt overwhelmed by the spaces and the amount of merchandise is a gross understatement. That IKEA experience was similar to my first trip to Toys 'R' Us in 1984 before my daughter was born. The giant toy retailer is said to be the first example of category killer, or a store that dominates its rivals in the marketplace through its vast offering of products in one domain, in this case, toys. Ironically, Toys 'R' Us is now said to be floundering because of the inroads made by Wal-Mart,[1] the behemoth general merchandise discounter, the ultimate in category killers. On that particular trip to the Toys 'R' Us store, I remember leaving completely overwhelmed, without a purchase. I knew nothing about merchandise for children, and I could not comprehend how it was possible to make a decision faced with that many possibilities. A colleague of mine in Rome, who is American by birth and whose spouse is Italian, told a similar story of the first time he took his wife to a Toys 'R'

---

[1] Spector, R. (2005). *Category killers: The retail revolution and its impact on consumer culture.* Boston: Harvard Business School Press, p. 182.

Us store in the United States. She left feeling overwhelmed as well; I don't know if she made a purchase.

My experience living for 4 months in the center of Rome (on the edge of the Piazza Navona) taught me a good deal about how Americans approach shopping. Why do we need an entire aisle of cereal when most grocery stores (markets) in the center of European cities have probably one-tenth the number. Despar, the grocery store where I shopped by the Pantheon in Rome, had fewer than 20 choices for cereal; the supermarket where I shop in New London, Connecticut, has more than 300 choices of boxed cereal by my count. Recently, the Aldi supermarket chain from Germany has been establishing a presence in the United States. What makes this development noteworthy is the marketing philosophy of the chain, which emphasizes carrying *fewer* selections, only about 1400 household and grocery items, than the stereotypical grocery chain. Limiting the choices enables Aldi to offer lower prices. Named Private Label Retailer of the Year in 2009, the headline of an article about the award says it best: "A frugal force."[2] In Ann Arbor, Michigan, Aldi is constructing a supermarket directly across the road from Plum Market, a decidedly upscale store with undoubtedly higher prices. In this difficult economy, a reasonable prediction is that Aldi will do well establishing a presence in Ann Arbor. As one of its dictums states, "Fancy stores have fancy prices. Keep it simple and save."[3]

Only in the last decade or so have social scientists begun to more actively examine the psychology of retail environments, adding to a body of research that had been the domain of researchers from the disciplines of business, marketing, and consumer studies. For example, when I checked the PsycINFO database on July 13, 2009, with the keywords "big box," only six entries were displayed, including an article on television (sometimes called a big box) and one on captive baboons (presumably housed in a big box). For the phrase "big box store," there were no entries.

It is not that social scientists have avoided the topic of such places as malls. On the contrary, in writing this book I can't remember how many times I came across articles about shopping malls as places to *recruit* people for research . . . on topics other than shopping. And the Marketing Research Association has spent a lot of time considering the "health" of consumer research in malls and what changes in the way people shop (e.g., more use of online approaches) may mean in terms of what is known as research

[2] Canning, K. (2009, April). A frugal force. http://www.shopaldismart.com/PL_Buyer .pdf?WT.z_src=banner&WT.ac=Banner-without-Alt-Tag.

[3] Welcome to Aldi. Our philosophy: "incredible value every day." http://www.aldifoods .com/us/html/company/Our_Philosophy_ENU_HTML.htm.

conducted through mall intercept (i.e., interception at the mall).[4] But as a focus of research, malls have been of little interest to social scientists. It may be that the topic itself seemed to have little academic sophistication. And more than one observer has noted the reticence with which the scholarly community has embraced the mall as a focus of study for academic journals.[5]

The academic community notwithstanding, this chapter will focus on the role of the physical environment in shopping, and in particular on the mall. Given the role of the Internet in our lives, the chapter will also examine the changes in the way we shop related to the role of e-commerce, as it is sometimes called. As the introduction to the book *Project on the City 2* states, "Shopping is arguably the last remaining form of public activity. Through a battery of increasingly predatory forms, shopping has infiltrated, colonized, and even replaced, almost every aspect of urban life. Town centers, suburbs, streets, and now airports, train stations, museums, hospitals, schools, the Internet, and the military are shaped by the mechanisms and spaces of shopping."[6]

Until I started to read material for this chapter, I had little idea that my personal experience with shopping dovetailed to a certain degree with the formative years of malls. I grew up in Ann Arbor, Michigan, about a 40-minute drive from Northland Center, located in Southfield, Michigan. This mall opened in 1954. Emil Pocock, a professor of history and coordinator of the American studies program at Eastern Connecticut State University, who has developed a number of useful Web sites about malls and shopping centers, reports that Northland was the largest mall in the world when it opened.[7] Victor Gruen, an architect and Austrian émigré and pivotal character in the history of shopping malls, designed the mall, working with representatives of the J. L. Hudson Company of Detroit to plan four malls in the suburbs of Detroit: Northland, Eastland, Westland, and Southland.[8]

Although Northland continues to function today, its physical presence (see Figure 5.1) clearly communicates a decline of its role in the community. This is a far cry from its role in the 1950s and 1960s. My brother-in-law grew up in Dearborn, Michigan (about 20 minutes from Northland), and

---

[4] Frost-Norton, T. (2005). The future of mall research: Current trends affecting the future of marketing research in malls. *Journal of Consumer Behaviour, 4*(4), 293–301.

[5] Bloch, P. H., Ridgway, N. M., & Dawson, S. A. (1994). The shopping mall as consumer habitat. *Journal of Retailing, 70*(1), 23–42.

[6] Chung, C. J., Inaba, J., Koolhaas, R., & Leong, S. T. (2001). *Harvard Design School guide to shopping.* New York: Tachen, Frontispiece.

[7] Pocock, E. http://nutmeg/easternct.edu/~pocock/.

[8] Gruen, V. (1973). *Centers for the urban environment: Survival of the cities.* New York: Van Nostrand Reinhold, pp. 23–24.

FIGURE 5.1. Northland Center

has fond memories of family shopping trips to Northland, which, in its newness and concept, was exciting and provided much more stimulation that the staid streets of Dearborn. My brother-in-law recalled a number of things about the mall, including the elephant statues, now in a grassy buffer on the perimeter of the Northland parking lot. With fond memories of these elephants, my sister and I took special care to photograph these statues for him. Following its construction, this innovative mall may have been viewed as the focal point of the community with arts, music, and special events. But today, in my opinion, Northland is dominated by its parking lots, a somewhat ironic fact given that many of its shoppers use public transportation. On the day my sister and I visited in June 2009, there were significant numbers of shoppers waiting for the bus and few cars in the vast parking lots.

Northland and Gruen's next mall, Southdale, was the collaborative effort of Gruen and the Dayton-Hudson alliance. In the mid-1950s a development company, the Dayton-Hudson Company, was formed by the Dayton department stores in Minneapolis and Hudson department stores in Detroit.[9] Southdale Center, the first enclosed mall in the United States, is located in Edina, Minnesota. Although Gruen envisioned an integrated area that

[9] Kowinski, W. (1985). *The malling of America: An inside look at the great consumer paradise.* New York: William Morrow and Company, Inc., p. 117.

would include housing and schools, that never materialized.[10] Northland was more consistent with the kind of integration that Gruen had envisioned. In the decade after Northland's construction, residential units, office buildings, health care and research laboratories as well as a hotel were constructed in the area around the mall, according to William Kowinski in *The Malling of America.* "It was the first real experiment in metro-nucleation planned around a shopping mall."[11]

But that kind of integration is atypical. As a prototype, malls have been characterized by access from major highway arteries but isolation from residential developments. Over time this combination has rendered the mall lifeless, a criticism being addressed by newer kinds of developments called "lifestyle" centers and mixed-use developments (more on those later).

I also have a number of personal memories of Hudson's department store. Growing up in Ann Arbor, Michigan, some 45 minutes from Detroit, one of my fond memories was our annual family outing to see Santa Claus in downtown Detroit (in the 1950s, Detroit did have a vital downtown). In Hudson's vast department store, Santa was located on perhaps the 13th floor, if memory serves me, and on the floor leading up to the official "Santa's lap" visit, there were aisles and aisles stacked with toys.

On the way back to the car, which we often parked in an underground garage at Grand Circus Park, we stopped at the Mayflower Coffee Shop on Woodward Avenue, about a block north of Hudson's, for a box of its wonderful glazed donuts. For the baby boomer generation, fond memories like these are likely to return if we take our children to reexperience this annual rite, but now such visits typically occur in a suburban mall. Ironically, researchers have shown that it is the parents and guardians of the children taken to see Santa who express happiness over the event; the vast majority of the children seem to be indifferent to the experience![12] Sadly, Detroit's population has dropped by as much as 50 percent since the Census of 1950.[13]

Other memories I have of visiting stores also point to the way the shopping environment and culture have changed in the United States. My mother occasionally went to a store named Muehlig's on Main Street in Ann Arbor. B. E. Muehlig's was what was known as a dry goods (and notions) store,

---

[10] Matthews, P. (2008, December 20). Matters of the mall. *The Press* (Christchurch, New Zealand), para. 16. http://www.stuff.co.nz/the-press/lifestyle/769797.

[11] Kowinski (1985), p. 118.

[12] Trinkaus, J. (2007). Visiting Santa: An additional look. *Psychological Reports, 101*(3), 779–783.

[13] Johnson, B. (2008, May 1). Baby boom nation. *National Real Estate Investor*, pp. 50–53. http://nreionline.com/mag/real_estate_baby_boom_nation_0501/, paras. 9–10.

primarily selling fabric. What fascinated me most about the store was its system of pneumatic tubes. These were tubes in which the sales clerk inserted your money and the bill indicating how much you owed; the tube was then whisked pneumatically to the cashier on a floor above, who then sent back your change and receipt. You may be familiar with the pneumatic tube system, but for a different reason. Pneumatic tubes are sometimes used on the exterior (outboard) lanes of drive-through banks.

Near Muehlig's on Main Street in Ann Arbor was Goodyear's, the quintessential department store. Most of the goods, for example, fine ladies' handbags, were enclosed in glass cases, and you had to ask to see an item. I wonder the extent to which such requests cut down on the number of purchases. Recently at a small store selling silk scarves in Florence, Italy, near the well-known church Santa Croce, the proprietor scolded me and another woman (with children) for "touching" the scarves on display. There was no handling the merchandise! In general my experience shopping in Italy suggested to me that the merchants were far less comfortable with the idea of customers handling the merchandise than is true in the United States.

Still other memories have to do with Sears and Montgomery Ward, which started as a mail order operation in 1872 and was similar to Sears; both had big catalogues. Montgomery Ward promised "satisfaction guaranteed or your money back" as early as 1875.[14] My mother, with five rambunctious children to clothe, often ordered items out of their large catalogues. Catalogue ordering was much easier than taking children into a store. Catalogue shopping is a form of what is known as remote shopping, and it mirrors the convenience of online shopping (discussed later in this chapter) in many ways. Another ritual many baby boomers may remember is the giant Sears toy catalogue, which occupied hours of time in the development of one's holiday "list."

THE EVOLUTION OF SHOPPING MALLS: THEIR BIRTH, DEATH, AND TRANSFORMATION

Although shopping centers can be traced to the early part of the 20th century, I want to start our journey in the mid-1950s. In the first chapter of this book, we saw what happened post–World War II, with the exodus of residents from the cities to the suburbs, spurred on by the expansion of those suburbs, precipitated by cheap land and the expansion of the highway system, among

[14] Latham, F. B. (1972). *1872–1972 A century of serving consumers: The story of Montgomery Ward.* Chicago: Montgomery Ward & Co., Inc.

other governmental initiatives. One argument has been made that until the 1960s, we as Americans had our needs met by the downtowns, and particularly Main Street, located near our homes. "But as Baby Boomers began migrating out of the cities by the 1960s, Main Street retailing faced a slow and painful extinction. . . . Americans fled to the wide-open spaces of the suburbs, thanks to new freeways and a boom in automobile production."[15] If downtown stores did not themselves establish a mall presence, they struggled, which was ultimately the case with Montgomery Ward, which lagged behind its peers, Sears and J. C. Penney, in building retail branches of its downtown stores.

When we look around, the variety of shopping venues available to us has increased dramatically since the mid-20th century, whether we think about malls in suburbs, power centers filled with big box stores, or lifestyle centers that look like the main streets of the 1950s. Writing about the baby boomer generation, author Ben Johnson asks, "Will malls be around 50 years from now?"[16] The answer may be "yes," but the form the mall will take in its next iteration (and it will not be its last) may look more like a nostalgic movie set for the Main Street of the 1950s than ever existed. Further, there may be fewer malls for the foreseeable future. Although a good deal of press during the recent economic downturn has focused on the home mortgage crisis, the commercial real estate market has been affected as well. Malls are part of that market, and they have been defaulting in high numbers, with delinquency rates at 7 percent, double the rate in the last year, according to news reports. Additionally, General Growth Properties, Inc. (GGP) filed for bankruptcy under Chapter 11. In the United States, GGP is the second largest owner of shopping malls.[17]

With regard to the development of the shopping mall, experts outside the United States who have also studied the history of the shopping center point to the impact of the automobile on the growth of shopping centers, noting that when housing spread away from the city center and people relied more on the automobile to get to work and complete tasks of daily living, the mall emerged. "Shopping [centers] are built for a car-driving population," in the opinion of Matthew Bailey, an academic in Australia whose Ph.D. involved the history of shopping centers.[18]

---

[15] Johnson (2008), para. 8.   [16] Ibid., para. 35.

[17] Zibel, A. (2009, July 10). Commercial real estate "a ticking bomb." *The New London Day,* Business, pp. C7–8.

[18] Campion, V. (2008, August 30). Fuel prices drive a corner shop revival. *The Daily Telegraph (Australia), 1-State Edition, Local,* p. 18, para. 4. http://www.news.com.au/story/0,23599, 24262391-2,00.html.

Writing in the *National Real Estate Investor*, Ben Johnson links the baby boom generation, the 75+ million babies born between 1946–1964 in the United States, to the growth of shopping malls and consumerism as a way of life, given the prosperity that the baby boomer generation has enjoyed. The article also points to the constant change in retail, which he compares to a living organism, with change a reflection of the dictates of the consumer. The article features John Bucksbaum, the CEO of GGP. Its real estate investment trust (REIT) has approximately 180 million sq. ft. of retail space and is among the country's top owners of mall properties.[19] There are an estimated 50,000 shopping centers in the United States today and more than 100,000 globally.[20]

THE FIRST MALLS

Northland Center, built in 1954 in Southfield, Michigan, is often credited with being the first real mall, at least one that would use the idea of an anchor department store and cluster stores around it. Northland was the work of Victor Gruen, an émigré from Austria with an architecture degree. At the time it was constructed, Northland was the largest shopping center in the world, at 1.2 million sq. ft.[21] With Hudson's department store as the anchor store, Northland marked a successful marriage between Gruen and the Dayton family and its developments. There were 110 stores covering two levels, with a department store in the center serving as anchor. Following the success of Northland, Gruen was hired by the Dayton-Hudson Company to build a mall in Edina, Minnesota, in 1956, Southdale Center, for which the Dayton department store served as one of two anchors.

Southdale Center in Edina, Minnesota, is claimed to be the first "true shopping mall" in the typical sense, in that the mall is enclosed.[22] What is said to have been one of the captivating parts of Gruen's design work for the interiors was "the way he used arcades and eye-level display cases to lure customers into stores almost against their will. As a critic complained, his shops were like mousetraps. A few years later the same would be said of his shopping malls."[23] Although this article in *The Economist* explains that an outdoor shopping center had appeared in Los Angeles in 1947, an outdoor approach would not work for the Midwest with its difficult winter

[19] Johnson (2008), para 3.   [20] Ibid., para. 4.
[21] Ibid., para. 14.
[22] Birth, death and shopping: The rise and fall of the shopping mall. (2007, December 22). *The Economist*, 385(8560), pp. 102–104. http://jowanderer.wordpress.com/2008/01/04/birth-death-and-shopping/.
[23] Ibid., para. 3.

climate, and Gruen approached that problem by roofing the structure and providing an HVAC (heating, ventilation, and air-conditioning) system that maintained the temperature at 75 degrees, reported to have been described as "Eternal Spring."[24] I was amused to read that among the things Gruen was described to have gotten "right" the first time was the use of a wayfinding device that featured animal signs as a means to trigger shoppers to remember where they parked [(a much more effective way than simply relying on standard alphanumeric approaches (e.g., B3)]. Another aspect of the mall deemed effective was essentially using a road that sloped so that the entrance could be achieved on two levels.

Speaking about the use of an atrium and density of the mall, packing in a relatively large number of stores in a small space, *The Economist* article states, "Oddly, this most suburban invention was supposed to evoke a European city centre. Hence Southdale's density and its atrium, where shoppers were expected to sit and debate over cups of coffee, just as they do in the Piazza San Marco or the Place Dauphine."[25] The article then describes the evolution (devolution perhaps) of the mall as I have observed in my own community. Parenthetically, I visited the Galleria Vittorio Emmanuelle II in Milan and the Galleria Umberto I in Naples (both of which date from the second half of the 19th century) in spring 2009. The Galleria in Milan is often pointed to as a precursor to our modern enclosed shopping centers, with its covered arcade and glass-domed roof. Originally its image was decidedly upscale, but I was dismayed to see that one of its current tenants is McDonald's, in a location at the junction of the galleria's two main corridors, prime real estate, as it were (see Figure 5.2).

Gruen, the article claims, citing Jeffrey Hardwick's biography of Gruen (*Mall Maker: Victor Gruen, Architect of an American Dream*), did not see his malls as a threat to the core of downtown shopping. In fact, as Hardwick explains, these malls often had outposts of downtown stores. But of course the malls did, eventually, hurt the core of downtown, although malls by themselves cannot be tagged with the demise of cities in the United States. In my own community, I remember the effect of the Crystal Mall, the first large enclosed mall in southeastern Connecticut (which has always been something of a retail backwater, in my humble opinion), which opened in 1984 with great anticipation. The Crystal Mall had 1 million sq. ft. of indoor retail space on two floors.[26] Today, Macy's has replaced Jordan Marsh and Filene's; J. C. Penney and Sears, among the original anchors, remain. The

---

[24] Ibid., para. 4.   [25] Ibid., para. 6.

[26] Dale, K., & Crompton, K. (2008, September 1). Chain retail for New London just a pipe dream, brokers say. *The Day*, pp. A1, A3.

FIGURE 5.2. McDonald's, Galleria Vittorio Emanuele II, Milan

Filene's space is now only partly filled by Bed, Bath, and Beyond and by The Christmas Tree Shoppes.

The effect of the mall was particularly poignant for a staid men's clothing store, Benoit's, which had a premier location in downtown New London but was lured to open a store in the mall. In this case, Benoit's did not retain its downtown location. Over time, the store failed. The rent at its large store at the mall outstripped its business, and additional expenses came from the greater number of hours, relative to its downtown location, that the store had to be open to conform to the mall's policies. Although it moved to a less expensive location in a mall less than a mile away, that move was doomed. The new location in the Crossroads Centre, a venue with Bernie's electronics and Bob's clothing store, was not consistent with the upscale image Benoit's had always maintained, to say nothing of the fact that this particular mall is not conveniently located in my opinion.

Gruen also had a hand in the urban plan of Kalamazoo, Michigan, in the sense that he recommended closing one of the major through streets, Burdick, to traffic to create what might be called a pedestrian mall, opened in 1959 and said to be the first pedestrian mall in the United States.[27] Many communities in the United States saw the pedestrian mall as a quick remedy

[27] Steinhauer, J. (1996, November 5). Downtown retailing trend again favors a car culture. *NYTimes.com.* http://www.nytimes.com/1996/11/05/business/downtown-retailing-trend-again-favors-a-car-culture.html?pagewanted=print.

for the ailing downtown economy, and as Gruen's biographer points out, it was much easier to close a street than to build a mall. But over time, these pedestrian malls failed, and many, like the one in Kalamazoo, were at least partly reopened to traffic. Writing about this pedestrian mall in Kalamazoo in the *National Real Estate Investor*, Johnson says that by closing the street to traffic, "in effect, Gruen was trying to bring the shopping center back downtown. As with Northland and the Southdale mall in metro Detroit and Minneapolis, only the retail portion of Gruen's vision was realized for the new Burdick Street Mall."[28]

New London, Connecticut, had its own version of the pedestrian mall, called Captain's Walk, which was created in 1973 and ripped up and reopened to traffic as State Street in 1991. Some have referred to the mall as a "semi-mall," in the sense that the entire length of the street was not fully closed to traffic.[29] A failed pedestrian mall, Captain's Walk was a victim of many things, including a poor choice about an extensive use of cobblestones, which made walking difficult, the lack of attractive parking offsite, the proportions of the walk that made it too long to traverse going uphill, and the competition from the new Crystal Mall. One online list of pedestrian malls in the United Sates lists 56 as at least partially reopened, including both the one in Kalamazoo and the one in New London, Connecticut; 9 as successful; and 7 as struggling.[30]

Interwoven with the flight of Americans to the suburbs, the growth in malls was spurred by the change in tax laws related to the depreciation of buildings, a change that, as we saw in the chapter on office environments, affected the construction of office buildings as well. There were also tax incentives in terms of the kind of financing offered. It was profitable to build malls.

Before reviewing the fall and rebirth of the mall (as we know it), let's look at what happens at the mall and some research on mall users.

WHAT TO DO AT THE MALL? ANYTHING YOU WANT

The mall has become a place of leisure for many age groups, replacing venues like the park or town square.[31,32] The mall has been associated with a lifestyle

---

[28] Johnson (2008), paras. 17–18.

[29] Rubenstein, H. M. (1992). *Pedestrian malls, streetscapes, and urban spaces.* New York: John Wiley & Sons, Inc.

[30] http://www.nfta.com/MainStreet/Appendix&20A.pdf.

[31] Berida, B. M. V., & Dimaculangan, S. F. C. (2008, October 17). Special feature: Modern shopping; City of malls, S2/7. http://nishberida.blogspot.com/2008/11/october-17-2008.html.

[32] Roberts, J. (1987). Buying leisure. *Leisure Studies, 6*(1), 87–91.

as well, called "malling."[33] With the combination of shopping and entertainment, malls have sometimes been said to provide "shopertainment."[34] The availability of entertainment rather than simply goods prompts repeated visits. There is even some suggestion that this idea of a malling lifestyle is emerging in places like western China.[35] Particularly with the recession of 2008, it seems that malls are welcoming a variety of activities; events ranging from concerts and karaoke to exercise, paintball, laser tag, ice skating, and wave-riding help get people through the mall doors. As one article suggested, "Maybe they'll shop later."[36]

Truly, you can do almost anything at the mall. At least in the minds of some, the mall has been elevated to a kind of status alongside the museum, in terms of its ability to offer consumption (of goods rather than art) and entertainment.[37] A sad commentary, in my view, is a statistic that reports that although gallery space has increased by 3 percent, the space devoted to museum stores in the United States has increased by 29 percent since 1992.[38]

Malls have expected activities like shopping at one end of the continuum, and at the other there are activities like having a root canal or an annual physical. The prestigious Mayo Clinic has leased space at the Mall of America and may offer such services as screenings, health and wellness assessments, and telemedicine.[39] In between the seeming behavioral opposites of shopping and health care are tarot card readings, haircuts, and pedicures. And of course there is WiFi. The mall provides a walking course for seniors who want to maintain their vitality and a social environment for teens as well. There are classes and fundraisers. For example, a homeless shelter in my community sponsors an annual fundraiser at our Crystal Mall (so named for the Waterford chandelier that hangs in its main concourse).

---

[33] Berida & Dimaculangan (2008), para. 9.

[34] Ganesan, V. (2007, May 30). Reaching for the mall of fame. *New Straits Times* (Malaysia), p. 48. http://www.ytlcommunity.com/commnews/shownews.asp?newsid=29592, para. 2.

[35] Tsang, A. S. L., Zhuang, G., Li, F., & Zhous, N. (2003). A comparison of shopping behavior in Xi'an and Hong Kong malls: Utilitarian versus non-utilitarian shoppers. *Journal of International Consumer Marketing, 16*(1), 29–46.

[36] Rosenbloom, S. (2009, July 12). Malls see plenty of action, but less of it is shopping. *The New York Times*, Metropolitan, pp. CT1, CT7, p. CT7.

[37] Prior, N. (2005). A question of perception: Bourdieu, art and the postmodern. *British Journal of Sociology, 56*(1), 123–139.

[38] Leong, S. T. (2001). . . . And then there was shopping. In C. J. Chung, J. Inaba, R. Koolhaas, & S. T. Leong (Eds.). *Harvard Design School guide to shopping* (pp. 128–155). New York: Tachen, p. 147.

[39] Chen, M.-Y. (2009, June 17). Mayo Clinic going to Mall of America. *McClatchy-Tribune Business News*. http://www.startribune.com/local/south/48279737.html?elr=KArks8c7 PaP3E77K_3c::D3aDhUxWoW_vcOiDUiacyKU7DYaGEP7vDEh7P:DiUs.

Personal grooming has its place at the mall, from something tame like a foot massage or hair straightening to something less tame (or potentially less relaxing)[40] like eyebrow plucking (via eyebrow threading). There is acupressure (with pressure instead of needles), ear piercing, exercise instruction, and therapeutic massage.[41] Most of these activities take place in the main concourse tied to pushcarts or freestanding kiosks of one sort or another. These kiosks, which tend to be owned by locals as opposed to retail chains, were given their start at Rouse's Faneuil Hall festival marketplace in Boston, and number more than 150,000, according to Paco Underhill,[42] who describes himself as a retail anthropologist and whose consulting business, Envirosell, examines what happens when people encounter products in particular spaces.

People watch television at the mall as well (consider the number of people who stop in any store such as Sears or Best Buy to watch sports on Sunday afternoon). And of course people exercise at the mall (e.g., they walk).[43] It is a place where health kiosks provide information about Alzheimer's disease.[44]

With the opening of the Mall at Wellington Green, PDQ Care (Patients Deserve Quality) has opened what it thinks is the nation's first walk-in clinic combined with pharmacy. This segment of the health care market will grow dramatically, it is predicted, offering nonemergency services at low cost. There were 126 walk-in clinics as 2006 started, and that number grew to more than 900 clinics in 2008. These in-store clinics are expected to be built by Wal-Mart and CVS/Caremark among others.[45] PDQ Care, Inc. is participating in such growth. One of the partners quoted in the article states, "Not only do we have a built-in customer base with an estimated 3,000 employees at the mall and surrounding businesses, but daily foot

---

[40] Flaim, D. (2008, December 11). Primp place: There's beauty in store at the mall. *Newsday*, Explore LI, p. B02.

[41] McIntyre, E. (2004). Therapeutic massage: An amazing modality. *Home Health Care Management & Practice, 16*(6), 516–520.

[42] Underhill, P. (2004). *Call of the mall*. New York: Simon & Schuster, p. 97.

[43] Eyler, A. A., Brownson, R. C., Bacak, S. J., & Housemann, R. A. (2003). The epidemiology of walking for physical activity in the United States. *Medicine & Science in Sports & Exercise, 35*(9), 1529–1536.

[44] Connell, C. M., Shaw, B. A., Holmes, S. B., Hudson, M. L., Derry, H. A., & Strecher, V. J. (2003). The development of an Alzheimer's disease channel for the Michigan Interactive Health Kiosk Project. *Journal of Health Communication, 8*(1), 11–22.

[45] PDQ Care, Inc (2008, April 28); Shopping for a check-up? PDQ care opens nation's first walk-in clinic and pharmacy in a mall. *Business Wire*, paras. 1–5. http://www.allbusiness .com/health-care/health-care-facilities-clinics/10181409-1.html.

traffic in malls is significantly higher than our retail competitors by 2 to 11 times."[46]

The marriage of medical care with declining use of malls has also led to the idea of using empty or largely empty malls as new "medical malls," a trend mentioned in Chapter 2, bringing health care to communities in which access to such care is limited. Prince Georges County in Maryland is one community considering this kind of mall conversion.[47] The article reports that although the concept of a medical mall has existed for about 2 decades, nationwide there are on the order of only 50 such malls.

Parenthetically, when communities have tried to cut back on early morning hours for walking (i.e., the hours before stores officially open), there has often been a backlash, with a petition to the mall owner, in one case the Simon Property Group, and associated newspaper coverage with the tongue-in-cheek headline "cane mutiny."[48] But the first amendment rights of free speech are not protected in malls, at least since the 1980s, although people often think about malls as a public domain. In the article about the change in mall walking hours at Jefferson Valley Mall, Pace Professor of Constitutional Law Ralph Stein is quoted saying, "There is no right whatsoever to access to the mall before it opens up. This whole business of mall walking in the United States is an accommodation for good will."[49] There was some reversal on the part of the mall regarding which spaces the walkers could use, but the earlier morning hours were not reinstated. Emil Pocock, who maintains a Web site on shopping malls, is quoted in the article as stating, "The irony is that the earliest builders of big malls, in the 1950s, actually conceived malls as the new public space for suburban communities, because there was a recognition that new suburbs didn't have natural civic centers."[50] And although those early malls included spaces targeted as public, for example, assembly halls, such spaces were eliminated when mall developers recognized revenue loss associated with those kinds of spaces.

[46] Ibid., para. 8.
[47] Wiggins, O. (2008, July 26). One-stop spot for health-care needs; officials say "medical malls" could make services more accessible, convenient. *The Washington Post*, Suburban Edition, Metro, p. C06. http://www.washingtonpost.com/wp-dyn/content/article/2008/07/26/AR2008072601657.html.
[48] Lombardi, K. S. (2008, March 2). In curbing walking sprees, a mall sets off protests. Section WE, *Westchester Weekly Disk*; County Lines, P1. Dateline: Yorktown Heights, para. 4. http://www.nytimes.com/2008/03/02/nyregion/nyregionspecial2/02mallwe.html.
[49] Ibid., para. 7. [50] Ibid., para. 16.

THE MALL OF AMERICA AND OTHER "LARGE" SHOPPING VENUES

In terms of expanding the kinds of things you can do at the mall, it would be hard to write a chapter on retail spaces without mentioning the Mall of America in Bloomington, Minnesota, a suburb of the twin cities of Minneapolis/St. Paul. The mall opened with great fanfare in August 1992. It is overwhelming, to say the least, with as many as 520 stores and 50 restaurants, according to its Web site in the summer of 2009. The mall also has an amazing array of entertainment, from theme parks with roller coasters to skating rinks, flight simulators, and an aquarium.[51]

Although the Mall of America is not the largest in North America (that title goes to the West Edmonton Mall in Canada, with more than 3,800,000 million sq. ft. of retail space, more than 800 stores, and World Waterpark, the largest indoor waterpark in North America, among other attractions),[52] the Mall of America is arguably the most well-known mall in the United States. Outside of the United States, one of the largest malls in the world (at this point the fourth largest)[53] and often written about is the Mall of the Emirates, in Dubai, which features an indoor ski slope, Ski Dubai.[54] I remember seeing the ski slope featured on the "Where in the World Is Matt Lauer?" series on *The Today Show* in 2007. In what some might see as a political irony, the largest shopping malls in the world are now being built in China.

WHO USES THE MALL AND WHY?

"Why is it that retail is so big," asks Paul Ballantine, an academic who studies shopping and consumerism. His answer: "Basically people want more and more. You have churches closing down and everyone goes to the mall on a Sunday morning."[55] In his book *Going Broke: Why Americans Can't Hold on to Their Money,*[56] my colleague Stuart Vyse has driven home problems that occur when such acquisition is fueled by access to easy consumer credit. Shopping malls play a role in exposing consumers to goods that they

---

[51] http://www.mallofamerica.com/#/about/about/information.
[52] http://www.westedmontonmall.com/.
[53] World's largest shopping malls. http://nutmeg.easternct.edu/~pocock/MallsWorld.htm.
[54] Ganesan (2007), para. 31.   [55] Matthews (2008), para. 49.
[56] Vyse, S. (2008). *Going broke: Why Americans can't hold on to their money.* New York: Oxford University Press.

then desire to purchase[57] but perhaps cannot afford. Researchers have even discussed our penchant for shopping and consumption in evolutionary terms, linking it to foraging, among other behaviors.

Who uses the mall and why? In addition to describing mall users in terms of the usual categories (i.e., sex, age, and income), one can describe the kinds of patterns of use people exhibit at the mall. This kind of description has been offered by a number of writers. Investigators repeatedly have asked the question why people shop and have examined as many as 24 motives for shopping.[58] From a rational economic point of view, we should all stay home and order everything online. That would save time, if not money. But we do not. The mall satisfies a number of psychological needs that have little to do with the actual purchases we make, and more to do with the pleasure we derive from the process of being there, including social needs.[59]

But people frequent the mall for different reasons. One of the most intriguing typologies emerges from research done at three different super-regional malls in the United States, with 600 respondents. The typology that emerged describes mall users as mall enthusiasts (24 percent), traditionalists (28 percent), grazers (20 percent), and minimalists (28 percent). Enthusiasts embrace the mall, with high levels of purchase and what is called "experiential consumption," essentially the notion that enthusiasts take in all aspects of the mall. Traditionalists also make purchases but are unlikely to consume the other aspects of the mall, such as eating, browsing, or use of other services (e.g., hair salon). The grazers do what you might expect from their label; they browse and eat, but they also make impulse purchases. Finally, the minimalists don't do much in any of the activity categories. What makes this research different, according to its authors, is the focus on the mall itself as a consumer habitat, rather than on the stores within the mall. Further, these categories were able to describe individuals across age and socioeconomic status, and in that sense they are fairly robust.[60]

---

[57] Erasmus, A. C., & Lebani, K. (2008). Store cards: Is it a matter of convenience or is the facility used to sustain lavish consumption? *International Journal of Consumer Studies*, 32(3), 211–221.

[58] Yavas, U. (2001). Patronage motives and product purchase patterns: A correspondence analysis. *Marketing Intelligence & Planning*, 19(2), 97–102.

[59] Uzzell, D. L. (1995). The myth of the indoor city. *Journal of Environmental Psychology*, 15(4), 299–310.

[60] Bloch, P. H., Ridgway, N. M., & Dawson, S. A. (1994). The shopping mall as consumer habitat. *Journal of Retailing*, 70(1), 23–42.

It should come as no surprise that women are more likely to shop at the mall than men. Underhill notes that men have been much more dominant as shoppers in the supermarket than in the mall.[61] Although men walk faster than women on a city street, he says, the opposite is true in malls, and it is women who dominate the mall, where they "inhabit the place with a true shopper's sense of purpose."[62] As William Taubman, COO of Taubman Centers, has indicated, the customer who comes to the mall is a "she," and she is interested in shopping. Parenthetically, Taubman is not convinced about the value of what has been labeled "shoppertainment," given his conviction that the "she" is fundamentally interested in shopping. Quoted in an article, he stated, "Our purpose is first and foremost to create a comfortable and safe shopping environment. . . . The US customer comes to the shopping centre for the brands. She is not necessarily interested in entertainment while shopping. . . . People have wasted billions of dollars on these developments, which now stand empty."[63]

MALLS HAVE PERSONALITIES

Does the image of the mall influence our perception of the stores housed therein and the likelihood that we will shop there? Yes. The mix of stores in any given mall, and often in a particular section of the mall, tells us something about image. At the Westfarms Mall in West Hartford, Connecticut, one prominent anchor is Nordstrom's, and at Nordstrom's end of the mall you see stores, such as Apple, that are complementary to the kind of price points Nordstrom's offers (including Collezioni Armani at the high end). This proximity focuses attention on the power of such complementary adjacencies. At the same time, keeping with its upscale image, high-end retailers such as Coach, Louis Vuitton, and Tiffany are sprinkled throughout the mall, encouraging people to delve further into the mall to pursue these pricey wares. Moreover, consistent with its image, the Westfarms Mall doesn't have a food court in the typical sense. The large center common space of the mall offers Starbucks surrounded by lounge seating and the customer service center.

Researchers have used self-congruity theory to explain that the perception of stores within a mall is influenced by the social class image of that

---

[61] Underhill (1999). *Why we buy: The science of shopping.* New York: Touchstone.

[62] Underhill (2004), p. 42.

[63] Radebe, S. (2007, October 12). Reinventing retail. *Financial Mail* (South Africa). Economy, Business, & Finance, p. 76, paras. 9–10.

mall.[64] In other words, not only do stores have images and personalities, but so, too, do the malls themselves. Self-congruity theory suggests that we like to see ourselves as more upscale than we are in reality. To that end, we might see ourselves having greater self-congruity and want to shop at a mall that is upscale rather than at one that offers lower-priced merchandise. Research advises that mall managers need to keep in mind the audience they target and shape the mall environment accordingly. For that reason, it is somewhat surprising that one of the major entrances to the Nordstrom's store at the Westfarms Mall is through an unattractive parking garage. Parenthetically, the entrance into Nordstrom's through the mall itself conforms to one of Paco Underhill's observations that one of the greatest synergies in shopping is between shoes and cosmetics. As he explains, women are most interested in their faces and their feet, and as you wait for the shoe salesperson to look for your size in a particular style, you can browse in cosmetics. Thus, as you enter Nordstrom's from the mall itself, the vast shoe department is to your left and the vast cosmetics department is to your right.

Beyond self-congruity theory and the demographic of gender, other demographic aspects, particularly use of the mall by different age groups, has tended to be of interest to researchers. The two groups that have garnered most attention are essentially at opposite ends of the age spectrum. Both, it could be argued, lack a base of power in society. These groups are teenagers and the elderly.

TEENAGERS AND THE ELDERLY

Teenagers are a core group of mall users, but one that not infrequently causes problems when groups of teenagers roam the mall without adults. Plenty of teenagers without supervision use malls responsibly, and they have money to spend. One market research estimate is that in 2006, teens had $153 billion of spending power.[65] Research in the 1980s indicated that teenagers typically went to the mall with friends, but not often with their parents. And a survey indicated that 63 percent considered themselves regular users of the mall and spent from 1–5 hours there at a time. Shopping was a reason for being there among only about half

[64] Chebat, J-C., Sirgy, M. J., & St. James, V. (2006). Upscale image transfer from malls to stores: A self-image congruence explanation. *Journal of Business Research, 59*(12), 1288–1296.

[65] Spending power of the teen consumer – US. http://www.marketresearch.com/product/display.asp?productid=1353518.

of the teenagers interviewed. This research[66] makes a case for the mall as a kind of third space for teenagers, a description used by others as well.[67]

But some teenagers are less responsible, involved in behaviors that range from simply making noise to shoplifting and fights, some of these actions precipitated by alcohol, and some malls have developed policies to limit the free ranging of teenagers. For example, at Delaware's largest shopping center, the Christiana Mall, policies as of July 11, 2008, include no solo minors on Friday and Saturday after 5 p.m., with security guards checking identification at the door after that hour; each chaperone can be responsible for a maximum of four teenagers.[68] The International Council of Shopping Centers, cited in the article on this Delaware mall, indicates that the Christiana Mall became the 55th mall in the United States with a policy requiring that teenage mall-goers have chaperones, at least during specific periods such as Friday and Saturday evenings. The Mall of America, the article reports, has such a policy. A look at that policy on the Mall of America Web site[69] in July 2009 revealed a Friday and Saturday night restriction; from 4 p.m. until closing, youth under 16 have to be accompanied by someone 21 years or older. More lenient than the Christiana policy, one adult may supervise up to 10 youths.

This idea of what is called an "escort policy" appears to have met with success. With more than 1000 enclosed malls in the United States, the number of malls with such escort policies for teenagers is relatively small, but this movement has made an impact, at least in terms of coverage in the press. Citing data from the International Council on Shopping Centers, this article reports that the Mall of America created the first such escort policy in 1996. The payoff (pun intended) for such a policy is literally a payoff, as malls with such escort policies have experienced increases in sales, decreases in retail fraud, as well as a reduction in loitering.[70] Data related to the effects of changes at the Mall of America are impressive. In 1995, the mall had as many as 300 incidents of such things as fights; following the implementation of the escort policy, the mall reported 2 such incidents.[71]

---

[66] Anthony, K. H. (1985). The shopping mall: A teenage hangout. *Adolescence, 20*(78), 307–312.

[67] Matthews, H., Taylor, M., Percy-Smith, B., & Limb, M. (2000). The unacceptable flaneur: The shopping mall as a teenage hangout. *Childhood: A Global Journal of Child Research, 7*(3), 279–294.

[68] Nunnally, D., & Pipitone, N. (2008, June 19). Del. mall imposes a curfew. *Philadelphia Inquirer*, Inquirer Business Homepage, p. B01. http://www.specialtyretail.com/news/2008/06/delaware_mall_curfew.

[69] http://www.mallofamerica.com/#/parental-escorts/home/parental-escort-policy.

[70] Nunnally & Pipitone (2008).   [71] Ibid.

As an adult, it may be easy to lump teenagers into one homogeneous group, but teenagers are no more homogeneous than any other age group. Moreover, in the research literature teenagers are not infrequently grouped into the subcategories of preteens (generally considered those between the ages of 9 and 12) and those between 13 and 19. And these groups differ significantly in the way they view the mall experience. Preteens, for example, are much more enthusiastic about all of the stimulation a mall provides, whereas students in high school tend to be more critical of the mall experience and feel that adults do not appreciate their intelligence. Many teenagers are sophisticated, and as the research indicates, they understand that retailers are "selling" to them.[72]

Why do teenagers go to the mall? Do their motivations differ by gender and ethnicity? The answer seems to be "yes." Essentially paralleling the research on adults, studies suggest that young women are more likely to be attracted to the mall by the opportunity to shop and as a diversion, whereas young men are more likely to be interested in the opportunities for social contact and eating that the mall provides. Moreover, White teens are more likely than non-White teens to be drawn to the mall for eating, whereas the opportunity for social contact and sensory stimulation attracted non-White teens.[73] And the mall appears to meet any number of social needs teenagers have and may in fact address two different aspects of loneliness, intimate and social. Intimate loneliness refers to feeling isolated from others, whereas social loneliness takes in not having people to talk to. Different aspects of the mall can address these issues for teenagers.[74]

The use of malls by teenagers is not limited to the United States. For example, malls in Zimbabwe with names like Westgate, replicating a design in Ottawa, Canada, are places where teenagers gather during school vacations.[75] Research cross-culturally suggests similar motives for shopping among teenagers. The idea that shopping brings pleasure was a core value that emerged from research on teenagers in India.[76] And teenagers in Brazil

[72] Stockrocki, M. (2002). Shopping malls from preteen and teenage perspectives. *Visual Arts Research, 28*(2), 77–85.

[73] Kim, E. Y., & Kim, Y.-K. (2005). The effect of ethnicity and gender on teens' mall shopping motivations *Clothing & Textiles Research Journal, 23*(2), 65–77.

[74] Kim, Y.-K., Kim, E. Y., & Kang, J. (2003). Teens' mall shopping motivations: Functions of loneliness and media usage. *Family & Consumer Sciences Research Journal, 32*(2), 140–167.

[75] Mupawaenda, D. (2007, August 18). Zimbabwe: Shopping malls – Relaxing spots for teenagers. *The Herald.* http://allafrica.com/stories/200708200212.html.

[76] Kaur, P., & Singh, R. (2007). Uncovering retail shopping motives of Indian youth. *Young Consumers, 8*(2), 128–138.

list shopping malls among their preferred places (at 19.6 percent), after the home (at 35.3 percent).[77]

But not only do young people "hang out" in malls; older people have similar penchants.[78] In what seems to be a play on words, the way the elderly have used the mall to meet some of their social needs has been called "mallingering," and there was a relationship between this mallingering and the satisfaction and degree of welcome these elderly felt about the mall; the greater the level of satisfaction with the mall, the greater the mallingering.[79] And of course the elderly use malls to address some of their health needs, especially in terms of walking for exercise. For some, the mall is a place where social groups have formed around walking as a form of rehabilitation after a heart attack.[80]

Older Americans shop, and they appear to be motivated to use malls to achieve two types of goals. One involves consumption (the value and service related to purchases) and the other involves the experience itself. In this regard, malls certainly have the ability to reduce the loneliness experienced by many older Americans.[81] And research conducted in Montreal also points to the role that the kind of indoor public space that one might find in a mall plays in addressing the social needs of the elderly. The elderly are disproportionately represented at the mall, particularly the percentage of elderly men who are alone at these centers.[82]

Who will drive the future of the mall? Will it be teenagers, sometimes referred to as the "Echo Boomers," who have grown up with the mall as much more central in their upbringing than was true of their baby boomer parents? Or will it be the baby boomer parents, with their substantially greater capacity for consumption? Regarding these Gen Xs and Ys, "They don't want what their moms and dads had, they want their own mall.... They want their own excitement. They aren't interested in just shopping, they want to be entertained.... They look at what the previous

[77] deAraujo Gunther, I., Nepomuceno, G. M., Spehar, M. C., & Gunther, H. (2003). Favorite places of adolescents in the Federal District. *Estudos de Psicologia, 8*(2), 299–308.

[78] White, R. (2007). Older people hang out too. *Journal of Occupational Science, 14*(2), 115–118.

[79] Graham, D. S., Graham, I., & MacLean, M. J. (1991). Going to the mall: A leisure activity of urban elderly people. *Canadian Journal on Aging, 10*(4), 345–358.

[80] Fletcher, S., & Macauley, C. (1983). The shopping mall as a therapeutic arena. *Geriatric Nursing, 4*(2), 105–106.

[81] Kim, Y.-K., Kang, J., & Kim, M. (2005). The relationships among family and social interaction, loneliness, mall shopping motivation, and mall spending of older consumers. *Psychology & Marketing, 22*(12), 995–1015.

[82] Brown, D., Sijpkes, P., & Maclean, M. (1986). The community role of public indoor space. *The Journal of Architectural and Planning Research, 3*, 161–172.

generations did as boring and slow. They want fast and cool," says the president of Jones Lang LaSalle Retail in Atlanta, quoted in an article.[83] If those comments are on target, then it will undoubtedly be the teenagers, the somewhat now and future consumers, who will drive the future iterations of malls.

THE END OF THE MALL AS WE KNOW IT?

The rumors of the death of the mall as a standard bearer of consumption may be slightly exaggerated, but not off the mark completely. There are even Web sites devoted to dead malls (e.g., deadmalls.com). In an article reviewing the expansion of the largest mall in Christchurch, New Zealand, the author presents the statistic that a mall opened in the United States about every 3 to 4 *days* during the peak development period, the 1970s and 1980s, a statistic that Paco Underhill has also reported. However, in the year 2007, not a single new mall opened in the United States, the first time that had happened since the 1950s.[84] Factors that seem to have influenced the mall's illness, if not death, include economic downturns, overbuilding, the reemergence of the city center, concerns about environmental issues, the backlash against big box stores and large chains (e.g., Wal-Mart) in general, and the rise of Internet shopping. But excess and its aftermath is not new to our generation, although the extent of it may be unprecedented.

But where some see death, others see an opportunity for rebirth, and for malls, that rebirth often takes the form of renovation. For example, the Lakehurst Mall in Waukegan, Illinois, is being reborn as Fountain Square,[85] consistent with the trend that seems to include the use of "square" and "center" in these renamings. As a quotation in one article boldly proclaims, "If you rebuild it, they will come."[86] The reporter provides both a timeline and a facility description of the evolution of the mall, starting with the economic boom following World War II, with the construction of strip malls in the 1950s, whose purpose was to support the fast expansion of suburban growth. The 1970s were marked by turning "inward," in the sense that climate control and food courts in indoor malls became more popular than open-air facilities. The author claims that climate control and food precipitated longer visits for shoppers. This form was the prototype until

---

[83] Johnson (2008), para. 33.   [84] Matthews (2008), para. 5.

[85] Schmidt, E. (2007, May 1). Wisconsin, Illinois projects; Re-dos help rejuvenate fad-ing shopping malls. *Retail Construction*, 14(5), p. 37. http://midwest.construction.com/features/archive/0705_feature4.asp.

[86] Ibid., para. 1.

the 1990s, "when New Urbanist thinking led to open-air malls called 'lifestyle centers' or 'town centers.'"[87] What we left in the 1950s, Main Street, we see again. The idea is that there is more to shopping than shopping, if you will. The shopping location, whether a mall, a lifestyle center, or a town center, has to be a destination. In fact, there are so many labels and versions of these new forms that no clear model has emerged as dominant. In addition to the lifestyle center, town center, power center, and hybrid development options, there is also a variant called an omnicenter, which includes discount tenants. And there are mixed-use developments, which typically include residential elements. "Diversity is the new byword. Developers are willing to mix and match practically any kind of tenant in creating shopping environments with an eclectic urban feel. They've got grocery stores and movie theaters and high fashion shops all jumbled together."[88]

This pressure to stay competitive has filtered down to my area. A Wal-Mart in the area feels the need to improve its image and renovate in this competitive climate.[89] And I have noticed that my TJMaxx in Groton, Connecticut, is undergoing a renovation (the store is only about 8 years old) to create a more upscale image, according to an employee with whom I spoke.

One view of what is happening to the mall is that the process is more evolutionary than revolutionary.[90] For example, the Nouvelle at Natick, the site of the former Natick Mall, constructed in 1965 and leveled and rebuilt in 1994, is now the home of 215 condominiums. The Natick Collection is the largest mall in New England, and its Web site states[91] that the mall has the largest skylight in New England. In the case of this current transformation of the Natick Mall, GGP is investing $370 million to see this next evolution in the life cycle of the mall, "applying the lifestyle-center model, where upscale retailers, sit-down restaurants and condos are built around what looks like a city street."[92] What an old mall can provide, it is argued, is a really good location, typically near a highway interchange, and a reasonably large parcel of land. The Natick residents, who are spending between $425,000 and $1.6 million (recent figures are not surprisingly lower, from the $300,000s to over $1 million, reported on the Web site in July 2009) depending on the unit size

[87] Ibid., para. 8.

[88] Murphy, H. L. (2007, February 1). Reinventing retail. http://nreionline.com/mag/real_estate_reinventing_retail/.

[89] Cronin, A. (2009, July 22). Norwich Walmart gets a new look. *The Day*, pp. C7–C8.

[90] Davis, L. S. (2007, September 30). When downtown is in the suburbs. *The New York Times*, National, Real Estate Desk, section 11, p. 6, para 4. http://www.nytimes.com/2007/09/30/realestate/30nati.html.

[91] http://www.natickcollection.com/html/mallinfo.asp.

[92] Davis (2007), para. 5.

and vista, gain a variety of amenities. These amenities include a gym, social club, rooftop garden, membership in the Massachusetts Historical Society, private mall entrance, and personal parking spot. As one resident is quoted as saying, "It's like having the city come out to the suburbs"[93] when walking downstairs takes you downtown. Reflecting on the likelihood that this kind of conversion will be replicated across the nation, one shopping center trade group member essentially said the redevelopment's degree of success would be the predictor, but also noted that with 1200 enclosed malls in the United States, it was unlikely that the Natick solution could be used in all instances.

In the article entitled "Birth, death and shopping: The rise and fall of the shopping mall," *The Economist* provides one version of the growth of the mall culture and then what is described as the ongoing demise of the facility type "the mall" as we know it. No, Americans have not given up shopping, although in this current economic downturn Americans have certainly cut back on their spending. Rather, the form in which the shopping takes place has changed. Often, the distance between a mall where shopping formerly look place and what has replaced it (if we set aside the issue of online shopping) is less than a mile.

A case in point is the Crystal Mall in Waterford, Connecticut, which has experienced a significant downturn since it opened in 1984 (including the apparent downgrading of the mall in terms of the items it carries, at least in this shopper's perspective) and what has appeared less than a half mile away, The Waterford Commons, a complex populated with big box stores. These stores are familiar to anyone, anywhere, who shops in America and include Dick's Sporting Goods, Borders, and Best Buy. A separate geographical cluster (off the same entrance) houses Panera Bread, Talbots, and Coldwater Creek, also familiar to shoppers across the United States. A limited number of consumer dollars cannot support all mall models. Big box power centers have substantially impacted the viability of older neighboring malls.

MALLS AND NEW URBANISM

One emerging version of the mall is related to the new urbanist movement, described in Chapter 1 of this book. In the wonderfully entertaining film *The Social Life of Small Urban Spaces*,[94] William H. Whyte, better known to some as the author of *The Organization Man*[95] and a research inspiration

---

[93] Ibid., para. 14.

[94] Whyte, W. H. (1988). *The social life of small urban spaces* [Film]. New York: The Municipal Arts Society of New York.

[95] Whyte, W. H. (1956). *The organization man*. New York: Simon & Schuster.

to Paco Underhill, talks about the characteristics of great urban spaces, highlighting such characteristics as seating, sun, and food. In the film, Whyte points out that people will pay "good money" for the experience of an old-fashioned street, which he says they find at Disneyland. In other words, people will pay good money for the experience of a community, at least what they remember as a community in small town America, perhaps with more than a dose of nostalgia. This experience of community is what new urbanists offer, and what a new version of the mall offers in such configurations as lifestyle centers and mixed use developments.

On some level, we are seeing a return to that desire to connect to other people in a way that resembles what used to be experienced as community life. "By the time of his death in 1980, mall pioneer Gruen had long since disavowed malls, feeling developers had misinterpreted his notion of building communities. He had envisioned a mini-city with a mall at its center, surrounded by interlocking social functions, including apartments, schools, parks and lakes."[96] In other words, Gruen envisioned what new urbanists now promote. And we undoubtedly are tired of the commutes many of us make to work, a factor discussed in Chapter 4, adding to the desire to live closer to where we work.

As *The Economist* article argues, we may want our shopping experience in a place that doesn't look like a mall, but rather like an old-fashioned street, and then gives the example of a shopping center in Los Angeles, the Grove, built to look like a town center and punctuated with fountains and real flowers and the ability to be outdoors as you walk from shop to shop or take a tram.[97] In the article, the developer of this town center, Rich Caruso, described what he builds as "streets," forgoing the term "lifestyle center," which is used in the mall industry. The article credits Mr. Caruso with such success with the Grove and similar ventures that in some measure he can be thanked that "every new shopping centre built in American next year will be roofless (and several traditional shopping malls will tear off their roofs). Open-air centres will appear not just in temperate places like southern California but also in muggy Houston and frigid Massachusetts."[98] Caruso integrates a variety of styles in his centers in the hope that they will create a "festive, holiday atmosphere" that promotes spending. He is also quoted as saying that his "creations are more 'real' and authentic than conventional shopping centers."[99] The article compares Caruso and Gruen, pointing to the social nature of humans as a species and arguing that as a culture we

[96] Johnson (2008), para. 6.   [97] *The Economist* (2007), paras. 21 & 22.

[98] Ibid., para. 24.   [99] Ibid., para. 25.

have failed to create the kinds of spaces that support those social needs. The two designers, it is argued, create these social spaces but emphasize different components. The analysis is kinder to Gruen, whose goal was to update the city center in America with a European flavor, than to Caruso. Caruso "has tried to re-create a kind of prelapsarian downtown where there is no crime or homelessness. His romantic evocations of city centers are possible only because people have forgotten what downtowns used to be like. And they have forgotten, of course, largely because of the suburban shopping malls that Gruen built. It was necessary to kill the American city centre before bringing it back to life."[100] Shades of Disney's Main Streets, anyone?

In something of an irony, in my view the lifestyle centers we now see were foreshadowed by what is hailed as the first suburban shopping district in the United States, Kansas City's Country Club Plaza, built in 1922. I visited this mall, south of downtown, in 2009 when the Environmental Design Research Association conference was held in Kansas City. I had trouble understanding why the architecture had a Spanish theme (fountains, court-yards, and red-tiled roofs) and looked something like San Antonio until I read that the development by Jesse Clyde (J. C.) Nichols was influenced by his travels to Europe and the southwestern United States. According to the map and dining guide to the plaza I read, the development was initially called "Nichols' Folly" because people had trouble seeing how the former hog farm and brickyard, permeated with stagnant water and shacks, could be transformed. This was "the nation's first master-planned suburban cen-ter designed to accommodate people arriving by automobile," according to the second paragraph of the plaza guide. Eventually apartments and hotels were added to the surroundings of the 15-block district with more than 150 shops, creating something like we see today in these new urbanist lifestyle centers. When I visited the plaza, it looked surprisingly modern, especially and unfortunately, in my view, because it contained all the usual retail sus-pects, like J. Crew, Barnes & Noble, the Pottery Barn, and Banana Republic. Also foreshadowing retailing today, the plaza prides itself on the number of special events it holds, particularly its lights, which glow from 5 p.m. to 3 a.m. Thanksgiving to mid-January.

This trend in recreating downtown or at least opening up the mall, turn-ing it inside out, is not limited to the United States. Although the president of an association for shopping and residential management was speaking about Malaysia, she might have been speaking about the United States when she said, "Twenty to 30 years ago, not only was the hardware/architecture

[100] Ibid., para. 27.

very different, shopping complexes were also called 'black boxes' as no one could see through the buildings or know the activities that were taking place there. Today, it is the other way around. Mall owners are bringing the life out of the box as in the case of al fresco dining."[101]

Many malls are struggling, and estimates from the International Council on Shopping Centers were that almost 150,000 retail establishments would be out of business by the end of 2008, with almost 75,000 predicted to close during the first 6 months of 2009.[102] But some communities are holding on to retail by focusing on the substantial ethnic diversity in their communities and appealing to that diversity. For example, in communities with large Hispanic populations, such as border communities in Texas, malls have taken on some of the persona of Mexican villages, with mariachi acts and butcher shops.[103]

The use of ethnicity to add interest and renew vitality is being used in strip malls as well. Strip malls such as the Flea Market Discount Plaza, in Manassas, Virginia, function as "de facto town squares for the Hispanic community" who have been drawn there in search of jobs and to meet other Hispanics. These strip malls offer what is essentially missing in suburban America, anything that resembles public space. These spaces are described as the "automobile-era version of Delancey Street on the Lower East Side," by one geographer who has studied communities of immigrants.[104]

MUNDANENESS: THE DANGER IN SAMENESS

One of the fundamental reasons that has contributed to the need for the mall to reinvent itself relates to a basic human characteristic: the desire for variety. I include the following quotation at length because I think it eloquently captures the problem of sameness in the retail landscape:

> The wandering continues, along U.S. Route 1 now, the old East Coast byway that hurries and halts for 2,000 miles from Maine to Florida. And a familiar sensation returns: We have never been here before, but we have been here before. To the left, the Wendy's, like a gingerbread house from a child's nightmare. To the right, the Burger King, like a highway restroom that sells hamburgers. And everywhere, the billboards and neon, the strip

[101] Ganesan, V. (2007), para. 21.
[102] Kavilanz, P. B. (2008, December 17). The dead mall problem. CNNMoney.com. http://money.cnn.com/2008/12/17/news/economy/retail_wasteland/index.htm.
[103] *The Economist* (2007), para. 20.
[104] Miroff, N. (2006, December 19). Bringing nueva vida to aging strip malls. *Washington post.com*, paras. 6, 9.

malls and parking lots, urging us to look here, here, no here, drive up, drive thru and, remember, drive safely.... We "find ourselves forging through familiar and hideous commercial stretches that all but dare us to guess the state we are in.... But why are these stretches almost uniformly ugly, so much so that most of us have conditioned ourselves not to notice...."[105]

Not surprisingly, empirical research attests to the fact that we don't like the way these commercial strips look.[106]

Over the years of my interest in architecture and the American landscape, one article that continues to make an impression on me is a piece by Calvin Trillin in *The New Yorker* titled "Thoughts brought on by prolonged exposure to exposed brick."[107] In this article he talks about the lack of differentiability among malls up and down the East Coast, many of them developed by the Rouse Company, well known for its festival marketplaces. The title of the article refers to the idea that after you sandblast the buildings and bring in the ficus plants and then populate the mall over time, even if not initially, with chain stores, you have lost whatever is distinctive about the place. There is no sense of place, in fact. Moreover, the lack of variety and diversity is dangerous. In an article I remember from graduate school days, "Man's efficient rush toward deadly dullness,"[108] the author argues from a biological standpoint that having diversity makes it easier to adapt when circumstances change. Consider what might happen when a particular kind of raw material is no longer available if all of the examples in a given category are constructed from that raw material. Further, diversity promotes stability and mental well-being. Having diversity spreads the risk across members of the species. In the present context, as fewer and fewer megaretailers control more and more of the landscape (and product lines) we are left with less choice. More is less.

In comments about the current problems with malls and about retailing more generally, lack of diversity is a theme. Research by the University of Pennsylvania and the Verde Group released in December 2008 speaks to the issue of repetition. Of every five complaints by shoppers about malls,

---

[105] Barry, D. (2007, December 23). A place just like every other place. Only not. National Report, *The New York Times*, p. 22.

[106] Herzog, T., Kaplan, S., & Kaplan, R. (1976). The prediction of preference for familiar urban places. *Environment and Behavior, 8*, 627–645.

[107] Trillin, C. (1977, May 16). U.S. Journal: New England. Thoughts brought on by prolonged exposure to exposed brick. *The New Yorker*, pp. 101–102, 104–107.

[108] Watt, K. E. F. (1972). Man's efficient rush toward deadly dullness. *Natural History Magazine, 81*, 74–82.

three of those targeted the repetition of stores and the "mundaneness" of malls.[109]

Airports, which advertise their shopping opportunities and are becoming recognized for shopping, face this same challenge – how to stand out. And this is big business, as projected sales for such airport shopping in 2000 were more than $1 billion.[110] Travelers are said to want something distinctive, a souvenir of their visit in that particular city, and not something that can be found at the local mall. " . . . the retail environment needs to be customized to the locale so the comfort of seeing familiar brand names is balanced by a sense of local charm, color and flavor, and the excitement and discovery of the new, even the exotic. It should give passengers a sense of place, conveyed through the [special] personality of the environment."[111] It's not that easy. On my last trip business trip home from the EDRA conference in Kansas City, I was hard pressed to find something at the airport that said "Kansas City" in a distinctive way, at least something that would pass through security, unfortunately not the case with BBQ sauce.

Mall developers and managers are investigating ways to bring diversity and "excitement" to the mall, and to that end they have examined what factors are likely to lead customers to stay longer and return (the literature refers to "repatronage intentions and outshopping"). Repatronage refers to the idea that you will return to that mall, whereas outshopping refers to the idea that you will shop elsewhere. The most influential factor appears to be the variety of tenants (including food, stores, and entertainment), followed by how involved shoppers are in the shopping experience, and finally the environment of the mall.[112]

This problem of variety is ubiquitous. I find it somewhat ironic that in an article about malls in New Zealand, the author makes a similar point, stating that malls built in New Zealand but developed by foreign owners have a certain universal mall style. The author then goes on to say, "You will search Westfield Riccarton in vain for anything suggestive of Christchurch. You could be in Auckland – or, indeed, Australia."[113] A professor who taught at Auckland University quoted in the article reflected, "Shopping malls are phenomenally boring. . . . What are your anchor stores? Invariably in New

---

[109] Matthews (2008), para. 24.

[110] DeLise, J. T. (2000, April 10). Elaborate retail environments taking off at U.S. airports. *Brandweek, 41*(15).

[111] Ibid., para. 5.

[112] Wakefield, K. L., & Baker, J. (1998). Excitement at the mall: Determinants and effects on shopping response. *Journal of Retailing, 74*(4), 515–539.

[113] Matthews (2008), para. 19.

Zealand, throw in a supermarket, a general merchandiser like a Warehouse or a K-mart, a department store which is inevitably going to be a Farmers, mix in 70 per cent or so of fashion stores, add a food court and movie theatres and, boom, you've got a shopping mall."[114]

But some do not see malls as these "archetypical globalized spaces."[115] Writing in the *American Behavioral Scientist*, Salcedo points out that where land is scarce in Europe and Asia, underground malls or vertical malls provide different models. Still, in my reading of the literature, the weight of opinion heavily criticizes sameness. Further, the majority of these diversity examples come from outside the United States. Within our borders, one would be hard pressed to make a case that challenges the overwhelming sameness we see, the sameness that Trillin described as early as 1977. Even Salcedo comments that "the architecture and design of malls seems to be quite homogeneous" but then observes that their capitalization is not. Salcedo reminds us that local customs can emerge through aspects of culture, from food selections (e.g., McDonald's selling wine in France), banning men from a mall in Saudi Arabia, and providing a church for Catholic masses in the Philippines. Regarding the combination of religion and commerce, the developer of that Philippine megamall, quoted in the Salcedo article, states, "The church is our best anchor store."[116]

Some mundaneness is related to the appearance of malls, especially their exteriors. In his volume about the mall, Underhill lays the blame for the exterior ugliness of malls at the feet of those who created the mall, the developers, and not at the feet of retailers. He argues that there is essentially a tragic and fundamental flaw in how shopping centers were conceived (or more importantly by whom). "I put a large amount of blame on the mall's fatal flaw – its lack of mercantile DNA,"[117] meaning that the malls were the children of developers, not merchants. Underhill points to the development of the great 19th- and 20th-century department stores by retailers, whereas malls are the products of real estate development companies whose major interest is using their land to maximize profit. Quoted in an article, Underhill says, "Aesthetic value is the last thing on anyone's mind when imagining a mall."[118]

One of the other problems in the blandness of malls is the lack of visibility of goods from the outside. Underhill says that the mall turned

[114] Ibid., para. 22.
[115] Salcedo, R. (2003). When the global meets the locale at the mall. *American Behavioral Scientist, 46*(8), 1084–1103, p. 1084.
[116] Ibid., pp. 1096–1097.   [117] Underhill (2004), p. 202.
[118] Matthews (2008), para. 41.

FIGURE 5.3. Pompeii "storefront"

many aspects of this early shopping pattern around; no longer was there the ease of parking, where you could drive right up to the storefront *and* see the merchandise in the window.[119] I am reminded of what I learned this year visiting the ruins of Pompeii, where the partial structures of stores were still visible, as were the indentations in their countertops where urns held liquids or grains for customers to see (see Figure 5.3). This visibility of goods, which adds visual variety, is a long human tradition, and a tradition that changed fundamentally when the enclosed mall was built and revealed nothing of its wares to the outside.

Underhill is particularly harsh on mall parking lots, as well he might be, arguing that no one has given thought to these vast expanses of asphalt. But he also points out the potential uses of such spaces for community fund-raising activities and meeting nodes, both in the parking lots and, of course, inside the mall. "This is where the mall-as-community shows its shiny, peppy face. If we were a village society, or even an urban one, these activities might take place at the schoolhouse, or the community center, or in the village green on market day. But since we're a predominately suburban nation, and suburbs tend to be short on gathering places, it all happens at the mall."[120]

[119] Underhill (2004), p. 19.   [120] Ibid., pp. 29–30.

Underhill recognizes that the cities presented plenty of dangers in the form of crime and poor health and housing conditions, but he also reminds us that when we abandoned the cities, spurred by federal initiatives related to highways and housing, the suburban answer to shopping was "a big air-conditioned vanilla box with all of the action on the inside."[121] I was disheartened reading an article that included the shopping mall in the same category as the Roman Forum, as a symbolic center of community life. In saying "Each society has buildings that epitomize its life,"[122] the author went on to say that Rome has its forums and coliseums; society in the early 21st century has the shopping mall. In a word – discouraging.

Underhill argues that the zenith of the mall has been reached and that we are, in a sense, postmall. We will frequent them, he says, but they are no longer the central form of shopping. "These shopping centers will never look as shiny and inviting and wonderful to us as they once did. We're never going to love them the same way again."[123] Underhill points out that the majority of the large malls in America were built more than 20 years ago. He goes on to observe that we may in all likelihood not find these malls of sufficient value to renovate them, which is not the case with many of our majestic public buildings – our post offices, department stores, and train stations – of the past.[124]

Does the criticism Underhill and others apply to the exterior of the mall extend to its interior? The term mall atmospherics has been applied to the physical design and decoration of the mall.[125] Not surprisingly in my view, consumers are likely to pay little attention to the interior decoration of the mall or the components that constitute its atmospherics. Even mall users who enjoy being in the mall, mall enthusiasts as they are called, do not seem to be aware of the architectural features and décor of the mall.[126] Those of us who spend our professional lives working in the field of environmental psychology are often disappointed that users have less enthusiasm for and awareness of particular design features of environments than do we, but that is to be expected. Most research, whatever the facility type, seems to show that people notice the environment when it falls below some baseline or

---

[121] Ibid., pp. 32–33.

[122] Stockrocki, M. (2002). Shopping malls from preteen and teenage perspectives. *Visual Arts Research, 28*(2), 77–85, p. 80.

[123] Underhill (2004), p. 201.   [124] Ibid., p. 203.

[125] Bitner, M. J. (1992). Servicescapes: The impact of physical surroundings on customers and employees. *Journal of Marketing, 56*, 57–71.

[126] Bloch, P. H., Ridgway, N. M., & Dawson, S. A. (1994). The shopping mall as consumer habitat. *Journal of Retailing, 70*(1), 2–42, p. 37.

standard, not when it surpasses that standard. If there is trash or buildings are not well maintained, our antennae seem to be stimulated; otherwise, the architectural and design nuances don't seem to register. We may be more aware of the variety of stores that a mall offers than its design.

THE SHOPPING CENTER AND THE ROLE OF THE BIG BOX STORE

I have already mentioned big box stores in passing but I am now ready to tackle the topic head-on. There are a lot of terms surrounding the idea that individual stores have grown large, more than 20,000 sq. ft. and substantially more, to capture the consumer market. You know these stores – Office Max, Staples, Dick's Sporting Goods, Best Buy, and Toys 'R' Us, to name a few. Big box stores generally focus on one type of product, whether home improvement, toys, or electronics. They are often referred to as category killers in the sense that they overwhelm their often smaller competition with price, extent of merchandise, and economies of scale, among other assets. The 1970s marked the emergence of a variety of larger stores, including big box merchandisers of a single category, the category killers, discount mass merchandisers like Kmart and Target, and warehouse stores such as Costco, Sam's Club, and BJ's Wholesale Club. There were also off-price merchandisers such as TJMaxx and Marshalls. It was a pretty simple formula: "Pile it high and sell it cheap."[127]

Then of course there is Wal-Mart. One name. You could write an entire book about the effect Wal-Mart has had on shopping, and not just in the United States. Wal-Mart stands alone. It is a big box, and it is a category killer, but not in the usual sense. It is the category killer of lower-scale merchandise, of the discount department store, of places like Ames, and Caldor, and Bradlees, which have gone out of business, and Kmart, which still has a presence. I had a special affinity for Bradlees; its first store was in New London, Connecticut. I was also fond of another discount shopping retailer, Caldor, which had a store near me where I took my daughter for a lot of her early childhood "portraits." Wikipedia maintains a list of now defunct shopping centers (by state) in the United States. It is a sobering and extensive list.[128]

Wal-Mart has dramatically impacted all aspects of shopping. Writing about category killers, author Robert Spector reports that through

---

[127] Spector (2005), p. xiii.
[128] http://en.wikipedia.org/wiki/List_of_defunct_department_stores_of_the_United_States.

consolidation and mergers, department store chains have shrunk to 7 from the more than 20 that existed in the 1970s.[129] Popular movie culture has also passed judgment on the category killer. You may remember the 1998 movie *You've Got Mail* in which Tom Hanks plays Joe Fox (Joe Fox III, actually), the discount store bookseller who forces The Shop Around the Corner, the store of Meg Ryan's character Kathleen Kelly, out of business. For me, at least one bright spot is that, despite its seeming ubiquitousness, Starbucks, a category killer of a different sort, has made no inroads in Italy and apparently has decided not to expand there.[130]

Social criticism of big box stores is widespread. The book *Big-box Swindle: The True Cost of Mega-retailers and the Fight for America's Independent Businesses*,[131] begins with a story about saving an independent bookstore in Menlo Park, California, and describes how communities around the country have banded together to stop the development of big box projects in their neighborhoods. Sometimes this fight takes place legislatively, with laws to curb store size or demand economic impact reviews, and to halt tax benefits that sometimes are available to chains but not to the independent retailer. The author maintains that it is not consumer choice, but public policy, that has driven the rise of big box stores. Both local and state subsidies, she explains, have been used by chains like Target, Lowe's, and Wal-Mart and goes on to describe that the tax benefits for these construction projects are called the "Geoffrey Loophole," named after what most parents will recognize is the name of the Toys 'R' Us mascot, the giraffe named Geoffrey. So the depreciation opportunities enacted by Congress in the 1950s opened the door for deductions on commercial properties. She lists the kinds of breaks they get: "... free or reduced price land...; property tax breaks; sales tax rebates; free infrastructure and other site improvements; low-interest, tax-free loads; and job training credits...."[132] Further, she says, another major benefit accrued in the form of tax incentive financing (TIF) districts; when bonds for site improvements are paid for by taxpayers. "TIF essentially allows tax-exempt, low-interest public capital to be used for private development, and further subsidizes that development with future tax dollars."[133]

[129] Spector (2005), p. 89.
[130] Scocco, D. (2007, January 15). Why Starbucks is not present in Italy? http://innovationzen.com/blog/01/15/why-starbucks-is-not-present-in-italy/; Burke, G. (2008, July 22). Starbucks in Italy? No, grazie. http://onethescene.blogs.foxnews.com/2008/07/22/starbucks-in-italy-no-grazie/.
[131] Mitchell, S. (2006). *Big-box swindle: The true cost of mega-retailers and the fight for America's independent businesses.* Boston: Beacon Press.
[132] Ibid., pp. 164–165.   [133] Ibid., p. 168.

The statistics she cites are sobering in terms of the number of independent retailers who have died off, at a time when in 2005 $1 of every $10 spent shopping on the product categories of food, toys, hardware, and clothing was spent at Wal-Mart. One of the descriptions she uses paints a vivid picture of the situation: "With 600 million square feet of floor space in the United States, Wal-Mart could fit every man, woman, and child in the country inside its stores."[134] Wal-Mart's distribution system and pricing strategy was documented in a PBS special called *Store Wars: When Wal-Mart Comes to Town*,[135] produced by Teddy Bear Films. On the company's Web site, the producer explains that the name Teddy Bear Films was chosen so that if Wal-Mart sued the company, the headline would read something to the effect of "Wal-Mart sues Teddy Bear." The largest property developer in the United States, Wal-Mart's "portfolio of real estate comprises about *3 percent of the world's total retail space,*" according to data cited in Spector's book on category killers.[136]

The documentary on Wal-Mart and other large retail forces focuses on the small town of Ashland, Virginia, population 7200, and the fight a segment of that population wages, and ultimately loses, against a Wal-Mart store. The vast majority of books written about big box retailing view it as the enemy, although Vedder and Cox's book *The Wal-Mart Revolution*[137] is positive about the benefits that accrue to the local economy and the consumer in general. State its authors, "Wal-Mart's critics, by and large, are simply wrong."[138] Although my book is about the built environment, not about politics and labor, it is hard to circumvent the intermingling of these forces. Writing about the category killers, author Robert Spector says that with "close to 2.5 percent of America's gross national product . . . Wal-Mart has an impact – either directly or indirectly – on virtually every other type of retail and retail-vendor business on the planet."[139]

The author of *Big-box Swindle* also notes that as retail continues to move farther from where we live, on cheaper land, we drive more to accomplish household shopping. She reports that the number of miles driven for these tasks is up 40 percent or more in the 1990s. I think this driving will decline and that we will increasingly use the Internet to replace some of the shopping

---

[134] Ibid., p. 12.

[135] Peled, M. (2001). *When Wal-Mart comes to town* [Film]. San Francisco: Teddy Bear Films.

[136] Spector (2005), p. 157.

[137] Vedder, R., & Cox, W. (2006). *The Wal-Mart revolution*. Washington, D.C.: The Enterprise Institute.

[138] Ibid., p. 6.   [139] Spector (2005), p. xv.

done at power centers (clusters of big box stores). I no longer drive to (or frequent) the power center near me, Waterford Commons, with Best Buy, Dick's Sporting Goods, and Borders, among others. This decision was cemented by the fact that Borders never seemed to have the books I wanted, which relates to the fact that independent stores are able to make their own decisions about what products they carry; at chains like Borders, these decisions are made up the corporate ladder, she argues. I will buy locally or order online.

All of these stores (category killers, discount department stores, warehouse clubs) created too much choice and not enough consumer dollars to support every single store. Another startling statistic the *Big-box Swindle* offers is that "since 1960, median family income, adjusted for inflation, has increased by about 80%, while the amount of retail space has grown 850 percent."[140] An article about the transformation of the mall observed that "there is as much retail space within a mile of the big malls now as inside them."[141] Literally tens if not hundreds of retail names (e.g., Ames, Caldor, Bradlees) have gone out of business, and we have less choice offered by fewer retailers, whether the product category is office supplies or home remodeling. The stores may be bigger, but as I pointed out earlier, there are lots of ways in which the takeovers and failures result in less choice for the consumer, not more. Wal-Mart's pricing strategy, which often initially undercuts prices of other retailers in a given category, such as toys or consumer electronics, is part of what has been labeled the Wal-Mart effect.[142] Wal-Mart has the power to essentially become a category killer in any consumer goods direction it pursues. The consumer's wallet benefits, right? At least in the short term, that may be the case. To its credit, Wal-Mart has no peer in its efficiency, particularly its distribution system. But in the long run, the decline in diversity is a problem, in my view.

When I look at my own community, among the large stores I see are Wal-Mart, Kmart, and Target; TJ Maxx, Marshalls, and Home Goods; and BJ's Wholesale Club. Not only have these stores defined taste through the goods they offer, but equally through their physical presence, which is monotonous and unattractive. And as much as I might admire the design aesthetic of some of Target's offerings, there is little in the nature of its setting, its exterior, and its parking to distinguish it from any other big box

---

[140] Mitchell (2006), p. 107.

[141] Albright, M. (2007, June 6). The morphing of the mall. *St. Petersburg Times* (Florida), South Pinellas Edition, Business, p. 1D, para. 11. http://www.sptimes.com/2007/06/06/Business/The_morphing_of_the_m.shtml.

[142] Spector (2005), p. 182.

merchandiser. I remember when CVS entered the Mystic landscape in the former A&P store at the end of Main Street; on its way in, two independent pharmacies in town went out of business. The one concession CVS made to its usual design was to retain the cupola from the old building. Otherwise, the store would be indistinguishable from CVS anywhere, USA.

Through the growth of the big box stores and discount retailers, the concept of the department store has lost its focus. Spector says that this weakness of department stores, which essentially have lost their identity, is hurting malls. Further, he cites the statistic that we are spending less time in malls, down to 2.9 hours/month in 2003 from 4 hours in 2000. Other retail concepts gaining more credence are dollar stores. People are frustrated with the time it takes to navigate and negotiate sales in large stores. Somewhat in response to that, he says, smaller versions of category killers are being built in neighborhoods and in urban environments where the product line can be fine-tuned to shoppers' interests.[143]

Just as Gruen put a roof over anchor stores and their packed retail neighbors and enclosed the mall, evolution of the shape of the mall continues. "Now it's mostly outdoors. It might have condos or office spaces. And it will be called something like a 'town center.'"[144] The mixture described in this article, including big box stores such as Costco and SuperTarget, placed in an outdoor setting, is described as a "super-regional open-air shopping center."[145] A new direction in shopping and in mall architecture, is emerging that mixes shopping and retail and office spaces, and, not infrequently, as in the Natick Mall, residences. This direction could be considered a reincarnation of the kinds of mixtures that Jane Jacobs talked about in *The Death and Life of Great American Cities*.[146]

But typically happening in the same space, or at least on the perimeter of the same development, is the construction of big box stores. "In one corner of the project, typically, there's a Main Street for smaller mall stores, boutiques and Starbucks. Some have offices or condos upstairs. The street is lined with what's called 'teaser parking' so motorists drive a lap before realizing the empty spaces are in a vast lot out back. But dominating center stage is a lineup of up to 15 big boxes."[147]

An example of this intermixing, and a model of what is and what is to come, is the Garden City Center on Route 2 in Cranston, Rhode Island, south of Providence just off I-95. One part of the center (see Figure 5.4) called The

---

[143] Ibid, p. 112.   [144] Albright (2007), para. 1.
[145] Ibid., para. 3.
[146] Jacobs, J. (1961). *The death and life of great American cities*. New York: Random House.
[147] Albright (2007), para. 9.

FIGURE 5.4. The Commons (foreground) and The Village, Garden City Center

Village is this kind of quintessential Main Street, with upscale boutiques such as Mel and Me, and chains such as Banana Republic, Starbucks, Williams-Sonoma, and The Gap. The logo on the Garden City Center Web site pictures a charming bandstand, reminiscent of something one might see in the park of a small town.[148] But the other part of this retail expanse, called The Commons, is the zone of big box stores, including Borders, Office Max, and iParty! Circuit City and Linens 'n' Things are now gone, leaving their store "scars" behind them (the labels on the facades that are still visible). Parenthetically, a Web site is devoted to such label scars and presents a retail history blog (http://www.labelscars.com). On the south side of The Commons, across the road, is an upscale mixed-use development called Chapel View. Built on the site of the former boys training (i.e., reform) school, the $90 million retail complex consists of 75,000 sq. ft. of office space, 35 residential condominiums, and more than 300,000 sq. ft. of restaurant and retail space, including a grocery store.[149] A Whole Foods grocery store is also within walking distance. The restoration of some of the stone dormitories and the chapel itself create an impressive effect. My sense is that the project will draw even more business away from The Commons, and eventually from The Village, in this evolutionary cycle of retailing.

[148] http://gardencitycenter.com/home.html.
[149] http://www.carpionatoproperties.com/article.asp?ArticleID=31.

MALLS OUTSIDE THE UNITED STATES

Although malls may be dying (and reborn in another form) in the United States, that is hardly the case outside of America, especially with regard to Asia. It is also the case that malls are still being built in substantial numbers in the West, including Australia and New Zealand. Those countries are behind the development curve probably by as much as 10 years, whereas in the United States the development trajectory has reached its apex and is dropping precipitously.

In researching this chapter, I was struck by the number of newspaper articles devoted to the development and growth of the mall outside the United States, particularly in Asia. That kind of growth peaked in the United States in the 1980s. Asia is "home to some of the top shopping destinations of the world – Dubai, Hong Kong, Singapore, Bangkok and even Jakarta."[150] But the challenges for malls outside the United States appear similar to those we have here: "a right tenant mix, architecture and added-value . . . unique selling points (USP) – a key challenge for the industry."[151] The president of Persatuan Pengurusan Komplek (PPK, the Association for Shopping Complex and High-Rise Management) is quoted as saying, "Product differentiation is a difficult thing to do, as such, there exists a 'copy phenomenon,' especially in Asia, due to a lack of research and development."[152]

Again, in a certain irony, the word concierge, which appeared in the medical industry (discussed in Chapter 2 of this book) and has its origins in the hotel industry, has also been used to describe the person who provides information at the shopping center. The concierge provides extraordinary services as a way to create differentiation, that is, what this shopping center offers that others do not.[153]

I wouldn't be surprised if countries building large numbers of malls experience the same kind of saturation that appears to have happened in the United States. In Istanbul's Levent district, for example, a 5-minute walk will bring you in contact with three malls, although one supporter points out that Turkey falls below the ratio of shopping center/person boasted by other countries in Europe.[154] But as I said previously, most articles dealing with the growth of malls feature countries outside of the United States. In addition to Turkey, for example, South Africa has experienced substantial retail growth, according to an article in 2007. Since 1999, the rate of growth

[150] Ganesan (2007), para. 3.
[151] Ibid., para. 11.
[152] Ibid., para. 12.
[153] Ibid., para. 14.
[154] In Turkish retail, how much is too much? (2007, March 19). *EuroProperty Magazine*, Country Survey, p. 38. http://www.accessmylibrary.com/coms2/summary_0286_30631167_ITM.

for retail space in shopping centers in South Africa has reached 8.7 percent per year; further, shopping malls accounted for 43 percent of the retail activity in the country, and 53 percent of spending on retail occurred in shopping centers.[155] However, it is interesting to hear the same kind of caution expressed about these malls that we hear in the United States, such as the need to innovate to keep customers coming back. An expert on South Africa's retail environment is quoted in an article as saying, "Shopping centres run a high risk of becoming sterile. There is a great need to spice up the shopping centre environment to make it a compelling visit for consumers."[156]

Cross-culturally there appears to be some overlap in the factors that influence mall use. Among these factors are distance from the mall and the image of the mall.[157] In fact, one issue of the *Journal of International Consumer Marketing* was devoted to a review of the kinds of factors that work to attract customers cross-culturally, including attention to price and the influence of salespeople.[158]

Although the idea of the mall may be global, there are cultural differences in the purposes that shopping serves cross-culturally. For example, in a comparison of U.S. and Chilean shoppers, the U.S. shoppers expressed a larger variety of reasons to shop, including a greater likelihood to be motivated by entertainment. Chilean shoppers, on the other hand, were far more likely to be motivated to shop by purchases.[159]

ONLINE SHOPPING

What is the impact of online shopping on the physical landscape of shopping? Will we need less space for buildings as we move to greater reliance on remote shopping? One article posed the contrast as "Bricks vs. Clicks."[160] Online shopping, or e-commerce as it is sometimes called (although e-commerce is a larger concept that involves the nonretail customer as well), involves the purchase of products remotely through electronic means. It has

[155] Radebe, S. (2007, October 12). Shopping centres; reinventing retail. *Financial Mail (South Africa), Economy, Business, & Finance*, p. 76.

[156] Ibid., para. 5.

[157] DeJuan, M. S. (2004). Why do people choose the shopping malls? The attraction theory revisited: A Spanish case. *Journal of International Consumer Marketing, 17*(1), 71–96.

[158] Kaynak, E. (2004). Editorial. *Journal of International Consumer Marketing, 17*(1), 1–5.

[159] Nicholls, J. A. F., Li, F., Mandakovic, T., Roslow, S., & Kranendonk, C. (2000). US-Chilean mirrors: Shoppers in two countries. *Journal of Consumer Marketing, 17*(2), 106–199.

[160] Bocanegra, L. (2000, May–June). Reinventing retail. http://www.ciremagazine.com/article.php?article_id=398, para. 6.

become big business, but not in all product areas, and consumers have some trepidation about issues related to privacy and security. In one survey, more than 36 percent of survey participants expressed concern about the security of their personal and financial data, and such concern predicted their online shopping use. Somewhat surprisingly, respondents who had been shopping online longer had greater concern about issues related to privacy.[161] The security of personal and financial data (e.g., sharing information with other companies, tracking shopping habits, cookies) will continue to temper the use of online shopping, but it has not prevented a dramatic increase in the medium, particularly for certain categories of goods, such as computers and electronics. There are other categories of goods, for example, produce, for which I think most shoppers still like to look and feel the items. In a *Business Week* article in 1995, Bill Gates predicted that one-third of our food retailing (groceries were a $400 billion business in the United States in 1995) would be done online by 2005. At the time Gates made that prediction, the article reported that fewer than 1 percent of groceries in the United States were bought from home, and typically over the phone, not the computer.[162] The prediction Gates made hasn't been realized. But there is plenty of growth in online shopping. There is no doubt that online retail spending is growing, from totals of $128.1 billion in 2001 to a projection of $147.6 billion in 2008.[163] In total online sales for 2007, the largest spending areas were computer hardware and software, at $24.1 billion, apparel, accessories, footwear, and jewelry (one category) at $23.2 billion, and home products ($18.8 billion). In total online sales in 2007, the smallest categories were sporting goods ($2.5 billion), consumer health ($4.2 billion), and flowers and specialty goods ($4.3 billion). We ordered $7.4 billion worth of groceries and pet food online in 2007.

If you examine these figures a different way, as a percentage of *total* retail spending, the picture is different for a number of categories. For computer hardware and software, we buy 43.2 percent of the items online; we buy 19.1 percent of our tickets online, and 16.3 percent of our books, music, and videos. These are the largest percentages by category. But we buy only 6.3 percent of our apparel, accessories, footwear, and jewelry online, and only 1.1 percent of our groceries and pet food online. In other words, I think we

[161] Miyazaki, A. D., & Fernandez, A. (2001). Consumer perceptions of privacy and security risks for online shopping. *The Journal of Consumer Affairs, 25*(1), 27–44.
[162] *Business Week* (1995, September 11). The grocery cart in your PC. http://www.businessweek.com/archives/1995/b344183.arc.htm.
[163] Table 1016. Online Retail Spending, 2001 to 2007, and Projections, 2008. http://www.census.gov/compendia/statab/tables/09s1016.pdf.

make purchases online that fit the qualities of the medium. You generally don't need to "touch" music or videos to make a decision to purchase the product. In contrast, I think most people like to look at the produce they are buying, as well as the clothing. Sure, if you know the particular brand and size of jeans or tennis shoes you want to buy, purchasing online is not a risk. But to purchase sight unseen in the apparel category is still a risk. In discussing the future of shopping, the author Julian Markham notes, "Human behaviour relies on the senses, and consumers are used to the see-feel-smell factor in making decisions based on their own psychological reactions to the inherent feelings generated by these experiences."[164]

Social commentators worry about the loss of a place for social discourse as we move more to electronic commerce. Tracing the locations of commerce from specialized squares in Roman life to the electronic present, a case has been made that we are losing a special means of communication as we move to electronic commerce.[165] Living near the Piazza Navona in Rome, I was a regular shopper at the nearby Campo dei Fiori open market, where vendors sold everything from food and flowers to sunglasses and thread (see Figure 5.5). I cannot imagine replacing this experience by shopping online.

As Gumpert and Drucker review, electronic shopping is not the first means to provide what they call nonlocal retailing. Baby boomers can think back to the Sears or Montgomery Ward catalogues, where the focus was the procurement of goods that were not available locally and ease of access. A second wave in the march toward e-commerce was retailing related to television, which was available around the clock in 1985.[166] Familiar to most of us are the two most well-known television retailers, QVC (Quality, Value, Convenience) and HSN (Home Shopping Network). Describing electronic shopping, Gumpert and Drucker say, "The format is simple. Hype the product, emphasize the special price, develop a special rapport with the audience, flash the 800 number."[167] They ask us to question whether we are losing something significant about our qualities as humans as electronic communication gains followers. "There is a fundamental difference between transaction and interaction. Community ties, a sense of belonging, ties to the familiar, are linked with interaction. Community is rooted in social intercourse that creates opportunities for transactions about

---

[164] Markham, J. E. (1998). *The future of shopping: Traditional patterns and net effects.* London: Macmillan Press LTD, p. 222.

[165] Gumpert, G., & Drucker, S. (1992). From the agora to the electronic shopping mall. *Critical Studies in Mass Communication, 9,* 186–200.

[166] Ibid., p. 190.   [167] Ibid., p. 191.

FIGURE 5.5. Campo dei Fiori, Rome

problems, issues, concerns of mutual interest, and commerce. . . . Can electronic shopping provide more than a variation on the theme of shopping?"[168]

We shall see. One of the new approaches to connecting commerce and community is through the use of social media connection sites, such as Facebook, Twitter, and MySpace. A number of retailers have Facebook pages and have used them to target subscribers and increase revenue. For example, Powell's Books, a large bookseller based in Portland, Oregon, posted a note on its Facebook page with an incentive for a $5 coupon on a subsequent online purchase if people signed up for its newsletter, which targets customers' specific interest areas. The 6-day promotion yielded 400 additional e-mail subscribers.[169]

Although the recession has slowed the growth of online retailing, it is not as decimated as the retail industry as a whole. Although I did not purchase a report on online shopping in the United States for 2009 (the purchase price was a hefty 2995 Euros), here are a few tidbits I gleaned from a brief summary on the Web. The categories that are not tech-related are growing the fastest; Amazon leads online retailing by a significant amount; concerns

[168] Ibid., p. 196.
[169] Retailer boosts online sales with specialty emails, social media (2009, June 25). *Business Wire*. http://proquest.umi.com/pdqweb?did+1761914031&sid=1&Fmt=3&clientId=13779&RQT=309&VName=PDQ.

about privacy and also objections to shipping costs hinder e-commerce; m-commerce, or mobile shopping (essentially shopping using your cell phone), is gaining a following.[170]

More than 10 years ago, observers thought that specialized online retailers, of which Amazon.com, at that time just a bookseller, was an example, would succeed where the online shopping mall had failed.[171] Ironically, in my view, in the subsequent decade, Amazon.com has become that online shopping mall, given all of the product categories it now offers, from books and Kindles, to home and garden and gourmet food. I especially like the category "Everything Else" in Amazon's drop-down menu of departments. Amazon.com probably qualifies as what is called a megastore, a "single site that sells a mall's worth of products but with the best specialized retailers' efficiency, discounts and streamlined buying."[172] But in 1997 when the article was written, Amazon was more focused, what the article describes as the "best-of-breed" model. One place where online shopping has made a major impact is the travel industry, where the erosion from e-commerce of the very thin margins is a substantial threat.[173] Many consumers who fly, for example, order their tickets online or at least search for tickets through such comparison sites as Kayak.com.

What does the future hold? Analysts from Jupiter Research, which focuses on the effect of the Internet and developing technologies on business, expect e-retailing in the United States to level off at 10–15 percent of the total retail sales in this country, "barring a dramatic change in the online shopping experience that promotes an inordinate spending shift among buyers."[174] Its report, *US Online Retail Forecast, 2006–2011*, also points to the influence of the Internet on what are called off-line retail sales. We are all familiar with the process, if not the terminology. What that means is that we use the Internet to gather information about pricing and availability and then purchase the item in question off-line, that is, not using the Internet. The research report predicts that by 2011 as much as 40 percent of U.S. off-line retail sales will be influenced by the use of the Internet prior to purchase. A technological relative of Internet retailing is what is called m-commerce, or

---

[170] Research and Markets: Online shopping – US – 2009. (2009, June 29). *Business Wire*. http://www.iqpc.com/News.aspx?id=132374808&IQ=marketing.

[171] The once and future mall: Internet shopping (1997, November 1). *The Economist* (US), 344, 64–66.

[172] Ibid., para. 4.

[173] Peet, J. (2000, February 26). Shopping around the web: A survey of e-commerce. *The Economist* (US).

[174] Jupiter Research forecasts that off-line retail sales influenced by online research will reach one trillion dollars by 2011 (2007, January 17). *Business Wire*, para. 1.

mobile commerce. Whereas 4 percent of the 500 top online retailers in the United States now have mobile commerce cites, analysts predict that figure to reach 50 percent in 5 years (by 2014).[175]

Underhill doesn't believe that cyber shopping will replace shopping done in real time and space. "Even if Web site shopping doubles the catalog's success rate, 80 percent of shopping will continue to be done in the real world."[176] But online shopping avoids what research has demonstrated to be the greatest irritant people report about shopping: high-pressure sales tactics.[177]

NEW DIRECTIONS

The 2008 recession provides challenges and perhaps new opportunities for retailers. As an example that is in some ways reminiscent of the approach taken by the Aldi supermarket chain, Office Max is opening smaller stores that focus on a limited selection of products popular with customers. These stores, with the name Ink Paper Scissors, are significantly smaller, about one-ninth the size of the normal Office Max stores. Some version of this focused, smaller approach has also been tried by RadioShack, Best Buy, Lowe's, and even Wal-Mart. "In some ways, retailers are going back to their roots, evoking the corner store."[178] And, evoking the idea of overstimulation, a psychological concept, the vice president of a marketplace management consultancy quoted in this article in the *New York Times* real estate section says, "There is such a thing as too much variety."[179]

Another new direction for malls may be the concept of one-stop shopping, where essentially every price point is represented, from dollar stores to Nordstrom's, in a hybrid center. These kinds of hybrid centers have a presence in Australia and Europe.[180] The idea is that there will be increased traffic from people shopping at these different price points, and they are not always different people. The highest rate of growth for customers of dollar stores in the United States came from households that earned a

---

[175] Clark, S. (2009, June 24). 5% of top US retailers have m-commerce sites. http://www.internetretailing.net/news/5-of-top-us-retailers-have-m-commerce-sites.

[176] Underhill (1999), p. 215.

[177] d'Astous, A. (2000). Irritating aspects of the shopping environment. *Journal of Business Research, 49,* 149–156.

[178] Shevory, K. (2009, May 20). Mini version of big-box stores. *The New York Times,* para. 15. http://www.nytimes.com/2009/05/20/realestate/commercial/20small.html?pagewanted=print.

[179] Ibid., para. 16.   [180] Spector (2005), pp. 177–178.

minimum of $70,000 in income, according to an A.C. Nielsen statistic Spector cites.[181]

A DEVELOPER'S PERSPECTIVE

In research for this chapter, I interviewed Daniel Sargis, from the Hartford, Connecticut, area, who is a principal in a development company involved in strip malls and more recently in health care facilities. When I asked him about the future of malls, he essentially agreed with Underhill that the mall as a concept is now passé, replaced by new iterations. Among other issues, he pointed to the problems malls have had as hangout spaces and also noted that the costs to maintain the large common areas ultimately must be passed on through the retailer to the consumer.

What does he see as the driving force behind the new physical models for retail? In a word – demographics, but demographics understood in the context of economic self-interest. In other words, the response to the question "What do we build and why?" is economically driven by demographics. His firm's foray into the construction of health care facilities reflects the national trend of meeting the needs of an aging population. As the baby boomers age, they (we) will need increased support services, primary among them health care. Providing more shopping opportunities close to retirement communities and assisted living facilities makes sense. For that reason, lifestyle centers may gain increasing traction, especially those geared toward retirement-aged individuals. Mixed-use developments incorporating housing, as in the Natick or Chapel View models, are also likely to be successful, although such housing has to be available at a wider range of price points at the lower end.

In Mr. Sargis's view, what we build has to make financial sense. Just as health care developers are now more willing to build facilities with patient single-room occupancy because a business case has been made for it (reviewed in Chapter 2), we may be willing to build smaller developments if a business case can be made for the profitability of such developments.

But he does not agree that the sense of community we seek can be recreated in these lifestyle centers. It is not the same as the kind of communities, like those in his youth, where neighbors actually exchanged recipes, or as Jane Jacobs recounts, where storeowners watched the neighborhood children. The sense of community in lifestyle centers is artificial, in his

---

[181] Ibid., p. 116.

view, in the same way that the Main Street of Disneyland is artificial, I would add.

With regard to the Internet, he views the three aspects of shopping, the physical, the paper (catalogue), and the Internet, as complementary. "They are all three players in the marketplace for the foreseeable future." His comment underscores the data cited earlier in the chapter that by 2011, as much as 40 percent of off-line retail sales will be influenced by data gathered on the Internet prior to purchase.

As a summary statement, he observed that evolution is always part of the retail environment. No one model will work in perpetuity, and developers will try new versions and duplicate the most successful configurations, as we now see in the growth and popularity of lifestyle centers and mixed use developments.

ENDING REFLECTIONS

Here we are at the end; in some ways we are back at the beginning, looking at what suburbia "has wrought." When I began this book, I had little under-standing of that interconnectedness, or of the role of the federal government in shaping our landscape. Sure, the impact of the federal highway system is easy to see. But the role of depreciation laws in fostering the growth of big box stores may be outside the knowledge base of most people not involved in commercial real estate.

In the *Harvard Design School Guide to Shopping*, one of the most poignant sections for me was a series of pages at the beginning of the book comparing the visual similarities of shopping spaces, from Fishkill, New York, to Las Vegas, Los Angeles, Amsterdam, Ontario, and Seoul, among others. The similarity of these spaces is overwhelming. Yes, they all bear the same lineage from the early marketplaces where a path is essentially lined with goods on either side. But in the process of globalization, we have lost a lot of what is unique about each place.

Writing this book has made me treasure what is unique about where each of us lives. When I visited San Antonio for the first time in 1994 for another EDRA conference, I was both delighted and shocked. The delight came along the San Antonio River, where the River Walk retail environment, developed in the 1960s, provides a spectacular way to combine nature and retail; the shock came from the retail environment within a stone's throw of the Alamo, a historic treasure. There is no way around it; the neighbor of the Alamo is a tacky retail strip of souvenir shops. We have the capacity to make retail environments that improve the visual landscape. If we do not, how will America look in 50 years?

I am reminded of the preservation of an area in Ann Arbor, Michigan, called Kerrytown, where some of the buildings date from 1874. This area is part of North Central Ann Arbor, which in the 1950s was populated primarily by African Americans and was slated for urban renewal. Federal dollars were to be used to raze and clear what was considered to be substandard housing; perhaps as many as 80 percent of the units were to be demolished. If residents refused, eminent domain was to be invoked. But there was no promise in the plan that the segregation in Ann Arbor's housing would end if this area underwent urban renewal. Only 15 percent of the residents wanted to move. In the end, the plan was defeated, and by the late 1970s the housing stock needing improvement was addressed, and the Kerrytown buildings began to be renovated into shops in an area scheduled to be demolished to make way for a motel or discount store.[182] What exists now is a vibrant neighborhood with an eclectic mix of stores, a community park (replacing the former junkyard), and a successful farmers market. There is a synergy between the market and shops, and people come together as a community at the Saturday morning market, as they have for generations.

I feel as if I am channeling William Whyte, who wrote, "I end, then, in praise of small spaces.... For a city, such places are priceless, whatever the cost. They are built of a set of basics and they are in front of our noses. If we will look."[183]

[182] Silberman, E. (1998, January). We almost lost Kerrytown. *Ann Arbor Observer*, pp. 31–34.
[183] Whyte, W. (1980). *The social life of small urban spaces.* Washington, D.C.: The Conservation Foundation, p. 101.

CLOSING COMMENTS

In a sense, there are two layers described in this book. One layer is our collective outer self, as defined by the buildings we construct. The other layer is our collective inner self, on some level related to these physical manifestations. America is vast, and in the 20th century we developed our transportation infrastructure to suit the automobile. To a great extent the highway system that supports the individual car is a product of incentives from the federal government. We drive; by and large we do not take the train or the bus, and we definitely don't walk. This is not "new" news; it is just not good news. In this book, data are presented that suggest that in many instances our bigger is better mentality has failed us. In the United States there are problems in commuting and lack of community, in educational achievement, in health (specifically obesity), in work–family balance, and in the malling of America.

Although this book focuses on buildings, beneath the bricks and mortar is a sense that Americans crave something they think they have lost, and they aren't sure how to retrieve it. What they seem to have lost is a sense of togetherness, and perhaps a sense of safety that comes from that connection. The absolute size of our nation has something to do with this loss, as does the infrastructure of roads and highways, and the creation of suburbia.

If connections to other people really do matter – and as someone trained in psychology, I think they do – we need to look at the kinds of physical environments that support making those connections. These kinds of spaces and places are more likely to be small than large. They are the new urbanist communities or small towns or even city blocks; they are the small health care facility, auxiliary structure, and the Planetree model; they are the school within a school; they are the reincarnation of the Main Street of the 1950s through lifestyle centers or reinvigoration of existing downtowns.

Data suggest that we need to build spaces that say to us, "I need to know how much you care before I care how much you know." These are spaces where the individual matters, and the physical environment can and does communicate these messages. It is not necessarily that smaller is somehow *fundamentally* better; what counts is the kind of interactions more likely to occur in smaller settings, as has been argued in the case of the small school movement.

Such messages about the importance of the individual come through environments that are human-scaled, welcoming, and approachable, just as Propst indicated when he reflected on schools. The theme that the built environment needs those characteristics emerges repeatedly across building types, particularly in situations where there may be stress, as in our health care facilities or schools. We see this theme in the preference for shopping environments that resemble small towns. Even in work environments, we see the need to offer spaces that support personal space and privacy as well as collaboration and community.

The landscape of the work environment recommended by BOSTI and others incorporates both private and public space. Technology further provides the possibility for many citizens to work from anywhere. Roads and suburbia have separated us, but technology can bring some of us together. In a fascinating way, it is in the area of the work environment where we see new ways of creating community and interacting, in the work-from-anywhere movement and the idea of ROWE (results-only work environment). Perhaps more than has been true for the last 50 years, many Americans have the opportunity to work from home some of the time, which may mean flexibility in where home "is."

In terms of my theoretical leanings in psychology, I am not a strict behaviorist, but I do think that reinforcement contingencies strongly influence behavior, and they are hard to ignore. For that reason, I think we will need help from our government to reshape our physical landscape. And it won't be easy. But we have seen instances where we clearly reconfigured the way we deliver services, for example, in the move toward consolidating schools in the second half of the 20th century. We can use contingencies to move in the other direction. It will take investing in mass transit, providing incentives for new urbanism and for small schools, and purchasing from small local business owners who stimulate responses other than "thoughts brought on by prolonged exposure to exposed brick."[1] Altering the attraction Americans have to "bigness" is a challenge; those who have *more* generally don't want

---

[1] Trillin (1977).

less, as we saw in the data about what might attract people to give up some of their land for proximity to new urbanist features. We have also championed the notion of economies of scale, whether we think of Wal-Mart, health care facilities, or the size of our public schools. And when we address problems in this country at the level of government intervention, we typically do it on a large scale and in a fairly uniform manner, as we did with the National Highway Act and the National Housing Act. But our tax dollars can work in a way to provide a variety of solutions across communities, as what is needed and what works in some areas of the country may be a poor match in others. But surely some incentives can target small solutions, such as neighborhood schools and small stores.

In helping us address issues in our physical environment, social scientists can play an important role. One theme that emerges from this survey of American building types is the importance of evidence in helping us make decisions about improving our way of life. No, the picture from evidence is hardly ever *perfectly* clear, and behavior is never completely predictable. After all, inferential statistical analysis, a primary tool of social science, is predicated on the notion of probability. But it's the best we have.

Not all research included here would pass muster as "good" research in the sense that some of the samples were hardly random or representative. But there is good research coming out of the evaluation of health care facilities, arguably a difficult place to conduct research, and there is a movement toward evidence-based design in which physiological measures often play a larger role and the reliance on self-report measures is reduced. Further, there are some convincing data emerging from research on the small school movement related to cost when the outcomes are rates of graduation and not simply attendance. Research from both the health care and school venues points to the importance of the person, whether it is the care provided in health care facilities that champion patient-centered care or small schools that create communities within larger schools.

When I began this book, we did not have the economic challenges from the recession of 2008 that we currently face. I don't know if the 2008 economic crisis will be any more of a wake-up call than the oil embargo of 1973 when gas was rationed. But my hope is that as we emerge from the 2008 economic "downturn" we seize the opportunity to consider whether this country can make public transportation a priority. There are many problems we face, from health care insurance to terrorism. It is easy to push aside the issue of our built landscape and continue to support a way of life where driving is fundamental to survival. The legacies of the built environments of the 20th and 21st centuries need not be indistinguishable.

I hope that we support a system where walking becomes a fundamental part of our lives even if homes situated in areas that promote walking sometimes cost a bit more.[2] Quoted in an article by Malcolm Gladwell, Victor Gruen, the "inventor" of the mall, imagined that the primary means of traveling in his plans for America's postwar urban landscape would be walking. "Nothing like walking for peace of mind."[3]

[2] Max, S. (2009, November). Home: The market. What you'll pay to walk everywhere. *Money Magazine*, p. 46.

[3] Gladwell, M. (2004, March 15). The terrazzo jungle. *The New Yorker*. http://www .newyorker.com/archive/2004/03/15/040315fa_fact1, para. 24.

INDEX